MW01089171

Despair and
the Return of Hope

Despair and the Return of Hope

Echoes of Mourning in Psychotherapy

Peter Shabad

Jason Aronson Inc.
Northvale, New Jersey
London

This book was set in 11 pt. New Baskerville by Pageworks of Old Saybrook and Lyme, CT, and printed and bound by Book-mart Press, Inc. of North Bergen, NJ.

Copyright © 2001 by Peter Shabad

10 9 8 7 6 5 4 3 2 1

All rights reserved. No part of this book may be used or reproduced in any manner whatsoever without written permission from Jason Aronson, Inc. except in the case of brief quotations in reviews for inclusion in a magazine, newspaper, or broadcast.

Library of Congress Cataloging-in-Publication Data

Shabad, Peter.
    Despair and the return of hope : echoes of mourning in
psychotherapy / by Peter Shabad.
      p. cm.
    Includes bibliographical references and index.
    ISBN 0-7657-0315-7
    1. Bereavement (Psychological aspects) 2. Loss (Psychology) 3. Reparation
(Psychoanalysis) 4. Psychotherapy. 5. Hope. 6. Existential psychology. I. Title.
    RC455.4.L67 S36   2001
    155.9'37—dc21   00-052203

Printed in the United States of America on acid-free paper. For information and catalog write to Jason Aronson Inc., 230 Livingston Street, Northvale, NJ 07647-1726, or visit our website: www.aronson.com

To my mother, Leslie

Contents

PART III: PSYCHOTHERAPY: THE QUEST FOR SELF-ACCEPTANCE

   Idealizing Transference and the Search for
   a Powerful Other   213

10 Confidence and Doubt: The Therapist's Sense
    of Lovingness and the Use of the Personal
    in Psychotherapy   241

11 Haunting Echoes of Personal Truth: The Pangs
    of Regret and Remorse   267

12 Self-Acceptance and the Generosity of
    Letting Go: The Experiences of Mourning
    and Growth   293

    References   315

    Credits   325

    Index   327

Acknowledgments

Through informal conversations, intellectual dialogue, and shared experiences, many individuals have had a hand in contributing to this volume. First and foremost, I would like to thank my patients for entrusting me with the most private of intimacies and allowing me to enter their lives. They have my deepest respect for the ways they have struggled with their disillusionments and sufferings in their search for hope and purpose in their lives. My gratitude also goes to the clinical psychology interns at Michael Reese Hospital and the clinical psychology graduate students at Northwestern University Medical School for their invaluable assistance in furthering the growth of this project.

Bob and Judy Shiffman, especially, were there to lend a boost to my morale when I most needed it. And as always, Carol Scally has been steadfast with her encouragement. Jody Messler Davies has been a valued, supportive friend, and more than once has contributed an apt turn of phrase to the creative process. By way of dialogue and friendship, passion and good humor, Spyros Orfanos has been an ardent backer of this book. Thank you to Cindy Sloan for making a difficult transition less difficult than it could have been. Jerome Kavka and Arnold Tobin have been generous in sharing the wisdom of their experiences.

A number of individuals have read and commented on different chapters of the book, and I am grateful to them. Stephen Mitchell provided helpful feedback to early drafts. Lew Aron, Nancy Burke, David deBoer, Gerry Gargiulo, Marilyn Meyers, Jeffrey Rubin, and Frank Summers have also contributed critical commentary, valued friendship, and morale boosting.

I am most grateful to Anne Marie Dooley for greeting my manuscript with enthusiasm. With her sensitivity, she has calmed an author's anxieties and given his "baby" a warm home. Thank you also to Jason Aronson for his valued feedback and support of the project, as well as to Judy Cohen for her labors and astute editorial comments.

I owe a special debt of gratitude to Cheryl Sporlein for typing many a draft of this book over the last decade. With unfailing patience, a strong work ethic, and a generosity of spirit, she has put up with the most impromptu requests.

This book would not have been completed if not for the abundant support of my family. I am grateful to Eugenie Gingold for providing the encouragement of a good-humored and wise "aunt." I am thankful also to Jeffry and Joshua Kulp and Barbara Neuman for welcoming me graciously into their family. Thank you also to Phyllis and Steven Shabad for their consistent support throughout the project. An added note of gratitude to my brother Steven for leading me to the works of Dostoevsky many years ago. A bone of gratitude goes to my dog, Teddy, whose sweet nature and lovableness keep me in consistent contact with the goodness in life.

I gratefully remember my father, Theodore, for providing me with a model of hard work and persistence. His ability to derive the most out of love, work, and play, while keeping his integrity and good humor, serves as a continuing inspiration. My mother, Leslie, was my first mentor and supervisor in psychology. Her love of ideas, and our early conversations about politics, philosophy, and psychology drove my curiosity to learn about people. Without her warmth and encouragement, this project would not have come into being.

I am very lucky to have two wonderful sons who have added indispensable balance and meaning to my life. Alex is deep and wise beyond his years, and has taught me how to be a better father. I have learned from Ben how to overcome odds with grit, determination, and good-natured spirit.

Finally, I would like to pay tribute to my wife, Elaine. During the writing of this book, she has reveled in its joys and shared in its miseries. With perseverance and fortitude, warmth and good humor, she has helped guide the book through its long journey to completion. Her abiding love, support, and companionship have been a constant source of strength and education for me.

Introduction

"He who dreads suffering already suffers what he dreads."

—Montaigne

"The only thing we have to fear is fear itself."

—Franklin Delano Roosevelt

When I was a small child I once had a nightmare after seeing the film *Snow White and the Seven Dwarfs*. Overwhelmed by the frightening profile of the witch looming large before me, I woke up and cried for help. My mother quickly came into my room, I told her about the dream, and she calmed me down. Immediately before leaving again, however, she said, "Think about the witch now, so you won't dream about her."

Little did I know then that my mother was introducing and initiating me into one of the most basic tenets of Freud's thinking. As a central part of my upbringing, she had, high school education and all, emphasized the main themes of Freud's (1914) paper on "Remembering, Repeating and Working Through": that which is not remembered, thought about, and spoken about is expressed compulsively in unconscious action. With the aid of my mother's informal teachings, I was nurtured early in life on the conviction that speaking of one's fears diffuses their potency. To this day I remain deeply convinced of the wisdom of the lessons I learned; they have become second nature to me.

From Freud onward, psychoanalysts have traditionally viewed illusions as wish-fulfilling fantasies that serve to buffer human beings against the miseries of facing reality more straightforwardly. Certainly there is a significant kernel of truth to the observation that all of us, to a greater or lesser degree, use the rose-colored glasses of denial to make our lives more bearable. However, in focusing so much on the escapist functions of our comforting fantasies, we lose sight of the fact that our less sanguine assumptions about the nature of reality also are forms of illusion.

On the basis of a single traumatic episode or a chronic pattern of traumatic experiences suffered at the hands of parents, we superimpose meanings and conjure up intimidating images about a whole world of unknown persons we have not yet encountered. These transferences of fear and despair, transposed from past experiences of suffering and projected onto the imaginary canvas of the future, could be called negative illusions. Negative illusions are deep-seated beliefs about the real world that are rooted in experiences of disillusionment. These illusions are insidious precisely because they are cloaked in the guise of truth; the pessimist claims he is not a pessimist, but a realist.

Behind a veil of mistrust our residues of bitterness do their destructive work. We brace for the worst, convincing ourselves that our repeated mantras of pessimism are the rational echoes of realism. When by some chance a piece of good fortune enters our lives and disturbs the fate to which we have become accustomed, we may not know what to do with what seems too good to be true. So we just wait anxiously for the inevitable other shoe to drop. In the meantime, we remain too enclosed in our private fatalisms to accept or take in with any sort of grace the unexpected bits of love that might fall our way.

The problem is that such fears of our personal phantoms can become self-perpetuating prophecies that plague us indefinitely until we come out of our defensive cocoons and learn something different. If only we were to call our ghosts into being and name them, we would realize how the terrible monsters that dwell within could be reduced to manageable size. Revealing our private madness to another provides a grounding of the real that calms our worst dreads. It is a terrible waste when we let our illusory despairs and resentments inhibit our passions, embitter our souls, and prevent us from becoming who we would become—sometimes not until it is too late.

It is in this light, I believe, that the existential juxtaposition of life and death is most relevant as a way of framing the human drama. The ever-present shadow of death lends a poignancy to the quest to live a realized, meaningful life. Despite the urgency we feel of having limited time at our disposal, our defensive efforts to immunize ourselves against experiences of painful disillusionment lead only to an alienation from those experiences and ourselves, and we find that as a result this tactic of exiling our sufferings, an integral part of our lives, to an internal netherworld boomerangs back on us. Eventually we are compelled to return to those aspects of ourselves that have been rendered dreamlike and unreal so as to bring them to meaningful life.

There is a profound tug-of-war in human lives between the repeated pull to commemorate earlier experiences of lonely suffering on one hand, and the urgent push to create and find new experiences in pursuit of our individual fulfillment on the other. This tug-of-war also reflects the tension between the psychoanalytic and the existential—between the unearthing of the inner demons that preoccupy us and the mandate to get on with our lives. Little do we realize that while we brace ourselves for the reappearance of the ghosts that haunt us, time does not miss a beat.

My primary reason for writing this book is to understand how our disillusionments and the walls that we resurrect to prevent a repeat of those experiences impede us from living fulfilled lives. I combine existential and psychoanalytic approaches to highlight the fact that we strive to rectify past sufferings and master internal conflicts always in the ever-lurking shadow of death. We cannot afford to let our fears of phantoms cripple our lives. In keeping with my belief that it is imperative not to lose sight of the larger picture, the sequence I have chosen for the chapters in the book roughly traces a person's journey through life—from innocence through disillusionment and finally to mourning and self-acceptance.

In Part I, "Huddling Together in the Face of Death," I describe the existential stage on which we play out our personal dramas. In Chapter 1 I discuss the impact that death has on the way we conduct our lives. Specifically, I examine the different implications that the relative awareness or denial of our mortality has for human relations. Living life unconsciously, as if we were never going to die, may lead to the depreciation of persons into objects whom we then dispose of and retrieve at our whim. Such exploitation eventually culminates in survivor guilt and the creative urge to make reparations to those who have been left behind.

In Chapter 2 I put forth a vision of what human development would look like in the ideal. In contrast to the traditional view of superego or conscience as an internal arbiter reflecting the moral norms of a given culture, conscience here refers to an inner knowledge that good can transcend the bad, that a bridge with another can be constructed over spaces and times of separateness. This knowledge spurs a gratitude and generosity that move the child to sustain the mother's life as she sustains his. Conscience thus is characterized by the ethic of mutuality. In this sense, a passion of gratitude and generosity infuses the child continually with the requisite courage to overcome the fear of the unknown and move toward a future in which he imagines a hoped-for other is awaiting him.

In Part II, "Disillusionment, Defense, and the Despair of Bitterness," I trace the onset of trauma and the disillusionments experienced at the hands of others, and the toll that self-insulating defenses then take on our lives. We retreat from helplessness and shame into fortresses of isolated self-enclosure. Convinced that the future will be but a revisiting of the past, we remain guarded against the vulnerability and unpredictability of offering ourselves for acceptance to others. These fears of openness mean that we have to memorialize prior experiences of suffering on our own by showing (repeating in action) rather than by telling them. Eventually the hopelessness of being developmentally enclosed and stuck may culminate in the characterological bitterness of resentment, envy, and spite.

In Chapter 3 I trace the onset of the traumatic disruption of a child's innocence. Rather than risk falling into a state of psychic desolation, children employ intensified mental activity to safeguard their survival. Out of fear, and governed by a desperate morality of survival, they begin to wear the mask of the enemy and to attack their own vulnerabilities. Although such counterphobic defenses as identifying with the aggressor may have the adaptive aim of securing survival, those same defenses also are a self-betrayal in that they tear apart a person's sense of developmental integrity.

In Chapter 4 I examine the human compulsion to return to a childhood innocence that has been fled rather than mourned and worked through. The detachment defenses used against experiences of disillusionment may lead to some degree of derealization in which individuals struggle with doubts as to whether their previous experiences really happened or not. Such persons may then feel compelled unconsciously to undo the trauma, and, as if for the first time, begin again, at a point before their innocence was ruptured.

In Chapter 5 I explore the way people lend meaning to experiences that have been rendered unreal through their symptomatology. Because most suffering is borne alone, its actual occurrence may then be doubted, with the consequence that individuals often attempt to bring out proof of their experiences through psychological symptoms. Symptoms thus have both the communicative and the commemorative function of securing a witness to one's story of lonely suffering, so as to give that story the conviction and dignity of having actually occurred.

In Chapter 6 I explore the passivity, resentment, bitterness, and sense of entitlement that can accrue when a person's hurts and burdens are neglected for too long. Due to self-protective defenses that inhibit an openness toward others, disowned wishes can become transformed into entitled needs. Such needs, with their implicit demands, do coercive violence to the give-and-take of human relationships, the credibility and authenticity of which depend on the freedom of each person to be him- or herself rather than the object of another. The implications that these tensions between wish and need, and thus between coercion and freedom, have for a psychoanalytic psychotherapy are then discussed further.

Chapters 7 and 8 follow up on these same themes of coercion and freedom. In those chapters, I explore the often self-destructive lengths human beings go to in order to preserve their integrity and dignity from the encroachments of others. Both chapters describe the havoc that is wrought when children are exploited narcissistically and objectified by parents. The despair of ever being able to break free to determine one's own destiny culminates in the passive fatalism and bitterness of envy and spite.

In Chapter 7 I use the metaphor of the evil eye to explore the pervasive role envy plays in human relationships. I focus especially on the separation envy of mothers who wish to retain possession of their children, and the child's consequent employment of various defensive ploys to ward off the covetous desires of the mother's envious evil eye. It is sadly ironic that it is those persons who stop their own growth in its tracks in order to placate the envy of significant people in their lives who then begrudge others the creative passion that they have denied to themselves.

In Chapter 8 I examine the phenomenon of spite as it is exemplified in the expression "cutting off one's nose to spite one's face." Drawing extensively from Dostoevsky's (1864a) *Notes from the Underground*, I suggest that the perverse and self-defeating quality of spite is a last-ditch attempt to preserve the freedom of individual dignity against the indoctrinations of others. Perhaps we can also see how, through one's self-injury and martyrdom, an attempt is made both to punish and to awaken the conscience of the exploiting other to one's own personhood.

In Part III, "Psychotherapy: The Quest for Self-Acceptance," I describe the way a patient may use the psychotherapy relationship to emerge from being an enclosed island unto himself, and take tentative steps toward mourning and self-acceptance. One primary source of a child's disillusionment has to do with not being able to give of himself successfully to the significant figures of childhood. Without being accepted, it is difficult to establish a sense of belonging and rootedness in those relationships. Throughout all the chapters of this volume, I emphasize that the degree to which we have succeeded in being of loving use and care to the significant people of our childhood goes a long way toward establishing a sense of confidence in our reparative capacities.

I think that this way of looking at the give-and-take dynamics of early significant relationships entails a potentially radical shift in the way we view a patient's transference relationship with the therapist. Whereas typically we think of the patient who comes for help as the receiver of the care and ministrations given *by* the therapist, it may be, as Searles (1975) suggested, that what is most therapeutic is the patient's feeling that he has given something of meaning *to* the therapist. The patient's sense of having enhanced the therapist's well-being also implies inclusive access and a crucial sense of belonging to the therapist's life. Ultimately it is this very personal sense of belonging to the therapist that may propel the patient's movement toward enlightenment, self-understanding, and self-acceptance.

My special concern here is that the relationship with the therapist be substantive and authentic enough—something akin to a psychologically minded I–Thou dialogue about the patient's life—so that the patient can use it to find hope in the possibilities of the real and unknown. Thus it is incumbent on the therapist to be hopeful and open enough to allow the patient to gain some access to him personally, and not merely stand on the ceremony of his professional role. In this regard, it is particularly important that the therapist understand not only his personal disillusionments—which often he is all too ready to do—but also the self-protective defenses he has resurrected against hoping for too much in his own life. I devote much attention to the way the therapist's defenses and unconscious attempts to master his disillusionments are embedded in his ideologies and values concerning clinical practice.

In Chapter 9 I delve into the ways patients attempt initially to flee the insulated burdens of self-recrimination by surrendering themselves to the authority of a powerful other. Here, the therapist's stance of anonymity and personal abstinence may collude with the patient's defensive wish not to know the all-too human being behind the therapist's personal mask. The chapter concludes with a discussion of how the therapist's view of the transference either as a freedom from or a freedom with has important differential implications for the therapist's use of herself as a person.

In Chapter 10 I explore how the intertwining disillusionments, values, and ideologies of therapists inform the way they practice psychoanalytic psychotherapy. The ways practitioners orient themselves to their bodies as well as their views of spontaneity and emotionality as compared to rationality all have important bearing on clinical intervention. For example, the fear of the unconscious and idealization of rationality that has been historically implicit in psychoanalytic ideology and technique may lead to the problematic outcome of self-consciousness instead of a more integrated self-awareness. When that happens, the premium that analysts place on thinking before acting can lead to an overemphasis on the trappings of their professional role at the expense of their personal effectiveness.

In Chapter 11 I discuss how a person's growing sense of urgency to lead a fulfilling life before dying may clash dramatically with a feeling of being stuck in the past. The insights gained from psychotherapy may become a double-edged sword when such an individual wakes up to missed opportunities long after it is too late to do anything about them. Many years of bracing fearfully against the shadows cast by his own phantoms can exact a heavy toll of regret and remorse. Rather than endure the pains of self-illumination, this person may seek to justify why he was compelled to commit his errors of omission and commission in the first place by repeating them again. In the end, one must acknowledge one's errors and use a generosity of spirit to forgive oneself and to reconcile with one's conscience.

In Chapter 12 I suggest that a generosity of spirit is precisely what is key in facilitating the letting-go process of mourning. Mourning does not have as much to do with adapting to external facts of loss and disillusionment as it does with reintegrating disillusioned wishes that have long been buried. Through this process of self-acceptance, the patient may be able to muster the generosity to own up to her wishes and to let go of the necessity that those wishes be fulfilled.

In the final analysis we are responsible for being true to ourselves and owning up to our desires, recognizing that we do not have the omnipotence to guarantee how those wishes may be met in the outside world. Perhaps a fundamental task of human life is to accept the limits of our mortal imperfection and to do the best we can given those constraints. Such self-acceptance provides a relief from being God unto oneself, and opens us up to our neighbors for help to complement and enhance the meaning of our lives. It is in the passionate exchanges of love, work, and play with others that one exercises the freedom, in Kierkegaard's (1843) words, "to choose oneself" (p. 219).

Part I

Huddling Together
in the
Face of Death

1

Death, Meaning, and Human Relations

Everything that we are in a positive sense is by virtue of some limitation. And this being limited, this being crippled, is what is called destiny, life. That which is missing in life, that which oppresses us, forms the fabric of life and maintains us within it.

—Emily Dickinson

The confrontation with death—and the reprieve from it—makes everything look so precious, so sacred, so beautiful that I feel more strongly than ever the impulse to love it, to embrace it, and to let myself be overwhelmed by it. My river has never looked so beautiful. . . . Death, and its ever present possibility makes love, passionate love, more possible. I wonder if we could love passionately, if ecstasy would be possible at all, if we know we'd never die.

—Abraham Maslow, from a letter written as he was recuperating from a heart attack

GARY: THE PROBLEM OF TIME MOVING ON

For the past five and a half years, I have seen a Pakistani-American man, Gary, in twice-a-week psychotherapy. As a first-generation, firstborn son of immigrant parents, Gary saw it as his filial duty to shield his parents' unacculturated innocence from the relative jadedness of their new culture. Through this process of protecting his parents, Gary became Americanized very quickly and was evicted prematurely from what never was a carefree childhood anyway.

Most of Gary's early years were devoted to some form of labor; schoolwork was first and foremost, along with careful planning for great achievement and success in the future. Any activities that took him away from this primary focus, such as playing with friends or watching TV, were considered trivial distractions or worse. But Gary also gave himself over to other, more private kinds of work; these were repeated efforts on behalf of his agitatedly depressed and often irritable mother. Indeed, Gary's career ambitions derived primarily from a wish to make his mother proud of him.

One scene from his earlier days stood out especially in Gary's memory. He recounted how as a child he would set up his homework on the dining room table, leaving his notebook open for all to see—just in case he was taken by surprise by his mother returning home from work. He would then grab a bag of cookies and turn on his favorite TV show, *The Brady Bunch*, all the while listening tremulously and alertly for his mother's impending arrival. On those occasions when Gary became too deeply immersed in the program, he would be startled by a loud thudding knock on the window. He would then quickly shut off the TV and be prepared to be reduced to nothing by her ridicule and sarcasm about his addiction to the "idiot box." When his mother walked in the door, he, humiliated, would stare down at the floor with his tail between his legs as he endured her scolding. The infliction of these indignities was not an uncommon occurrence. Later as a teenager when Gary would have too much fun with a friend or girlfriend or was generally too full of himself, his mother would deflate him quickly with a mocking, "Big man, eh?"

At other times, however, Gary imagined a different, more pathetic mother in need of his help. He recounted that he sometimes viewed her as a depressed, downtrodden woman, not unlike a pathetic bag lady he spotted at the Port Authority Bus Terminal in New York City. This potent mixture of maternal humiliation and pathos stimulated feverish scurrying on Gary's part both to alleviate his mother's unhappiness and to evade the thunder of her fluctuating moods.

From early childhood onward, Gary did all he could to lighten the load of his mother's life. On weekend mornings, he woke up especially early to wash the dishes and set up a bouquet of fresh flowers on the dining room table. He attempted to reduce her insecurities about her cooking by making a point of praising her meals in front of company. When Gary became older, he took great pains to make up for what he perceived to be his younger brother's insensitivity to their mother's plight. Unlike his more outgoing sibling, Gary made sure to remain near home—even during adolescence. On those few occasions when he went out with friends, he made it back before curfew without fail. Now as a young man, upon leaving his parents after a weekend stay, Gary speeds back three hours to his own apartment—without stopping to see hometown friends—to call his mother when he arrives so that she can go to bed in peace. In his constant devotion to her, he has differentiated himself proudly from his uninterested, rebellious brother and often absent father. Indeed he fantasized that his parents only had sex twice in their marital lifetime—and he was not even sure of that! He instead stood loyally by her side as her special hero and savior. Her wish became his command. Perhaps Gary's lifelong attitude could be summed up best in a statement that he made early in treatment, when he declared that he could envision no higher honor or pleasure than to refill his mother's teacup when it was empty.

Eventually, however, others had to pay for the numerous humiliations and loss of dignity that Gary suffered at the hands of his mother. At the outset of treatment, he described a volatile, sadomasochistic relationship he had with a young woman who was engaged to another man. He described his tempestuous moods, his rages, and the rough sex they shared. Sometimes Gary described his visits to a live pornographic theater to watch various female contestants engage in wet T-shirt contests. He recounted with relish how he took pleasure in the degradation of the women on stage.

Gary has a difficult dilemma. He likes to describe himself as a painfully lonely man who has romantic fantasies of a woman who will discover his special qualities and carry him off with her. He refuses to ask any women out on dates, insisting that they have to approach him first. The more attracted to and needful of a woman he is, the more enraged he becomes about his need of her. I pointed out to Gary that it seemed, much to his own chagrin, that he seemed determined to make war rather than love with the very women he yearned for most. Much of our work on this issue has consisted in examining the sharp demarcation Gary makes between his madonna mother and all other whore women. On one occasion, I asked him to imagine how he would feel if his mother participated as one of the contestants in the wet T-shirt contest. He responded half-jokingly that he felt like "punching me in the mouth"; eventually these exchanges became more humorous and playful, so that he, too, could play with the idea of aggression being directed toward his mother.

Gary has been a silently resentful man who is determined to get some restitution for missing the carefree pleasures of a normal childhood. When he returns home on weekends to see his parents, he attempts to catch up with an era that has passed him by. On these occasions, Gary attempts to freeze time and make it conform to his fantasies and demands. He fancies himself a child; once he slept at the foot of his parents' bed in a hotel room (despite his apartment being only thirty minutes away). Perhaps in some way he is hoping to catch a glimpse of them locked in embrace and thereby gain visual proof of the roots of his identity. Quite recently, Gary declared that on a forthcoming trip to Pakistan he would like to see where each of his parents grew up, as well as where they met.

Nevertheless, no matter how much he wills it to be so, the ongoing movement of time will not cooperate with his wishes for another opportunity to be a child. Feeling entitled and remaining passive, he waits indefinitely for the woman of his dreams to invite him on a date, but she never does. He cannot afford to realize fully the meaning of the phrase "seize the day" because that would undercut his project to get his just desserts. Instead he would have to face the fact that it is he who must, as he did in laboring on behalf of his mother, yet again make things happen in his life. While Gary waits, he misses out on the best years of his adulthood as he attempts fruitlessly to grasp hold of a childhood long since past. Gary has forgotten, as many of us do, that in this, our mortal life, the clock never stops ticking. I will return to Gary intermittently throughout the book.

DEATH: THE GIVER OF MEANING

As soon as we are born, we enter into a relationship with our death. From dust we come, we dance on this earth for a tantalizingly short while, and to dust we return. The seeming pointlessness of the whole endeavor seems a cruel mockery. For certain existential philosophers—and some acutely disillusioned teenagers and college students—the agonizing brevity of life seems to render all human striving absurd. Such sentiments have been well captured in Camus's *The Myth of Sisyphus*, in which a man labors endlessly to roll a boulder up a hill only to be faced with the continual prospect of it rolling back to the bottom.

The disillusionment inherent in such cynicism masks an underlying idealized vision of what life should be. Thus, for some, the inevitable finality of death is irreconcilable with the meaning bestowed by the glories of continuous life; it is proof that God is playing a cruel game at our expense. What if, however, we turn the whole question on its head and imagine for a moment what the utopia of a deathless life might entail?

Eissler (1955), for example, notes that, "if man's existence were not subject to death, he possibly would become a completely inactive being (p. 94)." Would we be as inclined to rise from bed in the morning or would we say "Maybe I will get up tomorrow instead"? What effect would deathlessness have, if we could say, on separating from a loved one, "I'll see you in a few hundred years" instead of "I'll see you tomorrow"? Because our perspective on time would change so profoundly, the greetings and partings of relationships would take on quite unpredictable meanings. What appears inevitable, however, is that in a world without death the quality of human relations would be altered radically and irrevocably.

As cold informs us about the sense of warmth and dark defines light, so, too, death serves as the background, the absence of life that complements life's presence. In the film *It's a Wonderful Life* (1946), James Stewart's character, George Bailey, briefly lives out a fantasy of what life would have been like had he never been born. After immersing himself in this nightmare of nonbeing, George returns to his life with deepened appreciation. His acute sense of the absence of life enables him to embark on a new beginning with renewed vitality.

In a short paper, "On Transience," Freud (1916) makes a similar argument:

> I could not see my way to dispute the transience of all things, nor could I insist upon an exception in favor of what is beautiful and perfect. But I did dispute the pessimistic poet's view that the transience of what is beautiful involves any loss of worth.
>
> On the contrary, an increase! Transience value is scarcity value in time. Limitation of the possibility of an enjoyment raises the value of the enjoyment. [p. 305]

Heidegger (1927) asserts that the awareness of death as an "ever present potentiality" leads to angst, or ontological anxiety.

Angst challenges us with an urgency as how best to use and trea-
sure each moment. It is because our time is limited that we are
required to set up a hierarchy of personal priorities and values.
Thus, Hoffman (1999) has said that "because of the value-lending
psychological function of death as a boundary, the ego senses a
kind of 'need' for death as an organizing influence and as the
background necessary for purposeful action" (p. 49).

An awareness of death brings a sense of urgency to the freedom to choose, and injects personal meaning into whatever choices
we make. By virtue of the relative brevity of our lives, we are obliged
to choose certain activities at the expense of others, and the company of certain persons instead of others. This intermingling of a
poignant awareness of life's fragility with the imperative of making very personal choices is fundamental to the loving appreciation of another person.

Rollo May (1969) suggests that when we fall in love we are
sensitized immediately to the potential absence of the other, which
enables us, in turn, to cherish the ongoing presence of the beloved. He says, "love is not only enriched by our sense of mortality, but constituted by it" (p. 102). One patient of mine noted that
he became tense when his girlfriend and soon to become fiancée
asked him if he thought that they would be together forever. He
began to feel trapped, and subsequently felt more alienated from
her. I suggested to him that keeping his distance may also be an
attempt to dissociate himself from the words "till death do us part"
that would be uttered at their wedding. To fall in love and to
commit oneself in wedlock puts one face-to-face with one's mortality.

Perhaps we could say that all our choices and commitments
serve what for Kierkegaard is the most fundamental of choices—
the choice of ourselves as manifested in our concrete actions. As
much as many of us would like to lead omnipresent parallel lives
in which we could be in more than one place at a time, we are
limited to one mortal body per customer. The limit of death, by
providing an impetus for choice, transforms the dream of having

any number of personal identities into the actuality of having but one. Our unfolding destinies, our life, and our death are irrevocable; in that sense, we are charged with the task of making our choices and commitments as authentically personal and meaningful as we can.

To what extent is it true that the scarcity of life enhances its value or quality? From the foregoing, it would follow that if one were to live thirty years instead of seventy, then that shortened life would become all the more precious. However, typically we believe just the opposite; as we see a person's lifespan shrink from thirty years to ten years to two years to a few days, we are increasingly challenged to retain a faith that such an extremely brief life has some meaning. Some individuals may become so despairing about the seeming pointlessness of an abbreviated life that they may come to feel that maybe it is better not to be born at all than to live for such a short while.

By focusing too much on quantity of time, however, we can miss the particular ways that death informs a life. Human development is a continual microcosmic interplay between life and death, between being and nonbeing, between the inherent quality of experience in the current moment and its surround; that is, each moment is circumscribed by ghosts of dead, previous moments and ghosts of yet-to-be-born future moments. Death or nonbeing complements the fleeting instantaneous life of each passing moment and highlights the intrinsic value of that moment. The moment that is experienced with authenticity and openness is illuminated ever so briefly—but indelibly—as it takes its rightful place within the integrity of our lives. To believe that meaning can only be derived from a certain quantity of time or a particular series of moments is to miss the dynamic, vital relationship between death and *this* moment in and of itself. Thus, the lives of stillborn children take on profound meaning as their names are engraved into the memories of their parents. If we would only let it be so, the intrinsic quality of a moment can live forever. In my view this romantic but powerful psychological notion is crucial to the process of mourning and psychic growth.

THE SENSE OF OVERWHELMING
HELPLESSNESS AND PSYCHIC NUMBING

It seems, however, that because of our human makeup, we have only a limited capacity to appreciate the raw impact that absence has on the presence of things we value. We cannot seem to sustain the intensity and urgency that comes with fully realizing the fragility of our lives. Maslow (1967) used the term *Jonah Syndrome* to describe this inability to bear the full intensity of life. He says: "We are just not strong enough to endure more! It is just too shaking and wearing. So, often people in . . . ecstatic moments say 'It's too much' or 'I can't stand it,' or 'I could die'" (p. 165).

At the peak of our most intensely happy moments, we are most vulnerable to our downfall. Thus Maslow says the Jonah Syndrome is "partly a justified fear of being torn apart, of losing control, of being shattered and disintegrated, even of being killed by the experience" (pp. 165–166). In this regard, it is worth noting that the French term for orgasm is *le petit mort* (the little death).

No matter how often we may tell ourselves to remain vigilant and to appreciate the presence of loved ones, inevitably we lose our resolve and lapse into unconsciousness. Perhaps that is just as well. If we were to stay ever alert to our ultimate fate, we would be overwhelmed by what we behold. In attempting to keep the idea of death in mindful focus and use it to enhance our lives, we are playing with fire. It is all too possible to become paralyzed into inaction by an obsessional fixation on the morbid.

I see a 31-year-old homosexual man in psychoanalytic psychotherapy who is struggling to commit himself to his lover. His lover recently discovered that he had contracted the HIV virus. The patient is so immobilized by anxiety and foreboding that he finds it exceedingly difficult to surrender himself to his lover's offerings of tenderness in the here-and-now. Thinking that if my patient could realize the quality of the relationship as it is proceeding it would alleviate his crippling anxiety concerning the future, I asked him at one point: "How does it feel for you when S. puts his arm around you?" He replied that he could not give himself over to the experience because he feels trapped and can think only of how he will be abandoned.

Whereas some moderate awareness of death seems to sensitize us to the distinction between being and nonbeing, and has a liberating effect on the conduct of our lives, a massive or profound exposure to trauma has the opposite impact. Robert Jay Lifton (1968) has used the term *psychic numbing* to describe the overwhelming disorientation and fragmentation experienced by atomic bomb survivors in Hiroshima and Nagasaki. Moreover, our sense of helplessness and insignificance is greatly exacerbated when recurrent experiences of loss and trauma deflate our constructive illusion that we are the pilot of our own destiny. When our deepest hopes are massively and/or chronically met with a nonresponsive silence, we may become frozen by overwhelming glimpses of our nonbeing. For the despairing, when all hope to overcome suffering is crushed, life loses its distinctive capacity to transcend death. For those who have been traumatized far too much, the distinction between death and the gift of life, now deadened, is no longer meaningful.

In this way, the seemingly conscienceless youths of our nation's inner cities, desensitized to the preciousness of life by pervasive deprivations, can gun down innocent bystanders at a moment's notice for no apparent reason. Such children, grown bitter and old before their time, are confronted daily with a helplessness to improve their lot in life. The humiliating powerlessness to overcome the accumulated frustrations, losses, and shame that results leaves such persons vulnerable to the existential indignity of being nothing but insignificant creatures that vanish in death. The struggle to be somebody thus gets conflated with the struggle to survive; not to be shamed—and not to succumb to the insult of disappearing "gentle into that good night"—becomes the ultimate aim. Perhaps it is not accidental then that in the inner city "dissing," or disrespecting, is a particularly provocative act. With its suggestion of insignificance and anonymity, disrespect carries with it a threat of meaningless oblivion. To kill the insulter is at one and the same time to fight for the dignity of one's name and for the preservation of one's life. When all hope to relieve suffering is dashed and nothing matters anymore, the pursuit of a transcendent life degenerates into a primitive battle for the pride of survival.

We can observe a similarly dulled sensitivity to the difference between pain and pleasure in so-called behaviorally disordered children who have immunized themselves to the series of punishments meted out to them by parents. In their determination to combat the humiliation of their beatings and not give the parent the satisfaction of seeing them shed tears, such children frequently use a defiant show of apathy to preserve their pride. One adult patient recounted to me how he would look up and smile while being spanked, which would only incense his father more. The problem for these children is that in the process of thwarting the sadism of their tormenters and becoming inured to their own pain, they lose a sense of compassion for all other tears of suffering as well. They can become numbed to the difference between good and bad, between pain and pleasure, and ultimately to the distinction between life and death.

It is quite tempting to evade the good in order not to be hurt by the bad that is bound up with that good; not to wish so as not to be disillusioned; not to receive and be wooed by pleasures that we fear we will eventually have to give up; and not to be born into a vivid, passionate life from which we must necessarily exit. As a patient once said to me, "I don't want to get too attached to you because I will have to leave you eventually."

We attempt to dampen down our creative passions to sidestep the loss and dissolution that are bound up with those passions. As Otto Rank (1936) notes: "The neurotic refuses the loan of life in order not to pay back the debt of death" (p. 126). For Rank, the defensive inhibition of our creative and self-creating capacities stands at the heart of neurosis; neurosis, because one must die anyhow, but now more despairingly after not having realized one's life.

In the retrospect of loss and disillusionment, and in anticipatory anxiety of further losses, we may shroud previous experiences in darkness, or we may shield ourselves from the pain that we imagine is soon to come. In the bitter aftermath of a significant relationship gone sour, we may attempt to distort or minimize the memory of better times that now seem only to lure us back into the dreaded trap of reliving the loss all over again.

THE VITAL LIE: COVERING UP INSIGNIFICANCE WITH THE MASKS OF NARCISSISM

Like the possum who plays dead in order magically to avoid a real death, human beings, too, engage in versions of psychological possum to deaden the natural expansiveness of psychic growth. Although this pattern is perhaps more glaringly apparent in those who have been severely traumatized, it seems that some degree of not caring or constriction of passion is built into the nature of the human beast. In our relationships we hold ourselves back in various degrees of reserve, since not all of them can be intensely deep or profoundly meaningful. We need intermediate friendships and acquaintances, as well as down time, to gain respite from the anxiety and urgent pressure of existing as creatures who are aware of their mortality. Perhaps only on the relaxed ground of forgetfulness can we act with any element of self-confidence and spontaneity.

It is frightening and humbling to pause and imagine how we, as members of the human species, fit into the infinite reaches of time and space; to consider, for example, that the whole of a person's life is but a micro-millisecond in the evolutionary development of the cosmos. We can easily be overwhelmed by the smallness and fragility of our individual lives, lives that seem in the face of the majesty of the universe to be nothing but an insignificant flickering in a sea of darkness.

Ernest Becker (1973), in his Pulitzer prize-winning book, *The Denial of Death*, describes how we all go to great lengths to minimize this sort of "creature anxiety" by narrowing our perceptual and imaginative worlds. In so doing, we can buttress our self-esteem against the vast, incomprehensible universe that dwarfs us. We make our respective worlds manageable by focusing on the concrete, practical problems that lie right in front of our noses.

As we narrow our life stage from the cosmos to planet earth, we are able to view ourselves as "human beings" who, at least, hold sway over all the other creatures on the planet. As this life stage contracts further to nation, we can identify ourselves as American citizens, with all the self-expansive glory that title evokes. When we reduce our life stage still further to city and to family, our sense of ourselves as influential persons increases dramatically. Finally, on the stage of romantic love our sense of significance can rise to transcendent heights; now we are the one and only in the passionately devoted eyes of our beloved. As we feel ourselves to be ever more important fish in a continually shrinking pond, we see how closely intertwined the relative size of a perceived ground (cosmos, nation, family) is with the sense of prideful significance or humbling insignificance of its figures.

Finding a place for our personal dramas on the manageable stage of our culture provides a protective buffer between ourselves and the overwhelming immensity and intensity of the larger scheme of things. Learning social conventions enables us to lower the high stakes in the game of life and death, and to retreat from uncertain, distinctively individual paths of developmental possibilities to more secure familiarities of cultural norms. In order to attain this sense of security, however, we often must adapt and immerse ourselves in the meanings of others at heavy cost to our own personal truths. Moreover, we must do so without fully knowing what we are doing and how much we need others to prop up our self-esteem, for that self-reflectiveness would defeat the whole purpose of the endeavor. Like the independence of a cat, we would like to present ourselves as proudly self-sufficient, seemingly indifferent to the invisible links of needed attachments on which we depend.

This use of another's meanings to lend ourselves a sense of significance prompted Becker (1973) to describe the narcissism of human character as a "vital lie"; vital, because this self-forgetful deception and ignorance as to the energies we really draw on enables us to go on living securely and serenely; a lie, because we do not want to admit how much our sense of individual significance depends on the meanings created by others. Becker puts it eloquently: "It is fateful and ironic how the life we need in order to live dooms us to a life that is never really ours" (p. 56).

When the seamlessness of a give-and-take with others is ruptured and the vital lie of self-sufficiency is exposed, and we get an unwelcome glimpse of our disconnectedness and acute need of others, we may experience a sudden rush of self-consciousness. Now unmasked, we are flooded with the mortifying shame of insignificance, as we see ourselves standing alone in our incompleteness. In the course of development, there are inevitable moments of transition during which human beings emerge from a cocoon of familiar relationships and experience a period of uncertain limbo before joining in a new network of relationships. Van Gennep (1908) called these transitions "rites of passage," and distinguished between a separation phase from an old entity, a liminal or transitional phase, and a phase of incorporation into a new entity. During certain points of development when the risk of isolation is especially great, such as in adolescence, we may be especially vulnerable to a self-consciousness concerning our reliance on others, especially our parents.

[handwritten margin note: like leaving school + starting a new career]

When adolescents attempt to navigate a path away from childhood dependence, they unconsciously borrow a sense of significance from the standards and values of peers, setting the precedent for the socialized construction of adult character. Reminders of childhood dependence may then be deflating precisely because they conjure up previous experiences of disillusionment and the humiliating incapacity to overcome those disillusionments. Thus, at the same time that we employ the adaptations and conformity of adult character in order to embed ourselves in the conventions of our culture, we eliminate from consciousness any deflating sense of smallness evoked by memories of previous disillusionments. In this sense there is a collusion between the socializing and repressive processes that enables us to relegate the vulnerable underbelly of past humiliations to unconscious oblivion. We use the self-forgetfulness of merging with others to flee from any awareness of our own relative incompleteness and insignificance as individuals.

It is understandable that we seek to evade the pressures of consciousness. To hold constant vigil on the larger meanings of life and death, and love and loss, would drive many of us insane. All too often, however, in efforts to preserve our security and sanity against the immensity of the existential, we go too far in over-protecting ourselves; we lose a sense of the passionate urgency inherent in living a mortal life. Eventually we may discover, to our chagrin, that our defensive tactics have backfired because in relying on them, we have succeeded only in depleting our relationships of meaning.

For example, when a man habitually puts any possibility of his wife's dying out of his mind, he makes sure that he does not become too acquainted with the fears and helplessness he would feel about losing her because then he would be humbled by an awareness of his dependence on her. As if to prove otherwise, he depreciates, scolds, and harangues her, all the while living under the illusion that he could never lose his wife. His poor treatment of her contributes still further to his denial of her death, since any thought that she could perish from this earth would flood him immediately with profound guilt and misgiving.

THE UNCONSCIOUS SENSE OF DEATHLESSNESS AND THE IMPERSONAL IN HUMAN RELATIONS

It is apparent that the way we fulfill our time with a loved one also carries with it the seeds of how adequately we will cope with the loss of that person. It is when we sense that our time with a significant other has not been and is not being realized that the loss of that person becomes ever more unthinkable, necessitating its further denial. And the denial of that loss, in turn, further postpones any urgency about fully appreciating the presence of the loved one.

Perhaps when we cannot distill a certain quality of intensity from our experiences on a conscious level, we attempt to make up for it in quantity; that is, we attempt to extend our time unconsciously, as if we were imploring the powers that be to compensate us for what was missed. Many therapists have had the experience, at the close of a therapy session, of patients who let it be known in one way or another that they are not prepared to leave yet. On these occasions it often has been my impression that patients feel that something fundamental about their experience had not been conveyed or understood to their satisfaction. Similarly, when we cannot find an essential quality of meaning in our experiences and they remain unrealized, we zealously pursue a quantity of life instead. This tendency is self-perpetuating, in that when we grab on desperately to a series of moments in this way, we may not pay sufficient heed to any one particular moment, thus furthering the cycle.

This cycle of sealing ourselves off from the quality of our experiences and compensating for that gap in quantity can intensify, especially when we have been exposed to our helplessness to overcome our losses and disillusionments. In the purposely forgetful, fractured aftermath of disillusionment, we lose our hold on our personal identities or continuity in time. That sense of continuing in time provides a meaningful rootedness or meant-to-be feeling that helps us weather the storms of constant change. Thus, invariably, we are drawn back to repair the blanks of meaninglessness in our lives. A continual desire to accumulate materials and power, and to see many new people in terms of one significant old one is insatiable, because quantification does not satisfy the need for the intense quality characteristic of earlier relationships and experiences. In this sense, perhaps not coincidentally, our unconscious immersion in the eternal circularities of the repetition compulsion can revolve endlessly around childhood fixations and developmental deficits. Maybe the lure in living unconsciously has something to do with Freud's (1915) pronouncement: "At bottom no one believes in his own death, or to put the same thing in another way, that in the unconscious every one of us is convinced of his own immortality" (p. 289).

To suspend an awareness of death, to be unconscious, is to live deathlessly. Time then extends indefinitely onward like a continually flowing river, untamed and undifferentiated. If we take this notion of unconscious deathlessness seriously, then the question I posed at the beginning of the chapter, of how life would be altered if there were no death, is not just a piece of imaginative whimsy. To the extent that we live unconsciously, we *really do* proceed in our relationships as if there were no death.

There is an ongoing tension in remaining openly alert to the meaningfulness of our significant relationships without slipping into either a pressured hyperconsciousness or a slumbering unconsciousness. If we are overcome with anxiety because of an acute awareness of the way the high stakes of presence and absence are played out at every moment in our relationships, we cannot derive any joy from them. On the other hand, we also can lapse easily into complacency and forget that a significant other may be gone someday.

The irrelevance of time to the unconscious places a fundamental limit on the degree and depth to which the finality of loss can be realized. There is a price to be paid for remaining in this unconscious sleep of denying our own death and the death of those closest to us. When the tragic dimension of loss is never fully internalized, when the potential final absence of a significant other is denied, our intimate relationships grow stale; we may take for granted that our loved ones will be around indefinitely.

I have wondered sometimes how long we would hold a grudge against a spouse if we were told that he or she would die the next day. If upon our hearing such news that grudge were to evaporate suddenly, as I believe many such grudges would, then we might conclude that we were playing a sort of unconscious gambling game with time. We were taking our chances that this person we cherish would not die in the midst of the tense silences. Some young adults, seeking to be free of parents with whom they are disenchanted, drastically reduce all contact with them. What would happen, however, while this young person occupies himself busily with the autonomous concerns of career and peer relationships, if his mother were to die of a heart attack? Nature is indifferent to our quest to fulfill our developmental prerogatives.

Somewhere deep inside of us we do not believe in the loss of the other, we will not accept it, we will not take "No" for an answer. This propensity of hope to spring eternal in the aftermath of loss also provides for a temporary resiliency, allowing us to bounce back and create further life for ourselves. Themes of restitution, restoration, and regeneration invariably accompany the loss experience. The mythological bird called the phoenix, rising from its own ashes, is an apt metaphor for the spontaneous unconscious tendency to resurrect replacements for valued people, places, ideas, or institutions. Freud (1908) has said: "Really we never can relinquish anything; we only exchange one thing for something else. When we appear to give something up, all we really do is adopt a substitute" (p. 145).

This process of unconsciously regenerating replacements for lost persons in our lives is at the heart of the transference. The illusion of the transference rests on denying the separate personhood of the therapist and re-creating the therapist in the image of a mother or father. The transference is not only a carryover of a familiar constellation of wishes and fears, representations, fantasies, and modes of relating, but is also an ongoing means of warding off the loss of the old and recognition of the new. By mimicking the ruthless movement of life marching on, the impersonal aspects of the transference, in which one person is interchangeable for another, become a means of perpetuating the omnipotent illusion of continuous survival.

When losses go on for too long or are too massive to bear, however, it may cause us to shrink back from the discovery of external reality and its time-bound world of living and dying. In reaction to a prolonged breakdown in the interchange of giving and receiving between ourselves and others, we curl in upon ourselves in a defensive stance of narcissistic self-enclosure. Without interpersonal openness, we are unable either to feel of effective use to others or to use the gifts we receive from others for our own growth. Rather than feel like an isolated, expendable creature, we react to any threat to our sense of significance by becoming more despairingly entrenched in a cut-off internal world of unconscious omnipotence, a world in which we make other persons over into our internal objects. Thus, the traditional psychoanalytic emphasis on the unconscious is reflected in the continuing use of terms such as "object" and "self object" to refer to persons. Without the civilizing influence exerted by a death-informed conscience and consciousness, it becomes all too tempting to cut a Faustian deal, and to use other persons, now transformed into internal objects, to patch together a narcissistic illusion of our own deathlessness.

The more we sense that our psychic survival is threatened, the more likely we are to fall back on our unconscious omnipotence and resort to a bottom-line or instrumental mode of relating to others. The embittering effects of our helplessness, despair, shame, and envy may accentuate this unconscious tendency to depersonalize human beings and to turn them into playthings that can be disposed of and retrieved according to our narcissistic whim. In the unconscious, the mutuality of Buber's (1958) I–Thou relationship may then be so depreciated that we may not view the other person as a singular Thou in and of herself, but only as one of many stepping-stones that can ensure our own survival.

Paradoxically, it is precisely because we do not accept the inevitability of death that we must strike down intimations of our mortality wherever we find them. To preserve our omnipotent illusion of continuous survival, we project our denied death onto other persons, who we then offer up as sacrificial victims to die in our stead. In this sense, human destructiveness has to do with destroying the impediment of death by disposing of others who carry our own mortality with them.

Becker (1975) thus suggests that the pervasive tendency to deny death is the mainspring of the human propensity to do evil. Evil here does not just have to do with actual killing, but also with the "soul murder" (Shengold 1991) of turning flesh-and-blood human beings into objects that are used as means toward our ends. Whether we are talking about the extreme case of Nazis turning human corpses into lampshades or ransacking teeth for gold fillings, or the much less extreme example of parents waking a baby up from a nap to display it to friends, we cannot seem to escape the universal potential of depersonalizing people by unconsciously extracting their souls from them and then feeding off their corpses (objects) to support our greater glory and survival.

In a more civilized vein, when we draw upon this self-preservative process of unconscious regeneration more resiliently, we are capable of transforming the defeat of loss into a source of strength and courage. Perhaps it was his indefatigable conviction of this power to regenerate that prompted Nietzsche to say, "Whatever does not kill me, makes me stronger." Klein (1940), too, has noted that suffering can lead to the further maturation of character, while Pollock (1989) has used the phrase "mourning–liberation" to describe the way we can use the mourning process as a springboard to creative and liberating expression.

SURVIVORSHIP AND THE URGE TOWARD REPARATION

If taken seriously, the incongruity of surviving and even benefiting from the loss of a loved one can be morally disquieting. Even the simple experience of enjoying and laughing at a TV comedy program six months after the death of a loved one may seem somehow inappropriate to the survivor of loss. How can I be laughing when I am never to see my beloved again? Perhaps what discomfits the survivor is that the amoral, unconscious process by which we impersonally regenerate replacements for persons can extend, in its extreme form, to the systematic, ruthless pursuit of Nazi-like ends. In this regard, it is significant to note Danieli's (1989) observation that for Holocaust survivors not to remember and grieve over the dead would mean to become the moral equivalent of the Nazis themselves.

Historically, the problem of survivor guilt has been studied in relation to the massive losses of Holocaust survivors. I would suggest, however, that the concept has far broader applicability. The unconscious tendency to regenerate hope in the wake of loss, and to use the death, decline, or misfortune of loved ones as a means to enhance one's own life characterizes the problem of survivorship, and complicates the process of coping with significant losses. To the extent that losses and separations are intrinsic to development, issues of survivorship are woven into the very fabric of the human endeavor.

Transitions between the end of one life and the birth of a new one can invoke such powerful self-recriminations of "separation guilt" that psychic growth may become a wrenching experience. Many people who come for clinical consultations have already initiated or are about to initiate developmental transitions in their lives. Such individuals often seem to be stuck in a developmental limbo between the old and the new, between remaining, for example, in a despised but familiar job or relationship and taking a leap of faith into the next unknown moment. Because such persons do not allow themselves to change and grow very easily, they may use life crises, character breakdowns, and accentuated symptomatology as opportunities to open themselves up to the process of further development. Sometimes it is only by becoming desperately ill to the point of saying "I can't take it anymore" that a person can acquire the requisite sense of moral right and accompanying courage to leap into the uncertainties of the future. It is as if we must first bear a sacrificial cross of suffering before proceeding with the "crime" of giving birth to new life for ourselves.

The tensions of survivorship are based in the discrepancy between the misfortune of the one left behind and the good fortune of the survivor who moves on, and are reflected in the envy felt by the less fortunate, the one who was left "for dead" and the guilt felt by the fortunate survivor. These tensions may create a movement toward equalizing the fortunes of both people, such that survivors may experience an urge to share or give back their good life, while envious persons have a corresponding urge to grab it away.

Consider the example of a young couple who are very much

looking forward to a party that their best friends are hosting on Saturday night. On Friday, the wife comes down with a fever of 101—not so high as to be dangerous, but high enough to prevent her from going to the party. How is this couple to resolve the predicament of their discrepant fortunes? Should the young husband say: "Honey, I love you very much. I don't want to go to the party without you and leave you all by yourself"? Or should the young wife say: "Dear, I love you. I want you to go to the party and have a good time. Don't worry about me. I'll be all right"?

Obviously, there is no correct answer to this value-laden dilemma. How we approach problems of this kind probably reveals much about our perspective regarding the relative virtues of togetherness versus individuation. Here, the tension of separateness is maintained by the guilt of the surviving individual who moves on or participates in the mainstream of life, and the imagined or real envy of the society or family or loved one left behind and left out. The urge to relieve the tensions of guilt and envy then contribute to a leveling process that is designed to equalize the fortunes of all. The construction of cultural norms and standards that ensure adherence to the loyalty ethic of all for one and one for all thus acts to minimize the likelihood of having to experience those emotions.

It is remarkable how rarely survivors seem to assume a generous love on the part of the one left behind, a love that would generate a feeling in the survivor that the best way to honor the dead is to live out the survivor's remaining life as fulfillingly as possible. Instead, many survivors imagine that, because of the possessive, envious quality of their love, the dead family members would begrudge them their continuing survival. Perhaps in the melancholic aftermath of loss survivors project their own guilty self-recriminations onto the dead, and then believe that the dead have envious designs to take their life back.

Innumerable Holocaust survivors have lost their entire families to the Nazi death camps. In their subsequent despair such individuals often deaden their pleasures and numb their passions, as if to placate the imagined envy of their ancestors by joining them in their lifelessness. Through actions that speak volumes, survivors share and duplicate the misery of their unfortunate loved ones to show and prove their devoted love. Such togetherness, felt to bridge the gap of separateness, even in death, takes on a higher value than the pursuit of an impermissably solitary life.

Perhaps if mourning were rendered mechanically perfect, the process of letting go of the old would resemble an assembly line sequence of requisite grieving, replacing one lost object with another more available object, and then getting on with one's life without a misgiving glance backward. However, much to the disappointment of the person who says "I thought I dealt with that already," the process of giving up the old and encountering the new often is fraught with messy emotional ambivalences and guilts that prevent us from tidily closing the book on our losses. Without this sense of closure, there is no real impetus to say our final goodbyes. And perhaps that is just as well. For now, the incompleteness of mourning, as manifested in the poignant residue of nostalgic memory, becomes a means of linking with and giving personal dignity back to the corpse that must be left behind.

Thus, loss often seems to have the effect of throwing a new light on our relationships after it is too late to change them. Freud (1915) describes how we derive this dawning awareness of death from our experiences: "It occurred when primaeval man saw somebody who belonged to him die—his wife, his child, his friend—whom he undoubtedly loved as we love ours. . . . Then in his pain, he was forced to learn that one can die, too, oneself, and his whole being revolted against the admission; for each of these loved ones was, after all, a part of his own beloved self" (p. 293).

Where once we might have repressed thoughts of our own mortality as well as the death of our loved ones, now in the undeniable wake of the loss experience, we become preoccupied with reversing time and making amends. As if desperately imploring fate for a second chance to undo what has been done, to transform our once depreciated object into a resurrected person once again, our fantasies become dominated by wishes to reconcile with the loved one who is now idealized from afar. In this sense, our survivor guilt contributes to a reparative urge to elevate the lost love object (in our memory) to the status of a person, and to do so in a dramatically appreciative fashion.

When guilt is retained, with all its nostalgic ruminations and idealized reminiscences, it may function as a partial atonement to the dead for our natural narcissism. By thinking about, preoccupying ourselves with, and commemorating the dead person, we literally give back moments of our life to the loved one left behind. In this way, guilt, the authentic feeling of conscience, prompted by a newly evoked awareness that we all walk on mortal feet of clay, becomes a means of civilizing an individual's unconscious desires for a solitary deathlessness by broadening them to encompass a wider social network of familial and cultural traditions.

To the extent that our creativity springs from the force of this unconscious omnipotence with its power to regenerate, we must donate our created products to our abandoned objects as a sacrificial toll for the right to further life and self-revelation. We thus pay as we go. For example, Niederland (1989) has documented the many ways specific creations of numerous artists, writers, composers, and poets reverberate back to the specific losses suffered by those individuals, and Aberbach (1989) suggests that a survivor's creativity may be used as a tool for searching for and linking up with a loved one who has died. In the same way, when an athlete dies suddenly in the middle of a sports season, the rest of the team may dedicate the remainder of the season to that athlete. If the team is successful enough to win a championship trophy, the team members may speak of sharing the trophy with the deceased athlete. We have no choice but to find more meaning in each other than we do in a lonely eternal life.

STEVEN: SURVIVOR GUILT OR LOVE?

No more is this life-and-death struggle of survivorship more evident than in the transition from one generation to the next.

Loewald (1980b) addressed the matter very directly: "If we do not shrink from blunt language, in our role as children of our parents, by genuine emancipation we do kill something vital in them—not all in one blow and not in all respects, but contributing to their dying" (p. 395).

At the same time that children grow and come into their own, their parents are often beginning to decline in their own lives. Children must then struggle with a separation guilt for leaving parents in a downward lurch, a guilt that parallels the survivor guilt that Danieli (1989) noted in Holocaust survivors toward their deceased families. The intergenerational drama of declining parents and ascending children thus brings the themes of envy and guilt of survivorship and reparation into sharp focus.

Steven is a 40-year-old man whom I have seen in psychoanalytic psychotherapy twice a week for almost two years. When he arrived at this first session, he shied away from my extended hand, saying that he did not want to give me his cold. With a pained, hangdog expression on his face, Steven then told me his story.

He had suffered from chronic depression for many years ("for as long as I can remember"), and currently he felt trapped and depressed in his marriage and medical career. He told me that in his early twenties he began a seven-year psychotherapy that helped him at the time, but that it had reached a point of diminishing returns when he decided to leave. He had gone into therapy after his mother committed suicide by carbon monoxide poisoning while he was a medical resident. When I said that it seemed that had been a major event in his life, Steven wearily but pointedly conveyed to me that her suicide was only the logical culmination of her whole life. She had been a very loving but very possessive and depressed mother. Soon after he left for college (his father drove him there while his mother remained behind), she became more depressed, suffering from assorted somatic pains, especially to her back. Finding no relief from doctors, she took her own life when Steven was 23 years old.

Steven had less to say about his father. He was a survivor of the concentration camps who had lost his entire family in the

Holocaust. He described his father as a "very nice man, but inef-
fectual as a father," who frequently took the path of least resistance
in family squabbles. Steven said his father also was depressed, although he tended to be more sociable outside of the family.

Much of Steven's complaint had to do with how he "fell" into
the life he had now. After three torrid, passionate, but short-lived
relationships that were permeated by his "over-excitement" and
the self-perceived incompetence of premature ejaculations, Steven
had consciously decided to find someone "less exciting and more
stable." He met his wife on a group tour and never missed an
opportunity to remind me that "he did not even notice her" at
first. After a courtship in which he perceived that she took the
initiative and he was only a bystander, they got married. It was only
when she became pregnant with their daughter that he realized
that he was not attracted to her and that she "did not have a lot
on her mind."

It was a similar story with Steven's choice of career. He became
a gastroenterologist, but claimed he did not know how he came
to be in medicine. He expressed resentment toward both of his
parents for not guiding him more actively into a career. He said
he did not feel much for his patients and did not think he was
very competent. Indeed, Steven often said he did not feel very
much at all for the people around him.

As themes of resentment and guilt about his mother's suicide
emerged early in treatment, Steven expressed irritation with his
previous therapist for not helping him cope earlier with this major loss. In each area of Steven's life there was a pervasive pattern
of inhibition and passivity leading to a ghost-like existence, only
to give way later to a sense of regret, resentment, and depression.

About nine months into treatment, Steven and I had a significant exchange. One day he came in and began his comments
by saying, "I don't know what your opinion is of these sorts of
things. . . ." He then proceeded to tell me he was thinking of attending an experiential weekend retreat, and he was wondering
what I thought about the idea. I replied that I usually was skepti-
cal about quick-fix programs, but that if he did not have very high

expectations, perhaps he might be able to get something out of it. In examining what I said in retrospect, I recognized that I have an almost constitutional aversion to programs that tempt people to take the easy way out and flee awareness through mass suggestion. I sensed also that Steven was probably searching for a sudden catharsis that would bypass the labor of words and his self-punitive consciousness and transform his inner deadness into emotive life. A few weeks later he went on the retreat and I wished him luck.

A few days later Steven began his next session with the statement "If you had seen me immediately after the seminar I would have looked very different. I almost feel like two different people the last forty-eight hours." Steven went on to tell me about the retreat, how he had shared his problems with the group, and how he had attained a genuine feeling of emotional release. The program culminated with a party where, to his delight, his wife surprised him as his "special guest." Steven then said that the elation of the weekend began to disappear on Monday, and especially on that Tuesday at work, the same day he was to see me that evening.

I returned to his first statement of the hour, "If you had seen me . . ." and suggested that he may have felt he had to relinquish his good mood very quickly for my sake and that he may have interpreted my reservations about his participation in the seminar as my jealousy of a rival therapy program. Out of loyalty to me he had made sure that he gave up whatever therapeutic gains were gotten without me and that were a betrayal of our relationship. Those were also the stringent conditions of possessiveness that he perceived his mother exacted in exchange for her loving him passionately. In this way, he brought his "gift" of morbid identification with his mother's deadness into our relationship and attempted also to give me a reparative gift of his misery so as to join me in my forsaken state. As long as he derived no joy from his heretical experience of independence, I would have no reason to feel angry at his betrayal. Steven took what I had to say under advisement, but agreed that it was strange how quickly the elation of the weekend disappeared right before he was to see me.

In letting Steven know what I thought of the weekend seminar I opened up the transference to his stringently constricting compulsion to take care of me. Perhaps, I suggested, knowing about the suffering of others did not necessitate his doing something about it, especially to the point of sacrificing his own life self-destructively. Love need not be expressed by keeping a person in distress company out of guilt for leaving the nest. Steven and I discussed how it may be possible to love with compassion and even experience sadness for others without joining them in their bereftness.

THE REPARATIVE NEED OF CHILDREN TO GIVE BACK TO PARENTS

A child now is faced with a dilemma of the first order: to carve out a solitary path separate from the indoctrinations of parents while healing the rupture left behind. In this respect, the parental acceptance of a child's offerings helps facilitate a reconciliation or reunion with the parent. In a sense, a child's gifts may provide a mother with compensation for the "sin" of separating from her. By accepting or internalizing those gifts, the mother enables her child to redeem his trophies in exchange for separating from her and giving continual rebirth to new life for himself.

We typically think of unconditional acceptance as something that children receive *from* their parents. However, at the same time that children are receiving such acceptance, they also are being accepted or received *by* their parents as a "gift from heaven." Thus, when patients complain that no matter what they do they cannot gain a parent's approval and it never seems to be good enough for the parent, they may be conveying that they had not been accepted or received as a gift.

When a parent is able to receive the offerings of a child graciously and show appreciation, a developmental flexibility and dynamism may be created that enables the child to move both closer and further away from the parent. From this perspective, development proceeds not only by way of the oscillating rhythms of regression and progression, but also through a give-and-take with the previous generation. And just as under ideal developmental circumstances, it is difficult to distinguish the movement of progression from "active" regression (Loewald 1980a), so too it is not easy to differentiate who is giving and who is receiving in a loving interchange between parent and child. The rhythms of progression-regression and giving-receiving thus may be interwoven so as to propel the developmental process forward. For example, the hard-earned accomplishments and created products of the progressive, self-expansive phase of the developmental process (first stick figure drawings, first bowel movements, school grades, career successes, one's own children, an authored book [!]) derive much of their value as trophies brought home during the regressive self-surrendering phase of the process and offered as sacrificial gifts to parents and/or their transferential surrogates. Thus, Klein and Riviere (1953) emphasize that guilt and the urge toward reparation are fundamental incentives to creativity and to work in general.

The gracious acceptance of these gifts enables the child to gain access to the inner space of the parent. In the aftermath of taking leave of a parent, the child's offering, as a stand-in for himself, is intended, at least symbolically, to heal the wound created by his departure and make the relationship with the parent whole again. Once the child is internalized by the parent and thereby gains a sense of belonging, he may feel worthy enough to internalize the emotional fuel necessary for his own further growth.

We often think of narcissistic adults as individuals who have developmental deficits, people who are emotionally empty because they have not received enough early mirroring (Kohut 1977). Such persons often feel that they have not been recognized or received as treasured gifts in and of themselves, but rather that they were exploited as disposable objects. Mirroring itself is a process of simultaneous giving and receiving. When viewing the developmental process from this perspective, we realize how essential the parents' capacity to receive their children's offerings graciously is to the development of healthy self-confidence and the creative unfolding of the child's identity. Winnicott (1954–1955) suggested that the infant cannot truly receive until first giving to the mother.

Yet for parents who are insulated self-protectively behind their characterological defenses, the vulnerability required to receive from another may be a daunting emotional challenge. Genuine receiving is a complex and active process that requires us to risk opening up to another person. In contrast, as Winnicott (1960b) made clear, people can give compliantly and obligatorily with the mask of a caretaking False Self without ever making themselves vulnerable to others. Indeed, sometimes compulsive giving may be a means of foreclosing an anxiety about receiving.

We frequently hear our patients speak about the caretaking heroics of their depressed mothers—women who were able, more or less, to sublimate their masochism in the generous deeds of self-sacrificing motherhood, but who did not allow themselves to receive or enjoy the offerings of love from their children. And yet the mother's acceptance of her children's gifts is precisely the price that must be paid in order for them to separate from her with secure and good conscience. In such circumstances, when a mother does not appear to appreciate or benefit from her children's gifts in any lasting way, children may feel an increasing paradoxical pressure to give up more of themselves in order to separate from the mother's unhappy state.

In leaving a piece of himself behind, a child is able to anchor himself securely in time and place, thus reducing the anxiety of separateness and guilt for leaving the parent. Fairbairn (1941) states that the parents' acceptance of their child's love enables the child to renounce infantile dependence without misgiving. And Winnicott (1954–1955) emphasizes that "the small child must go on having a chance to give in relation to guilt belonging to instinctual experience, because this is the way of growth" (p. 271). It is this sense of guilt consequent upon separation that prompted Loewald (1980b) to observe, "The self, in its autonomy, is an atonement structure, a structure of reconciliation, and as such a supreme achievement" (p. 394).

The lifelong process of separating and individuating is motivated, perhaps paradoxically, by an aim to reconcile with others.

In a sense, we could say the movement of development itself is impassioned toward an other who we imagine is awaiting us in the future. Our life derives its continuing meaning to the extent that it can be fashioned as a creative gift to be surrendered to this imaginary other. Carse (1980) puts it succinctly: "Our life is not our own in the sense that it belongs exclusively to us; however, it becomes our own to the degree that we share it, make a gift of it to others" (p. 5).

2

Conscience and the Ethic of Mutuality: Human Development as a Passionate Labor of Gratitude

If one does not hope, one will not find the un-hoped for, since there is no trail leading to it and no path.

—Heraclitus

To begin with oneself, but not to end with oneself; to start from oneself, but not to aim at oneself; to comprehend oneself, but not to be preoccupied with oneself.

—Martin Buber

LIVING FOR SOMETHING
BEYOND ONESELF

As members of one human race, we all own and belong to each other to some degree. We recognize the same strivings and inhibitions, the same pleasures and griefs in others that we are so well acquainted with in ourselves. If it were not for these identifications with the experiences of other people, neither the most loving acts of generosity nor the most hateful acts of spite would be possible. For better and for worse, we share in a common bond of humanity that provides a universal mirror of conscience for all of us.

In psychoanalytic theory, the terms *conscience* and *superego* typically have referred to the internalization of cultural norms for what is good and bad. In this view, morality is predicated primarily on an identification with the inhibitions and prohibitions set down by primary caretakers. Often what prompts these identifications are *fears* of consequences such as abandonment, disapproval, and retaliation. Thus, this morality of the superego is based on the coercive threat of consequences.

Here, I am seeking to understand a different source of ethical action, one that has its basis in gratitude and generosity and is manifested in the spontaneous *wish* to offer oneself and one's creations to others. Whereas the superego is derived more narrowly from the relative mores of a given culture, the ethical knowledge of conscience—that suffering can and should be redeemed—emerges from the experiences of want and fulfillment. As such, it is an ethical knowledge that is at once very personal and universal.

Erikson (1964) uses the terms moral and ethical to differentiate these contrasting orientations:

> I would propose that we consider moral rules of conduct to be based on a fear of threats to be forestalled. These may be outer

threats of abandonment, punishment and public exposure, or a
threatening inner sense of guilt, of shame or of isolation. . . . In
contrast, I would consider ethical rules to be based on ideals to
be striven for with a high degree of rational assent and with a
ready consent to a formulated good, a definition of perfection,
and some promise of realization. [p. 222]

Fromm (1947) has, in a similar way, distinguished between
"authoritarian conscience" and "humanistic conscience," stating
that humanistic conscience is "the voice of our true selves that
summon us back to ourselves, to live productively, to develop fully
and harmoniously, that is, *to become what we potentially are*" (p. 163).

As the wish to give of ourselves to an imagined other in the
future provides us with sufficient courage to propel development
forward, our personal truth or conscience guides the construction
of our individual destinies. By choosing to highlight the way psychological growth emerges from the smooth working of mutuality
in giving and receiving, I am describing a somewhat ideal world.
It is my belief, however, that we cannot adequately study how and
why things go wrong in people's lives until we cultivate a vision of
healthy development for ourselves.

While we share a deeply felt sense of purpose and destiny with
our fellow human beings, we also strive not to sink into a faceless
sea of collective anonymity. We play and work, we create and destroy to make a name for ourselves and to contribute uniquely to
the human endeavor. The recognition and acceptance of our
unique offerings engenders in us a sense of worth or personal
dignity of having a special part to play within the whole.

In this regard, the crucial element needed for an individual
life to have meaning beyond the bare bones of existence is to have
something to live for. A person may adapt and survive through
any number of terrible experiences, but those adaptations take
their toll, because to be a mere survivor of trauma may distort what
it is to be a person. The notion of a meaningful life that transcends
the self is not merely an existential appendage that becomes relevant only after our most basic needs are met and biological sur-

vival is secured. To attempt to disentangle the urge for transcendent meaning from the entirety of a human life is misguided. Living for something or someone other than oneself is fundamental to being human.

In concrete terms, this existential motivation to find one's individual place within the collective is manifested in a reciprocity of giving and receiving between oneself and others. In the previous chapter I suggested that children have a fundamental need to give of themselves and to be received graciously by their parents. At one and the same time that parents internalize their children's offerings, they also enable the children to secure a niche connecting them to the larger human enterprise. In feeling that they are contributing to their parents' intimate life, children attain an initial sense of transcendent meaning, a sense that their life has usefulness for something outside themselves. Whereas Winnicott (1969) emphasized that children must learn eventually to use their parents creatively as objects, I would add that they also must come to feel that they are cherished gifts who are *of use* or *useful* to their parents. Angyal (1965), in speaking of what he calls homonomy, says "To be, to exist on this level, is to mean something to someone else" (p. 18). He goes on to say that "the need to belong is expressed concretely in being of some use or service to another person, group or cause" (p. 21).

When all goes well, the mutuality of giving and receiving between parent and child seamlessly regulates the generosity and grace with which each takes the other into their respective worlds. This mutual exchange propels development forward as children gradually construct a sense of an individual self from their internalizations. This individual self in turn retains its lifeline to the collective by being internalized by the parent. As the child remembers the parent with a gift shared from her developing life, she is depositing a small memento for the parent to hold and remember her by as well. When a child is about to explore new surroundings, for example, she may place her belongings on her parent's lap for safekeeping. Parents frequently become receptacles of objects their children want to dispose of temporarily, but not to throw away. The parent's reception and holding of such offerings chronicles a history of the child's experiences, preventing them from dissolving into oblivion. The parent's internalization of these gifts thus enables the child to lay down and secure the roots of continuous experience that are intrinsic to the foundations of a personal identity.

BEYOND OMNIPOTENCE: NAVIGATING BETWEEN THE FAMILIAR AND THE STRANGE

As subjective agents of our lives, we embellish, minimize, dramatize, inhibit, and ultimately fashion a meaningful story from our experiences. In acts of constructiveness or spiteful destructiveness, our lives resemble works of art in which we are continually re-creating the realities that we encounter. Rank (1936) made the notion of living as an artistic process of self-creation a centerpiece of his will psychology. Each day brings with it hope for a meaningful "new beginning" (Balint 1968), an opportunity to create ourselves anew.

In and of itself, however, this creative process is incomplete. We require an audience to provide purpose for our dramas of self-expression. Thus, we do not create our narratives in a void, but always within the meaningful context of a relationship with another. In addition to actively transcribing our experiences, we also reenact those transcriptions in our relations with others, indelibly altering the meaning of the original experiences. A toddler who is comforted because he cried after banging his head on a door will have a very different experience than a child who has not been consoled. A parent's ability to respond to her child's sufferings has a profound impact on the evaluative meanings that the child imposes both on the original hurt of banging his head and his subsequent tears. If his cries are not heeded, the toddler is more likely to become more ashamed and self-conscious of the implicit plea for help conveyed by his tears. In this sense, a child's attitude toward his own sufferings as being good or bad is itself a transcription or internalized reflection of the quality of significant relationships.

It is through the validation provided by another person, one who remains outside what Winnicott (1960a) terms the "area of omnipotence," that we may discover something enduring in our experience. When someone else confirms that our creations are not just hallucinations, it is possible for us to step away from the second-guessings of self-enclosed isolation, of wondering whether an experience is nothing but our experience. The frenetic quality of chasing our own tails may finally be calmed only when we can find a mirror of who we are outside of ourselves. Just as Peter Pan emerged out of the Never-Never Land of fantasied possibilities to retrieve the lasting stability of his inescapable shadow, we yearn for some sort of real limits that would circumscribe and complete ourselves. The sense of safety and the calming effect provided by a holding environment derives from this sort of containment of our limitless, omnipotent fantasies.

One of the most important elements of psychotherapy occurs when, in the presence of another person, a patient can express a private image or thought out loud. This process of self-revelation transforms the patient's perspective on what he is saying, making it seem irrevocably real. It is precisely because of this overt, shared quality of the spoken word that many patients would prefer to avoid speaking of their dread. It is one thing to ponder the loss of a loved one privately, and something quite different to acknowledge that loss to another person. Recently, a 44-year-old married man told me—for the first time in ten months of treatment—that he has been suppressing homosexual fantasies since he was a child. As long as he kept his shame-ridden thoughts unarticulated, he could take comfort from the belief that they were just fantasies, that they were just part of a mental game he played with himself. In the aftermath of confessing his secret, he noted that "somehow, now it feels more real."

A child's sudden encounter with the new and strange, however, can threaten to disrupt his sense of continuity with chaotic disorientation. The transition from a familiar inner world of fantasy to an unpredictable external reality can be so abrupt that some reassurances from the yet-to-be discovered world are needed. In a sense, we provide these reassurances to ourselves through the ways we perceive and encounter others. Thus, as the ubiquitous phenomenon of the transference demonstrates, we seem almost instinctively to re-create what is novel in terms of something with which we are already well-acquainted. As Winnicott (1951) notes, "Sooner or later in an infant's development there comes a tendency on the part of the infant to weave other-than-me objects into the personal pattern" (p. 231). With the aid of imagining, thinking, and fantasizing, the child links up these new objects with his earlier patterns of experience, thus creating transitional objects out of what initially seemed strange.

These transitional objects, and the accompanying gradual buildup of an imaginative, intermediate space, buffer the encounter between self and other with soft, permeable boundaries. In this space, which Buber (1958) calls "the sphere of the between," there is a continuous interchange between what is inside and what is outside via projection and internalization. Thus, Loewald (1962) emphasizes that "on this level, we cannot speak of externalization (projection) and internalization as defenses (against inner conflict or external deprivation), we must speak of them as boundary creating processes. . . ." (p. 266).

Because this boundary is not hard-edged and impenetrable, the shift from internal to external is not abrupt and discontinuous; it is a vital, mutually interpenetrating "potential space" (Winnicott 1971) of give-and-take in which creative living occurs. It is only when our perceptions and creations have applicability outside the circles of our own making that we may arrive at a sense that our experience is real, or feel a sense of realization. The creations that we offer that are then received by others are a vital demonstration of this process of realizing our experiences. Through this give-and-take, our influence and impact on others reassures us continually that we are not alone, that we have not merely conjured up the world in which we live. Thus, Diane

Margolis (1998) states, "when we give gifts, we break down . . . boundaries and create, instead of me and you or mine and yours, us and ours" (p. 109).

As we create what we find and find what we create, we gradually attain a sense of the real, *but at our own pace*. These resonances of the familiar provide us with sufficient reassurances so that we can venture out and create anew. Perhaps paradoxically, it is when parents respect and take seriously the created illusions and dramas of their child's play by joining in, that the child, in turn, upon becoming an adult, feels sufficiently generous to come out of the world he knows and to acknowledge the realities of others. In this regard, Jerome Miller (1988) speaks of generosity as a form of hospitality and receptivity to otherness.

This sort of generosity is essential to psychological growth. Children, buoyed with courage by repeated interchanges of give-and-take with significant others, can voluntarily let go of their established personal pattern and risk losing themselves in the unknown. Along these lines, Mitchell (1988) points out that healthy narcissism reflects a balance between illusion and reality. He sees the process as one in which "illusions concerning oneself and others are generated, playfully enjoyed, and relinquished in the face of disappointments" (p. 195).

Each such separation, however, is contained immediately by an ever-expanding transitional space in which new experiences with others are re-created in terms of what is familiar. New illusions are then created out of the dissolution of old ones. Thus, Winnicott (1971) notes that "it could be said that with human beings there can be no separation, only a threat of separation" (p. 108). This transitional space between the subjective and the objective is enriched continually by experiences that are initially beyond the child's creative imagination but then infused with it. The realization of experience, then, is an ongoing process comprised of gradual disillusionments and encounters with bits of new reality that are re-created in the image of a continually evolving personal pattern.

As Winnicott (1951) aptly reminds us, "It is assumed here that the task of reality acceptance is never completed, that no human being is free from the strain of relating inner and outer reality and that relief from this strain is provided by an intermediate area of experience" (p. 240). For Winnicott (1971), this intermediate area of experience is a "potential space, one that can become an infinite area of separation, which the baby, child, adolescent, [and] adult may creatively fill with playing" (p. 108). In this regard, Horton (1981) suggests that transitional relatedness is a lifelong developmental process.

DEVELOPMENTAL HOPE AND BUILDING THE BRIDGE OF CONSCIENCE

To understand better the developmental inspiration and evolution of this paradox of creating what we find and finding what we create, I would like to refer to the first building block of originality, "the spontaneous gesture" or "gift gesture," a term coined by Winnicott (1956). Winnicott (1951) suggests that when "the mother places the actual breast just there where the infant is ready to create, and at the right moment" (p. 239), the infant begins to develop an illusion that there is an external reality that synchronizes with its own imagined creations. Here at the very beginning of life, the external reality of the mother's breast that is "found" corresponds very closely, almost exactly, with what the child conceived.

The mother's finely attuned appreciation of the baby's spontaneous gesture is her way of granting a gracious reception to the original gift of her baby's birth. Her capacity to accept her gift— by meeting the infant's spontaneous gesture—also has to do with her finding the child she physically and imaginatively conceived. This first welcome mat is the ground for the infant's "basic trust" (Erikson 1950) in the world's receptiveness to its search for belonging. In this way, a child's sense that there is a particular niche suited to him and awaiting his arrival lends meaning to the impetus to create and grow. As Dinnage (1978) points out, "the key to the making of things is concurrence; when what the child expects and what the world offers intersect" (p. 370).

Each time the baby discovers in the outside world the gratification of which he himself conceived, the unknown becomes more inviting; it is a mirror of his own creation. The baby, however, cannot remain for too long in the illusion that the world is just a figment of his creative imagination. As Winnicott (1951) says, "*if all goes well* the infant can be disturbed by a close adaptation to need that is continued too long, not allowed its natural decrease, since exact adaptation resembles magic and the object that behaves perfectly becomes no better than an hallucination" (p. 238). To begin to realize his experience, the baby must, at least momentarily, emerge out of his illusory universe. Thus, as Winnicott (1951) notes, "*If all goes well* the infant can actually come to gain from the experience of frustration, since incomplete adaptation to need makes objects real" (p. 238).

What then moves the child toward an ever-increasing, but never completed acknowledgment of reality? Toward some degree of appreciation of the independent, separate reality of others? To answer these questions, I would like to refer to Winnicott's (1967a) lucid description of the time factor when a baby is separated from its mother: "The feeling of the mother's existence lasts x minutes. If the mother is away more than x minutes, then the image fades and along with this the baby's capacity to use the symbol of the union ceases. The baby is distressed, but this distress is soon *mended* because the mother returns in $x + y$ minutes" (p. 97).

What is the baby experiencing during those extra "$x + y$" minutes, during that interval when the mother's image is fading?

As if he were entering a chasm yawning menacingly between the safety of two cliffs, the infant momentarily falls into the space of the not-self, a space in which the virtual synchrony of creating and finding is temporarily broken. What was originally the flush, glorious pleasure of the baby being sole author of his life now becomes the solitude of lonely searching for the mother's reply. Yet this immersion in the depths of solitude also brings an increasing acquaintance with the abyss of nonbeing. As long as the mother remains absent, the infant exists outside the bridge of creating and finding, stuck in the limbo of the emptiness in between. If the baby were to continue to grope in silence for a prolonged period of time, he would experience what Winnicott (1967a) refers to as "unthinkable anxiety," a sense of desolation that would paralyze any further creative initiative.

With the mother's return, the baby's search is contained by her renewed presence. The temporary disruption in his sense of continuity is restored to the mutual interplay of creating and finding again. But not before the anxieties of early searchings and yearnings have sensitized the baby to the experiences of nonbeing and absence, and perhaps to suffering in general. Bridging the gap to the mother instills the hope that such sufferings can be redeemed, that bad can be made good again. Thus, as Erikson (1964) states, "Hope is the enduring belief in the attainability of fervent wishes, in spite of the dark urges and rages which mark the beginning of existence" (p. 118).

If a bridge to the mother were not discovered and the baby's sufferings continued indefinitely, the despair of madness and bitterness would overwhelm the hope to find the good. For inner-city youths who have been inundated and surrounded by violence and poverty, and who have no obvious escape route by which to improve their lives, it is a daunting challenge to retain hope without the experience of fulfillment. By contrast, sometimes children who have been pampered with overly uneventful, comfortable childhoods may lack the impetus and passion to venture beyond their safely insulated worlds. Without the challenge of want, the foundation for the realization of experience with a genuine other would not be laid down. Gaddini and Gaddini (1970) note that where the mother is intrusive and ever present, there is no impetus for the child to develop symbolic representation or creative thinking.

As the cycle of the mother consoling the baby's sufferings is repeated, the child begins to internalize a knowledge of the good, of the ideal, that is grounded in his actual experiences of want followed by fulfillment. It is this inner knowledge that a bridge may be built with an other over a gulf of nonbeing that forms the basis of conscience. Thus, the term conscience derives from the Latin, *con-scientia*, "knowing together" or "knowing with." In this regard, Erikson (1964), too, speaks of the infant's initial experiences of the caretaking person as a "first knowledge, the first verification, and thus the basis of hope" (p. 117).

FROM SYNCHRONY TO MUTUALITY: GRATITUDE AND THE GENEROUS RELINQUISHMENT OF THE MOTHER

The mother's resonating reply to the baby's wants, internalized as a voice of conscience, spurs a grateful impulse to respond to the mother in kind. Klein (1957) has said that a sense of gratitude reflects an introjection of the good object that if strong enough, can offset the infant's envy and greed. A child's gratitude may spur the wish to nurture the mother generously, as she nurtures him. This may be illustrated in such situations as when a child spontaneously places a spoon in his mother's mouth while she is feeding him. In this small interchange of give-and-take we see an embodied illustration of the ethic of mutuality, the Golden Rule, "Do unto others as you would have them do unto you." This maxim of reciprocity lies at the heart of conscience, as now the baby is moved to sustain his mother's life as she sustains his.

In this way, from the very beginning of life the mother's responsiveness to the spontaneous gesture of the infant infuses development with a definite ethical cast. All ensuing experiences are filtered through a sense of want (bad) and/or fulfillment (good). In referring to the mother's fundamental recognition of the child, Loewald (1978) says, "This primal reflection and recognition brings about a *conscire* within the infant–mother psychic matrix and gradually becomes a crucial constituent, a potential of the child's individuating experiencing" (pp. 13–14). Loewald suggests that *conscire*, or knowing together, is a prelude to conscience and forms a basis for the morality of mental development.

For the individuating child, the dialectic of want and fulfillment is played out most crucially in the alternative rhythms of appearance and disappearance. In a well-known example concerning this theme, Freud (1920) noticed how his 18-month-old grandson threw a wooden spool with a string attached over the edge of his bed. Each time the string disappeared, he would let out an o–o–o–o sound. He then pulled back the spool and yarn and exclaimed "*da*" (there). Through his play, Freud's grandson began to internalize the rhythms of appearance and disappearance.

We might think of Winnicott's (1969) notion of the infant's destruction of an object and the object's survival of that destructiveness in connection with Freud's grandson. For Winnicott, it is "the destruction of the object that places the object outside the area of the subject's omnipotent control" (p. 90) because, in a psychological sense, the object has disappeared. In this regard, the survival of the object is analogous to the reappearances of the string for Freud's grandson.

Just as the infant's experience of want leads him to an appreciative gratitude when discovering fulfillment, his experience of loss enables him to feel grateful when the mother reappears. This gratitude spurs a passion of generosity that moves the baby to let go of her again. Paradoxically then, internalizing the mother's presence stimulates a generosity to give her away. In his brilliantly evocative book, *The Gift*, Lewis Hyde (1979) points out that it is only when a gift actually becomes ours that it can be released or passed along.

From the infant's point of view, we might think of separation-individuation not so much as the child taking leave from the mother but as a progressive relinquishment of omnipotent control over her. In this regard, the infant's gradual destruction of his omnipotently held mother is an act of generous relinquishment and granting of autonomy to her. In the spirit of mutuality, the baby's incremental acceptance of the mother's separateness is a generous response of reciprocity to her giving and nourishing his burgeoning life.

Developmentally speaking, this gradually increasing recognition of the mother's personhood is the only way to go. Thus, as Benjamin (1988) points out, "The need of the self for the other is paradoxical, because the self is trying to establish himself as an absolute, an independent entity, yet he must recognize the other as like himself in order to be recognized by him. He must be able to find himself in the other" (p. 32). Winnicott (1969) notes that when the object is destroyed it "develops its own autonomy and life, and (if it survives), contributes into the subject, according to its own properties" (p. 90). Lynch (1965) makes a similar point: "This relationship of hope and help must be one of mutuality. I must not be in such a relationship to objects that I vanish out of the picture, I am destroyed. And the reverse is also true: ideally the object in coming to one must find itself. It is the hope for this mutuality that is the secret of all our hopes" (p. 44).

THE CALLING OF CONSCIENCE: DEVELOPMENT AS A GRATEFUL MOVEMENT TOWARD AN AWAITING OTHER

If we view conscience as an internalized voice of knowing together that we project into the future, we may imagine a reverberating echo or calling out to us in return, as if from the wilderness. The calling of conscience reveals the original template of knowing together in this linking of present with future. With increasing faith that the experience of separateness will be bridged, the infant can begin to move from a synchronous relationship with the mother to one of mutual recognition.

As the child repeatedly separates and relinquishes and then re-finds the mother, his gratitude inspires him to transform the empty spaces between them into a creatively fashioned gift for her. Hyde (1979) terms this process a "labor of gratitude." He states,

> I would like to speak of gratitude as a labor undertaken by the soul to effect the transformation after a gift has been received. Between the time a gift comes to us and the time we pass it along, we suffer gratitude. . . . Passing the gift along is the act of gratitude that finishes the labor. The transformation is not accomplished until we have the power to give the gift on our own terms. [p. 47]

The impassioned movement of gratitude to respond in kind
to the calling of conscience drives development forward courageously, making it possible to bear the inevitable transitions and
losses of psychic growth. We can understand this movement toward one's calling more clearly if we think of it in terms of a young
toddler who is just learning how to walk. Perhaps the first time
the toddler stands on his feet, his mother calls out from the other
end of the room, "Come here, honey, here I am." As he takes his
initial tentative steps toward her, she continues encouragingly, "You
can do it, that's it." The toddler, in turn, beams with pleasure at
his newly discovered competence. This sense of accomplishment
and the incentive to move toward his mother's voice derives much
of its meaning from her appreciative recognition of his creative
feat.

After the toddler reaches her in a warm, happy embrace, the
mother now walks around the corner, out of clear sight and calls
her child's name from there. His memory of her pride in him
inspires the child to search for her again over the uncertain spaces
separating them. Eventually, as her voice becomes internalized as
his own calling, he can move toward others. In this regard, Gaddini
and Gaddini (1970) have also noted the role of the mother's voice
as a transitional phenomenon.

Erikson (1964) declares that "the mutuality of adult and baby
is the original source of hope, the basic ingredient of all effective
as well as ethical human action" (p. 231). Through the ethic of
mutuality, in which the child is moved to respond to the mother's
ministrations in kind, we can discern a close link between conscience and responsibility. In heeding the voice of conscience, we
come to know that "no man is an island, but a part of the main"
(Donne 1624). To be true or responsible to ourselves is to be
answerable to others. We are to care for one as we care for the
other. In the book of the Upanishads, the universal structure of
mutuality comes through clearly: "he who sees all beings in his
own self and his self in all beings."

Often there is a clear link between harming another person
and not remaining true to oneself. Buber (1965) describes this

interpersonal sense of responsibility eloquently: "Existential guilt occurs when someone injures an order of the human world whose foundations he knows and recognizes as those of his own existence and of all common human existence" (p. 117). Perhaps it is this interdependent bridge of conscience, of knowing together, that Martin Luther King Jr. had in mind when, in describing the oppression of black people, he expressed concern for the spiritual degradation of their white oppressors.

In the silently reflective aftermath of doing malicious injury to another, the perpetrator, if open to his conscience, feels the backbite of remorse. In committing such harm, he knows that he has not held true to the memory of his own suffering; he had not heeded faint whispers attesting to his knowledge that suffering can and should be redeemed. In this sense, a mother's gentle admonition to her child, "you know better," may be a reminder of obscured hope following acts perpetrated out of despair and bitterness.

HEEDING THE VOICE OF CONSCIENCE AND CULTIVATING A PERSONAL TRUTH

The relational basis of conscience, of knowing together, binds an individual's personal truth to the universal ideals of the Golden Rule. Guided by this knowledge of conscience, we trust that we will find a credible mirror of our own being in the unknown, in the unscripted freedom of others. With hope in hand and animated by the passion of gratitude, the ethic of mutuality thus weaves together the development of a singular destiny with the interdependent human fabric of which it is a unique part.

Hyde (1979) says, "An abiding sense of gratitude moves a person to labor in the service of his *daemon*. The opposite is properly called narcissism. The narcissist feels his gifts come from himself. He works to display himself, not to suffer change" (p. 53). Hyde defines "daemon" as that which "comes to us at birth. It carries with it the fullness of our undeveloped powers. These it offers to us as we grow, and we choose whether or not to accept, which means we choose whether or not to labor in its service" (p. 53).

Hyde's notion of the daemon follows in the tradition of a number of existential philosophers who have suggested that human freedom resides not so much in our limitless possibilities as in choosing whether to accept some essence or destiny in ourselves. Ortega y Gasset (1964) puts it this way: "Life means the inexorable necessity of realizing the design for an existence which each one of us is . . . our will is free *to realize or not to realize* this vital design which we ultimately are. . . . Life is essentially a drama because it is a desperate struggle—with things and even with our character—to succeed in being in fact that which we are in design. . . ." (p. 118).

For Buber (1952), destiny is not a design but a calling to respond to the outside world. In this sense, every human being, having something unique to contribute, is called to respond and fulfill his potentiality. Tillich (1963) clarifies this intertwining connection between conscience and responsibility as an impetus to self-realization:

> A moral act is not an act in obedience to an external law, human or divine. It is the inner law of our true being, of our essential or created nature, which demands that we actualize what follows from it. . . . And an antimoral act is not the transgression of one or several precisely circumscribed commands but an act that contradicts the self-realization of the person as a person and drives toward disintegration. [p. 20]

By discovering and re-creating others in the image of what is familiar to us, we pay continual homage to our respective life stories, to our evolving sense of personal integrity. In so doing, we hold true to our particular "going-on-being" (Winnicott 1956), or to what Bollas (1989) terms our "inner idiom." Thus, destiny lies neither in the distant past nor the distant future; it is not set at birth nor determined by our ultimate destinations. The evolution of a destiny is a dynamic process that is enriched continually by difference, by novelty, by the unpredictability of others. Our personal truths are found and re-created in interactions with the freedom of others.

A human life may be viewed as a creative medium that is both inspired by and generated toward an other. A passion of generosity, or the impetus to give ourselves over to others, underlies the creative process of human development. When others accept our creatively fashioned gifts, we find a real mirror to our spontaneous gesture. In this sense, our gifts and their reception are the meaning-making commerce through which we emerge from our spheres of omnipotence. A resonating reply from an other consecrates our dramatic stories by completing the circle of meaning from without.

Finding ourselves through the reception granted by an other breathes life into or inspires a constructive illusion of our singularity. This sense of singularity provides us with the indispensable meaning and courage to move on with our lives. When our uniquely generated gifts are accepted, it enables us to embrace our singular destiny rather than become resigned to the fate of possessing but one limited life. Through the relational bridge of conscience, we creatively transform our life from one determined by the capriciousness of fate into a destiny that is actively chosen.

This choice of onself can be seen as akin to Erikson's (1950) concept of Ego Integrity. Erikson describes ego integrity as "the acceptance of one's one and only life cycle as something that had to be and that, by necessity, permitted of no substitutions" (p. 268). Paradoxically, the achievement of this sense of integrity is not gained in and by that life alone, because ego integrity refers to a sense of having lived one's life according to one's conscience. That is, a sense of integrity in relation to oneself is at one and the same time keeping faith with others and the cosmos.

It is when we have the firm conviction of our singular integrity—a sense of ourselves as unique individuals living at one time and one place—that we are prepared to greet the arrival of our greatest challenge, death. For the person with a sense of integrity, death is not an absurd fate detached from the remainder of his life: it is *his* death, it belongs to his life. In surrendering the generated gift of an integrated life to an imagined other in death, he anticipates finding a meaningful climax to his creative strivings.

Through the developmental rhythms of creating and finding, the sacred foundation of a lasting monument may be shaped from our experiences. Perhaps we could say that it is this process of forming a sacred monument of one's life that constitutes our singular destiny. Out of one's well-consummated creative fires a unique gift for the cosmos has been offered. Thus Becker (1973) concludes *The Denial of Death* with a statement of moving eloquence: "Who knows what form the forward momentum of life will take in the time ahead or what use it will make of our anguished searching. The most that any one of us can seem to do is fashion something—an object or ourselves—and drop it into the confusion, make an offering of it, so to speak, to the life force" (p. 285).

Part II

Disillusionment, Defense, and the Despair of Bitterness

3

Selling One's Developmental Soul: Self-Betrayal and Wearing the Mask of the Enemy

Me and death would be friends because I would kill people for him so he wouldn't take my soul.

—Lamar, 14 years old

Could this be the contrary nature of the soul meeting the sorrow of the world halfway, an instinctual knowledge that we cannot bear the pain of things until we somehow *resemble* them?

—Phil Cousineau, *Soul*

For whosoever will save his life shall lose it. For what shall it profit a man, if he shall gain the whole world, and lose his own soul?

—Mark 8:36

JIM: BECOMING WHAT YOU HATE

Jim is a 52-year-old man suffering from anxiety and depression. He complained that he could not seem to derive pleasure from his life. When, in our initial meeting, he asked whether I would be employing some form of behavior therapy, I suggested that such an intervention might compound the problem of his feeling mechanical and joyless. Maybe, I said, psychotherapy could help Jim view himself less like a performing machine and more like a human being.

Jim's father had left his mother while she was pregnant with Jim. She had already given birth to and raised Jim's two older sisters, the youngest of whom was seventeen years Jim's senior. From Jim's point of view, he was born into the unwelcoming arms of a bitter woman who was intent on making her son pay for the sins of his father. Jim spoke about his father abandoning his mother while pregnant with him with characteristic self-deprecating sarcasm: "Yeah, what a coincidence."

Without the welcome mat of a warm reception granted by a wished-for mother, Jim's life, from its inception, became a struggle to prove he was worthy of inclusion in the human race. Only perfection seemed to be enough to keep his mother's unrelenting criticisms at bay. From very early on, driven by fear, Jim tackled the project of being perfect as a serious, humorless task required to earn his keep. Striving to reach his goals with a preoccupying sense of purpose, he felt he could not afford to play around with other ways of looking at things, other more forgiving ways of living his life.

Each small success, each perfection attained, bought only a momentary peace, before once again he had to prove himself worthy to his demanding inner demons with ever more good works. As is often the case in the aftermath of trauma, the stakes of life and death invade even the trivial and the playful with their

transferential ghosts. Recently, Jim reported that he would ha-
rangue himself mercilessly if he had a less than perfect round of
golf. For the weary there is no rest. Jim had become his mother;
he saw the enemy, he made it his own, and now she dwelt within.
As long as Jim held on tenaciously to his self-enclosed world of
slave master and terrorized slave, his life could never be more than
one of treading water. To swim to something greater, something
transcendently meaningful in his life would necessitate opening
up with hopefulness to his need of another—and risking that he
would drown in the spaces in between.

Three years ago Jim finally opened up from his rigid stance of
self-enclosure in a men's group where men like him also stripped
away their masks to reveal their various degradations and shames
to each other. These men became bound together not only by their
mutual confessions of emotional nakedness, but also by a group
norm of cure that held that they did not have to feel ashamed of
themselves any longer. The problem was that Jim replaced the
norms set forth by his mother by borrowing the meanings set down
by the men's group. Because there is a group pressure to not feel
ashamed (Jim says it is a "no-no"), he is placed in the paradoxical
position of experiencing a sense of shame relative to the group
for feeling ashamed. He has transformed the arbitrary, consensu-
ally agreed upon meanings of his men's group into the guiding
objectivity of a new ego ideal to live by. By mistaking the consensual for the power of the absolute, Jim is able to flee from a di-
minished, exposed sense of self, hammered down by constant self-
criticism, and hide himself in the more expansive power of the
group.

This search for objectivity in group norms is relevant also to
individual psychotherapy. The shamed patient seeks to hang on
to the meanings conveyed by the therapist as a new standard of
perfection to live by. In this regard, Jim and I explored his continual stance of apology to the world, and his adherence to the
different expectations set forth by his various therapies. When I
inquired of him "What do you want?" Jim was stuck dumbly inarticulate, as if the notion of his own desire was quite alien to him.
Long ago, Jim had lost sight of his own path.

Jim's desperate quest for acceptability is not an uncommon malaise; it brings out in bold relief what is common to all of us. In spite of our laborious attempts to escape the experiences and relationships we have suffered from the most, we find ourselves strangely haunted by what we thought we put behind us. We come to resemble what we hate. We scream at our beloved children with the exact same words that our parents shouted at us; yet these rantings are but an externalized echo of the recriminations we direct at ourselves.

In this chapter I will begin to trace the course of disillusionment and to explore how our defensive adaptations to our disappointments often accentuate and perpetuate our problems. In the process of bracing for a repeat of our worst experiences, we develop a kind of tunnel vision dictated by a survival mandate: something bad is better than nothing. By adhering too strictly to our self-enclosing defenses, however, we lose the guidepost of our desires and the capacity to re-create our lives. Whether in relation to ourselves or to our children, we become our own worst enemies.

DISILLUSIONMENT: THE RUPTURE
OF INNOCENCE

One essential constituent of healthy development lies in the capacity of the child to retain some sense of integrity or organismic wholeness as he proceeds through life. Initially, the mother's meeting of the infant's "spontaneous gesture" (Winnicott 1956) establishes a synchrony and then a mutuality between what is created and what is found, as well as a fluidity between a wish conjured up and a wish fulfilled. This fluidity fosters a constructive illusion of continuity, or what Winnicott calls "going-on-being." The philosopher Henri Bergson (1889) refers to this unconscious sense of continuity as a sense of duration.

The baby's created image of the mother is substantively nurtured when the baby is able to find some resemblance to that image in the real mother of the external world. This interplay of creating and finding himself through the reflected eyes of the mother contains the lonely process of searching. The baby's sense of omnipotence, thus reinforced, lays the foundation for a positive superstition: "What I wish for, I shall find." This positive superstition underlies the baby's innocence.

Innocence refers to the child's elemental conviction that he is welcome in a world that is benignly disposed toward himself. It is a constructive illusion that enables the baby or child to place his well-being trustfully in the protective arms of parents waiting to receive and care for him. Innocence thus consists of an unconscious, carefree sense that no matter which pathway one creates for one's developmental quest, the responsive home of a receptive audience is to be found at the other end. With each cycle of creating and finding, bridged by the giving of himself and acceptance by others, the child gradually gains a sense of belonging to the human endeavor. The reception of a child's uniquely fashioned gifts implicitly deems him worthy of entering into his significant relationships, as well as inclusion in humankind more generally. In this sense, a child's uniquely shaped offerings are a means of entering and exiting relationships with his individual dignity intact.

Implicit in this reliance on the receptivity and protection of others is an unconsciousness of impending threat. It is precisely this unawareness or innocence of evil that insulates an illusory sphere of going-on-being in which the child can play and explore in a carefree way. This sense of continuity then provides a secure base so that the child can remain open to the transformational possibilities of each new moment and space between himself and others. In relatively healthy development, this naturalistic buffer of innocence gives way only gradually to the disillusioning acknowledgment of unpleasant realities.

What occurs, then, when this sense of innocence is disrupted before its time? What happens when any number of impingements, frustrations, traumas, or prolonged separations prematurely evict a child from his private Garden of Eden? When the baby's created image of a wished-for mother does not match the reality of the real mother, the baby must begin to cope with the times and spaces between wish and reality. However, rather than conceiving of this separation between mother and child as an overtly physical one, perhaps we could describe problems in the quality of human relating with more phenomenological accuracy if we view the baby's initial experience of an alienating separateness as a widening discrepancy between the wished-for mother who is created and the actual mother who is found.

Perhaps we can better illuminate the baby's experience of the spaces separating creating and finding if we view it metaphorically as a solitary journey across a desert. At first, the baby relies on the internal compass of a maternal oasis to direct his quest. His hopeful conviction of reaching his destination provides the fuel of meaning necessary to supply his searchings. What occurs, however, if the child continues his journey across this private landscape without finding the mother he seeks, instead falling through the cracks between himself and others and remaining for too long in the chasm of nonbeing? Let us return to Winnicott's (1967a) description of a baby's experience of being separated from his mother as the time of her absence is extended: "In $x + y$ minutes the baby has not become altered. But in $x + y + z$ minutes the baby has become *traumatized*. . . . Trauma implies that the baby has experienced a break in life's continuity. . . ." (p. 97).

As long as the baby, toddler, or child continues to search for the created mother who is not there, he faces the prospect of encountering an unending solitude over infinitely empty expanses. When the baby's wished-for image of the mother is not supported by the experience of finding her really, the baby's creation remains just that: a hallucinatory image of a maternal oasis without substance—a mirage. When the internal compass of a hoped-for image of a mother breaks down, the guiding purposefulness of searching gives way to the vague aimlessness of mental wandering. Gradually, the infant's experience of absence may become increasingly flavored by a desperate *fear* of not finding the mother rather than by the *wish* to find her. A baby's too close encounter with a prolonged unresponsive silence to his yearnings forms the basis of negative superstition: "What I wish for, I fear I will not find." This experience is akin to the panic evident on the face of a young child who is stricken with the acute homesickness of waiting for his mother to pick him up from nursery school.

As the child becomes increasingly lost and disoriented, his whole being may be permeated with what Winnicott calls "unthinkable anxiety." André Green (1978) has noted: "Absence, paradoxically, may signify an imaginary presence or else unimaginable nonexistence" (p. 184). The madness of coming face to face with a mirageful silence is captured by Winnicott's (1967b) description of a patient who reported looking in a mirror and seeing nothing. Green (1978) refers to this as a "negative hallucination." This eerie intimation of nonbeing is similar to the experience of a very young child who loses his mother suddenly to death. In losing his secure footing, as if the rug were pulled out from under his feet, a child may lose his basic orientation to reality. From his viewpoint, a motherless world may feel like an interminable nightmare from which he longs to awaken.

This state of being is so unbearable that Winnicott (1967a) suggests "primitive defenses now become organized to defend against a repetition of 'unthinkable anxiety'" (p. 97). Perhaps it is in part because of this defensive determination to prevent a repeat of an encounter with nothingness that Winnicott (1967a) suggests

> the vast majority of babies never experience the $x + y + z$ quantity of deprivation. This means that the majority of children do not carry around with them for life the knowledge from experience of having been mad. Madness here simply means a *break-up* of whatever may exist at the time of *a personal continuity of existence*. After "recovery" from $x + y + z$ deprivation a baby has to start again permanently deprived of the root which could provide *continuity with the personal beginning*. [p. 97; original italics]

Trauma ruptures the illusory space that binds creating and finding, and that forms the innocent core of the baby's unconscious continuity of being. It is the defensive reaction to trauma, however, with its foreclosure of further openness and vulnerability, that seals off any possibility of restoring innocence to anything resembling its original form. In this sense, it is the combination of trauma and defense, of rupture and foreclosure that leads to the state Winnicott describes as a permanent deprivation of the root which could provide continuity with the baby's personal beginning.

INTROJECTING FRUSTRATION:
ADAPTATION AS A COUNTERPHOBIC
DEFENSE

Rather than face the madness of searching in a mirror for himself and seeing nothing, the baby adapts to the rupture of his innocence by taking the matter of his biopsychological survival into his own hands. This he does with the aid of counterphobic defenses. Whereas phobia entails a retreat from danger, counterphobia, in contrast, involves a movement toward precisely that which is most threatening or frustrating. As such, it is a means of adaptively rendering passive into active, of defending by taking the offensive.

In "Project for a Scientific Psychology," Freud's (1895) early notions of the ego originating as a defensive buffer against unpleasure reveal his awareness of a counterphobic means of adapting to frustration. Insofar as unpleasure remains the only means of education, the adaptation-seeking ego learns about reality by introjecting frustration. Later, the "non-occurrence of the expected satisfaction, the disappointment experienced" led to the development of the reality principle (Freud 1911, p. 219). For example, whereas at the initial stages of life, five minutes of the mother's absence might be too much to bear for the infant's instantaneous appetites, by the sixth month of life the baby, with the aid of his burgeoning ego functions, has made the alien foe of time delay his own by now delaying gratification himself. Here, Freud's early view of the ego very much resembles his later concept of the superego (Freud 1923).

The dynamic of the superego, in contrast to the hope-filled openness on which conscience is based, is one driven by a terrorizing fear of nothingness. The baby instinctively imitates and takes in the powerful enemy of the impinging reality that is present rather than the friend of a hoped-for ideal that is not. In this sense, the superego, formed with the mandate to watch over the child's survival, is based on the notion that something bad is better than nothing. To ensure at least some kind of secure place in the world, the child seeks to follow, to mimic, and to introject the powers that be. The young child whose wishes to be hugged and kissed good night are repeatedly ignored by his parents may eventually take in the enemy by ridiculing himself ruthlessly for still wanting something unattainable from his parents, with the result that he, too, will repress or ignore those same wishes.

What is introjection? How deeply do we internalize or introject frustration? Freud (1911) notes that the infant "treats unpleasurable stimuli as if they were external" (p. 220). Many years later (Freud 1930), he describes a tendency "to separate from the ego everything that can become a source of such unpleasure, to throw it outside and to create a pure pleasure-ego which is confronted by a strange and threatening outside" (p. 67). The implication here is that frustration is not internalized very deeply, if it is let in at all.

Loewald's (1962) concept of degrees of internalization helps shed light on this question. Loewald suggests that parental introjects shift in their degree of internalization between a deep ego core and the periphery of an intrapsychic space, which Loewald refers to as the "ego system." From Loewald's perspective, the superego, created out of the residue of disillusionment, exists on the periphery of the ego system at a safe distance from the child's deep ego core.

Unlike the relatively simple coping mechanisms of fight or flight, introjection is a rather ingenious means of gaining ego mastery or control over an external threat. It gives the appearance that frustration is being accepted, but without letting its meaning penetrate too deeply. Wearing the mask of the enemy in this way enables the child to co-opt and innoculate himself against the full potency of a traumatic experience by titrating the degree to which it is internalized. In speaking of the neurotic, Ferenczi (1909) describes introjection as a "kind of diluting process by which he tries to integrate the poignancy of free-floating, unsatisfied and unsatisfiable unconscious wish impulses" (p. 47).

Out of the child's mandate to care for himself emerges a pragmatic soul that ensures that the blank face of annihilation be avoided at all costs. Rather than wait indefinitely for a wished-for mother to materialize, the infant, sensing threat to his survival, instinctively makes do and adapts to the mother who is there instead. He attempts to gain mastery or a type of ownership over the frustratingly real mother by bringing her into the "area of omnipotence" (Winnicott 1960b). There, the child imposes his own introjective structure and meaning upon his experiences of impingement by creating what Winnicott termed a False Self devoted to the care of the mother's needs. This attempt to introject and co-opt the emotional potency of the frustratingly real mother carries with it a heavy cost to the child's sense of integrity and continuity, as is implied in the distinction Winnicott (1960b) makes between the True Self and the False Self. For although the False Self may be a necessary adaptation to impingement in the most biologically elemental sense, in another, almost Faustian sense, the counterphobic construction of the False Self belies a selling of one's developmental soul for the purposes of preserving one's survival.

From an evolutionary viewpoint, and insofar as quick, decisive action is adaptive, we could say that the counterphobic defense of bracing for and introjecting the primary source of threat enables the fittest to survive. The organism that is sufficiently pragmatic to adjust to an inhospitable environment is the one that emerges victorious. In this regard, the word *adaptation* itself, frequently used to indicate the achievement of mental health by those who prize the practical, is a remnant of Darwin's theory of natural selection. Yet even if we conclude that the chances for survival or adaptation are enhanced by counterphobic defenses, we certainly cannot assume that the same is true of the quality of life. When we view human beings primarily as biological organisms geared toward their survival, we lose sight of the human striving toward a meaning-filled existence. In the helping professions, it is especially important to be mindful of and address the higher aspirations (and the curiosity) that are integral to a fulfilled life. Indeed, the <u>very</u> <u>same protective mechanisms that insure survival often are antitheti-</u> <u>cal to the openness required for the individual pursuit</u> of mean- <u>ing in the company</u> of others. Those same processes that enable a person to adapt or to adjust to the exigencies of his environment may also <u>tear apart mind from body.</u>

WHEN THE MIND BRACES FOR DISAPPOINTMENT

Winnicott (1949) observes:

> Certain kinds of failure on the part of the mother, especially erratic behavior, produce over-activity of the mental functioning. Here, in the overgrowth of the mental function reactive to erratic mothering, we see that there can develop an opposition between mind and the psycho-soma, since in reaction to the abnormal environmental state the thinking of the individual begins to take over and organize the caring for the psyche-soma, whereas in health it is the function of the environment to do this. [p. 246]

As human beings, we introject and elaborate on our experiences of trauma, thereby transforming the meaning of those experiences in memory. When these meanings are projected onto the imaginary canvas of the future, a transference of trauma, or an anticipation of threat, forms out of the reflected shadow of past disillusionments. Once the unguardedness of innocence is ruptured in this way, the virginal expanses of the future are sullied by haunting afterimages of earlier experiences. Just as the Garden of Eden was spoiled after its inhabitants ate from the Tree of Knowledge so, too, once a child is evicted from his unselfconscious state there is no turning back; no matter how much he may endeavor to make it so, genuine innocence, once lost, is not retrievable. Never again, in the open interplay of giving and receiving with others, will he be able to ground himself without some mental vigilance. The future, now and forever, will be circumscribed to a greater or lesser extent by a fearful bracing for the dangers that have been transferred to its blank screen. As Adam Phillips (1995a) says: "In fear we assume the future will be like the past. . . . Fear, in other words, makes us too clever or at least misleadingly knowing . . . in fear the wish for prediction is immediately gratified; it is as though the certainty—the future—has already happened" (pp. 58–59).

Mike is a 44-year-old married man with two young children who has suffered from lifelong symptoms of anxiety, depression, and fears of death. Sometimes his death anxieties have been so great that, paradoxically, he entertains thoughts of suicide to escape them. Mike's history is replete with experiences of physical abuse at the hands of his father. On a number of occasions, Mike's father, without warning, would slap him across the face. He recounted that this arbitrary doling out of violence at a moment's notice often occurred at the dinner table. Once Mike proudly displayed a model ship to his father that he had worked on for two months, saying, "Look, this is the *Santa Maria*." His father responded by smashing the boat and saying, "Now it's junk."

Recently Mike disclosed that his fears of death intensified when he was less depressed, as if he were "bracing for impact." Indeed he said the worst way that he could imagine dying was to be run over by a car without forewarning. He said he could not stand the idea of being unaware of when he is going to die. I suggested that perhaps his fears of death had less to do with death per se and more to do with a fear of being re-exposed to the impact of his father's fits of violence. To counter his lack of preparedness for his father's unpredictability, Mike braces for impact at every moment through his self-deadening symptom of depression. If he deadens himself first, how can anything harm him? It is only when he entertains the possibility of a better life that he is filled with terrible death anxiety over his vulnerability to his father's envy and violence.

In this way, the precocious intensification of mental activity may become a primary means by which anticipated threats may be engaged ahead of time. Phillips (1995b) writes that, "because the mind comes in afterward—after the trauma— . . . it always runs the risk of being a preemptive presence. The mind object, that is to say, has always unconsciously identified with the traumatic agent (or rather, events) that first prompted its existence. *The mind that attempted to repair—to compensate for—the trauma becomes the trauma itself* (p. 238, original italics). Through the immediacy of such forethought, the future is reached instantaneously. From an early age, a child learns to use his mind to protect his emotional nakedness so that he is never caught off guard again. The counterphobic process of mentally leaping into the future is thus a means of bracing for disappointment and subjecting the helplessness of undergoing disillusionment to the omnipotence of mental control (Shabad and Selinger 1995). All incoming experiences are filtered through this braced mental activity. It is perhaps in this sense—of the child reinventing himself mentally after the death of innocence—that we can understand Winnicott's (1967a) assertion that such a baby "has to start again permanently deprived of the root which could provide continuity with *the personal beginning*" (p. 97).

The problem here is that the more the child relies on his own mental resources to watch over and cope with threat, the more he turns away from others. For the precociously developed mind, born out of the ashes of a dead innocence, a good-enough environment is no longer good enough. In turning toward himself for self-sustenance, the child also is seeking to evade the disillusioning imperfections of human relations. Thus Winnicott (1949) notes, "the mind has a root, perhaps its most important root, in the need of the individual, at the core of the self, for a perfect environment" (p. 246).

JANE AND DORIS: IN SEARCH OF PERFECTION

Recently, a 30-year-old woman, Jane, called me up and asked if I could see her 13-year-old daughter Doris for psychotherapy. She said that they had been to five previous therapists, and that this was the last chance before she sent her daughter away to a residential treatment setting. Jane also told me that she was engaged to be married. I suggested that she come in together with her live-in fiancé and daughter for the initial session.

During that first meeting, it became apparent that this family was sitting on a powder keg of resentments and tensions. While the fiancé sat back impassively and watched, Jane recited a litany of complaints against her daughter: she was running around with the wrong kids, she was getting involved with drugs, her grades were falling, she still had unresolved issues concerning her estranged father's unreliability, and that she, Jane, had "had enough." The daughter, Doris, alternately teary and sullen, tried to defend herself, saying she had begun to hang out with kids who do not get into trouble, and that it was hard to do anything with her mother watching over her all the time.

As treatment proceeded, I saw Doris both individually and together with her entire family. Although Doris suffers from melancholia in connection with feeling rejected by her father, as well as normal adolescent issues of how she fits in with her peers, a major aspect of her problems has had to do with living up to her mother's perfectionistic expectations.

For Jane, however, perfection was the only chance of redeeming what had been a brutal childhood. Jane's mother, diagnosed as schizophrenic and hospitalized on numerous occasions, had been both verbally and physically abusive and neglectful. Jane had had a good relationship with her father as a young child, but did not see him for three years after her parents were divorced when she was 8 years old. She remembers that whenever she got angry at her mother, her father would say, "Oh, Mom is just crazy. You can't do anything about that." Jane grew up very fast; she became involved with drugs when she was 11 years old and had a baby at the age of 16.

With the birth of Doris, it seemed all that was missed with her own mother got transposed into Jane's expectations of an idealized relationship with Doris. Doris and she would have a closeness that would redeem the failures in her relationship with her own mother. Although Jane gave up hope that her own mother could ever fill her needs, she did not give up on the needs themselves; with an intense demand for righting the wrongs of her life, she "substituted one object for another" (Freud 1908) and transferred her hopes to Doris.

For Jane, however, there was no such thing as an adequate relationship with Doris. Any error, failure, or deficiency on Doris's part only filled Jane with a panic that this prince of a perfect relationship would turn into the pumpkin of her earlier relationship her mother. This sort of fragility and anxiety reflects, I believe, Jane's barely perceptible sense that the first relationship was not worked through and mourned but rather survived and escaped. Jane's emotional memories of abuse and abandonment lurk silently in the background, ready to prey on her relationship with Doris into a reliving of her previous traumatic experience.

Increasingly, as Doris makes choices and mistakes that are not to Jane's liking, or within her control, Jane is faced with a dilemma. When Doris forgets a bus pass and misses her bus, or when she fusses and complains while on vacation with her mother, or when she skips a tutoring session during summer school, Jane flies into fits of rage, anxiety, and fear, declaring "I hate her" or "I can't stand her" to her fiancé (and now husband). He sometimes becomes concerned that Jane is "losing it." As Jane is forced to relinquish the possibility of her ideal Doris ever coming to pass, she has to face her own trepidations that her adult life is fraudulent and that everything may now revert back to her childhood nightmare. She cannot stand the idea that Doris may gum up her life and get pregnant "like I did." Much of the resentment that went unexpressed toward her own mother because "she was crazy" has been transferred to the new relations that have so disappointed her. For Jane, there is nothing in between; only the redemptive perfection of a new relationship or the inevitable imperfection of disappointment that reverberates back post-traumatically to the old relationship.

When Jane came in by herself recently, she recounted how she had no feeling toward her mother. Yet I pointed out that she had so much intense feeling toward her daughter. I asked her only to wonder and be curious about this strange contradiction. I let her know that I thought that she has tried her best, tried almost too hard to forge a great mother–daughter relationship, because she herself had never had one with her own mother. She wistfully said that she had "worked so hard" at this relationship, and then it seems that Doris whines about what she does not have and does not appreciate what Jane has done for her. She hates Doris's ingratitude. I suggested that she may envy Doris her opportunity to have had her, Jane, as a mother, when she is fully aware of the abusive mother she herself had to cope with as a child. In accordance with her relinquishment of an ideal Doris, Jane says that she has "given up" on her. In her calmer moments, she seems to know that she just needs "some space" to calm down and reorganize around a more authentic Jane and Doris relationship. Or perhaps Jane just needs some perspective on her relationship with Doris to finally mourn and disentangle herself from her memories of her relationship with her own mother. She has the chance now to confront and live through her anxiety, so that when she loses a fantasied control of another person it need not mean that the relationship reverts back to one like she experienced with her mother. Jane has the opportunity to grow and to learn that waking up to the real world is a lot better than suffering through a nightmare.

SHAME AND THE MORALITY OF SURVIVAL

After losing trust in the reciprocity of giving and receiving, a child can no longer take for granted a sense of belonging, and a self-consciousness of her isolation and incompleteness may begin to emerge before its time. In this regard, the rupture of innocence may be experienced as a psychic dying, a feeling of being an insignificant creature sinking helplessly into an abyss. The dread of re-experiencing this mortifying sense of acute shame infuses the child with a perfectionistic morality of survival. From the child's perspective, the standard of perfection is required because the error of falling endlessly through the cracks would be quite costly. The ruthlessness of natural selection takes no prisoners. Only the fittest survive and failure is punishable by death, or worse—the dreaded reliving of trauma.

For the traumatized child, there is no middle ground between life and death, between the perfection of surviving intact and the error of disintegrating extinction. Enduring the life-and-death stakes of such trauma may cause the child subsequently to view her world through the rigid either-or lenses of strong versus weak, and of success versus failure. Here the strong win the ultimate battle for survival over the weak who die out as extinct losers, and the struggle for power, as exemplified in the maxim "might makes right," guides a desperate quest for survival and significance. With the stakes so high, the strict morality of the superego ruthlessly takes its measure of both the self and the other.

On the basis of such a morality of survival, we construct narcissistic power hierarchies in which we distinguish between those persons who possess the qualities we find desirable and those who do not. These hierarchies enable us to cultivate the pride and strength of significance and keep the weakness and shameful vulnerability of reliving trauma at bay.

Above all, shame is a morality of pragmatism. For example, if a patient were to ask a therapist if she is married, and the therapist were to give a definitive answer, the patient would most likely not experience shame. However, if the therapist were to evade and parry the question with a return question, such as "What makes you curious?" the patient may become self-conscious and say, "I shouldn't have asked." Although the morality of asking the question remains the same whether it is responded to or not, the patient may feel as if she did something wrong if she is not given an answer. In this sense, shame has less to do with right or wrong and more to do with the bottom line, and with how things turn out, so to speak. Moral judgments based on shame have the purpose of ensuring that further experiences of vulnerability do not get repeated. Hence, weakness is coded as bad and strength as good.

Victims of bigotry sometimes turn on themselves with recriminations, even though the fault lies with the bigot. Individuals who are emotionally abused or berated in relationships make excuses for the abuser, while criticizing their own actions. The moral masochist may need the success and power of the sadist to compensate for her own sense of unworthiness. The might makes right morality of survival is characteristic of sadomasochistic relationships, which are based more on power and control rather than the mutuality of love. Because the moral masochist identifies with and attempts to merge with the larger-than-life dominance of the sadist in such relationships, we could say that both participants share a morality of survival in which the value of power is elevated.

From the first encounter with overwhelming frustration, a counterphobic process to meet and take in the enemy is set in motion. But the child's movement to merge with the source of her frustration has a disintegrating effect on her sense of integrity and of "going-on-being." In attempting to accommodate to her disillusionments, the child betrays herself by shifting her self's center of gravity and set of identifications from inside to outside, from the subjective experience of helpless yearning to an identification with the more powerful negation of those yearnings, and from a rootedness in her body to an identification with vigilant mental activity. Thus, Winnicott (1949) notes that, under abnormal circumstances, "one can observe a tendency for easy identification with the environmental aspect of all relationships that involve dependence, and a difficulty in identification with the dependent individual" (p. 247).

THE TRAUMATIC THEME: CUMULATIVE DISILLUSIONMENT

In clinical practice, I have been struck by how many patients seem to imitate those qualities of their parents that they could least tolerate. Such patients may report how they shout at their children in precisely the same fashion and with the exact same words that their parents scolded them. This sort of imitative behavior reflects, I believe, the counterphobic defense of wearing the mask of the enemy that I described earlier. The parroting of one's parents shows that something had not been metabolized, worked through, mourned, and left behind. Because many of these patients typically grow up in intact, two-parent households, I came to the view that these unmourned, unintegrated experiences from childhood derived from the [psychic loss] of a physically present parent (Shabad 1989).

Unlike a physical loss that occurs at a specific time and place, psychic loss refers to a subjective experience of loss without any obviously objective referent. In "Mourning and Melancholia," Freud (1917) captures the subtle, often unconscious aspects of psychic loss: "The object has not perhaps actually died, but has become lost as an object of love. In yet other cases one feels justified in concluding that a loss of the friend has been experienced but one cannot see clearly what it is that has been lost, and it is all the more reasonable to suppose that the patient cannot consciously perceive what he has lost either" (p. 245).

In the same paper, Freud also states that "the occasions giving rise to melancholia for the most part extend beyond the clear case of a loss by death, and include all those situations of being wounded, hurt, neglected, out of favor or disappointed" (p. 251).

The psychic loss of a physically present parent evolves out of the chronic disillusionment that the ideal parent who is conceived of and sought by the child is not the one who is encountered daily in the real world. In contrast to the acute and overt trauma of physical loss, the experience of psychic loss derives from relatively intangible trauma extending over many years, the residual effects of which are felt only after the fact. Kris (1956) describes "'strain trauma' as the effect of long-lasting situations which may cause traumatic effects by accumulation of frustrating tensions" (p. 73). In this sense, strain may be viewed as the result of ill-fated efforts put forth by the child to change the real parent into his image of an ideal parent.

Khan (1963) uses the term *cumulative trauma* to describe "the significant points of stress and strain in the evolving mother–infant relationship" (p. 55). Although Khan emphasized early mother–infant interaction as the major determinant of cumula-

tive trauma, the concept of cumulative trauma could be extended
to refer to trauma that accumulates throughout childhood and in
relation to any significant familial figure. Indeed, the traumatizing aspects of cumulative trauma may derive precisely from this
demoralizing quality of repeated frustrations.

If, for example, a father sits silently in his armchair one night
without speaking to his son, most likely the son will not be traumatized. But if night after night, year after year, the son is ignored
by that same father, the cumulative experience of being ignored
eventually may take on the emotional significance of a trauma. The
traumatizing aspects of such accumulating frustrations derive from
the child's everyday exposure to the constancy of a parent's characterological faults, which are enacted continually on the child.
Kohut and Wolf (1978) note that narcissistic injury results from a
"chronic ambience created by the deep-rooted attitudes of the self-
objects" (p. 417).

Previously (Shabad 1989, 1993a) I have used the term *traumatic
theme* to describe a patterned imprint of ongoing frustration that
emerges from the concrete interactions between the child and the
most problematic aspects of the parent's character. Administering
the silent treatment when angry, making petty criticisms, being
persistently intrusive, breaking promises, or calling a child stupid
may all constitute traumatic themes of varying severity. A mother's
histrionic displays of helplessness or a father's explosively drunken
rages may also leave a cumulative template of trauma on the developing child.

In addition, since we are speaking about child-rearing, it is
inevitable that cultural norms and personal values will have a great
influence on what we consider to be a traumatic theme. Most of
us, for example, would say that it is preferable for young children
to be tucked in and kissed goodnight by their parents. After such
youngsters pass a certain age of innocence they are weaned away
from their bedtime rituals, at which point they might just wave
goodnight and put themselves to bed. What if, however, as occurs
in some families, the children are never tucked into bed? Does
not being kissed goodnight consistently constitute a traumatic
theme, if even of a milder sort? Or is this parental lack part of a

more encompassing pattern of unaffectionate behavior? What of families that mark the passage of their children's birthdays with only the most minimal of celebrations? Is this just a less than ideal form of child upbringing? Or will such a child be at a distinct disadvantage in appreciating and celebrating the human drama, especially the drama occasioned by the anniversary of his own birth? Will such an individual then subsequently have difficulty celebrating the little pleasures and passions of life in general, always experiencing them with an invisible reserve?

The chronic quality of the traumatic theme derives from split-off, unmourned aspects of the parent's background and character that are then repeatedly enacted on the child. As a consequence, the helplessness engendered in the child by these chronic experiences originates directly from the child's ongoing inability to change the parent into a desired figure. As such, the traumatic theme is a slowly evolving blueprint of disillusionment before the powers of fate, as personified by one's parents and as uniquely shaped by one's developmental history.

INCOMPLETE MOURNING: THE SUBTLENESS OF PSYCHIC LOSS

The intangible, incomplete quality of chronic disillusionment can hinder a mourning process that is typically based on the relative finality and closure of physical loss. In the physical absence of a real parent, hope springs eternal that a wished-for parent can be found. The idealized image of this imaginary parent, formed during the real parent's periodic physical absences, becomes increasingly difficult to maintain in the face of the very real reappearances of the same frustrating parent. Mahler and her colleagues (1975) have noted that when this mother, or what Bowlby (1958) calls the "mother in the flesh," returns after separation, she is seen as intrusive and remains an "unassimilated foreign body." Each time such a parent reappears, then, the idealization and consequent internalization of the parent's image is thwarted and the mourning process is brought to a halt. Without the sense of closure that may be derived from a final physical loss such as death, continually resurrected hope is locked together in eternal embrace with endless disappointment.

If we return to the boy who is ignored by his father, we can see this cycle of hope and disappointment more clearly. This small boy has not received much attention of any sort from his father. But because on this particular day he has received a "B" in math (unusually high for him), he believes that maybe today his father finally will have some warm, kind words to say to him. He eagerly awaits his father's arrival from work. When his father does come home, however, he nods perfunctorily and grunts unintelligibly to the news of his son's grade. He then becomes engrossed in his daily newspaper and turns on the TV. He breaks the monotony of television watching only to remind his son to take the garbage out before going to bed.

Each day while his father is at work the boy's wish grows in the father's absence: maybe today things will be different. Perhaps if the father's absence were to become permanent at this hope-filled point in time, his son would be able to freeze the sequence of memory frames at that moment and internalize the idealized image of a rarely seen, caring father. This internalization of a benevolent father could then form the basis of a constructive illusion that would help sustain the boy's courage and willingness to grow into manhood himself. Instead, the treadmill-like quality of wish and disillusionment protracts the child's frustration and helplessness torturously. It is only in later years, when we observe repeated urges to undo and master the traumatic theme, that the experience of psychic loss can be reconstructed. Thus, the term *psychic loss* is used here post-traumatically to describe the picture of unfulfilled longings and the sense of incomplete mourning often observed in clinical practice.

The disillusionment of psychic loss accumulates slowly, covertly, and without end. Because we are speaking of a chronic sense of loss, there is no objective reference point by which to validate the child's feelings. Although the continued physical presence of the parent would seem to contradict the child's experience of loss, it is on the contrary, precisely the reappearing physical presence of the real parent that fuels the child's disillusionment. It is this pernicious, hidden quality of psychic loss that makes it so difficult to grasp and that delays its conscious realization. Unlike the overt, objective fact of physical loss, psychic loss is a subtler, more unconscious sense of deprivation. Consequently, the child's ability to convey his sense of loss is likely to be muted and postponed as well. Without a conscious recognition that something has clearly been lost, the child is unable to express "the overt yearning for the lost object" that Bowlby (1979) sees as necessary to healthy mourning. Because of the essentially private, experiential quality of psychic loss, the child often is not able to convey what he is going through. This contributes to a sense of solitary confinement that makes its eventual communication all the more necessary. Until then, within the private recesses of his imagination, the child is more prone to magical fantasies of restitution, more sensitive to those fantasies never coming to fruition, and more susceptible to the formation of defenses that would shield him from his helplessness.

GIVING UP THE IDEAL AND SETTLING FOR THE PRACTICAL

In a series of landmark studies, Robertson and Bowlby (1952), and later Heinicke and Westheimer (1966), observed the attachment patterns of 2- and 3-year-old children who were placed temporarily in a residential nursery. At first, they noted much separation anxiety on the part of the children, which they termed *protest*. The frantic searching behaviors of this first protest phase gave way gradually to a low-keyed grief which the researchers referred to as *despair*. Eventually, some of the children turned for comfort to their nurses; this adaptation, however, was not made without cost. For when the mothers of these children returned from their absences, all the children exhibited some form of detachment behavior, whereby they either seemed not to recognize the mother, or turned and walked away from her. Bowlby and his colleagues concluded that after a prolonged or repeated separation during the first three years of life, this third phase of defensive detachment can persist indefinitely.

In the case of psychic loss, because the cycle of wish and disappointment is so demoralizing, it is difficult to bear with the sadness and vulnerability of wanting something badly when it is to no avail. Rather than experience the shame of being frustrated repeatedly, many children probably move to this defensive stance of detachment much more quickly than they might in reaction to a physical loss. After awhile, the child comes to believe that it is not the real parent who is the primary source of torment, but rather his own misbegotten wish for a more ideal parent that leaves him so helplessly exposed to repeated disillusionment. Rather than continue to search for this created, wished-for parent and find nothing, the child detaches from wishes that lead only to perpetual disappointment.

The distinction between bearing with vulnerability or detaching defensively from it can be observed in the contrasting styles of leave-taking—long good-byes and short good-byes. During a long good-bye, persons who are being left often try to stretch out the leave-taking as much as possible. They may become tearful or clingy or dramatize how difficult it is to separate in one way or the other. After the loved one departs, these are the individuals who stay in contact over distant spaces and times. The saying "absence makes the heart grow fonder" well describes the person who embraces long good-byes.

Other individuals do not seem to tolerate a protracted anticipation of loss very well. Although such persons may be depriving themselves of precious minutes with a person whom they love dearly, they cut the leave-taking short. In quickly disengaging themselves, these persons attempt also to detach from the wish to hold on to the loved one; they leave before they are left. They do not write letters or make phone calls over long distances because that would arouse the pain of yearning in the face of loss. Instead, they are often pragmatic, even opportunistic persons who have learned to adapt and enjoy whoever is there if they can't be with those who are not. The saying "out of sight, out of mind" characterizes the detachment of short good-byes. Loewald (1962) has described this defensive dynamic as an attempt to deny loss by denying that the other person still exists or did exist.

Joffe and Sandler (1965) note that defensive detachment reflects a type of resignation that is an "attempt to do away with the discrepancy between actual self and ideal self" (p. 409). Instead, the child settles for its actual self. It has been my impression that this defense of giving up the ideal and settling for the practical is a pervasive phenomenon. It is manifest when we brace for disappointment, and pretend to ourselves that we do not want what we think we cannot attain.

THE RETURN OF THE REPRESSED: FROM DETACHMENT TO IMITATION

To the extent that each of us experiences psychic loss, we form a personal construct of helplessness corresponding to that loss. Rather than reintegrate and mourn this core of disillusionment, we seek to escape from it when we emerge from childhood. In a fundamental sense, the defensive aspects of our adult characters are created counterphobically in reaction to this dark underbelly of childhood helplessness so as to prevent a repeat of our worst experiences.

In seeking to evade further disillusionments, however, we pay a heavy price. By detaching from our desires and their corresponding ideals, we lose a sense of our integrity. We become a house divided against ourselves. This defensive foreclosure of vulnerability is a betrayal of a self whose lifeblood depends on keeping meaningful links to significant others open. Our development, and its emotional refueling, depends on a reconciling interchange of give and take, in which our offers to be of use are recognized and accepted. To detach ourselves from all that we desired from our parents cannot help but cripple our unfolding. Singer (1971) thus concludes, "Those concerned with the origins of psychopathology and with efforts to rekindle emotional growth must give serious attention to the possibility that the most devastating of human experiences is the sense of uselessness" (p. 65).

However, there is no escape. As Freud (1917) said, "The shadow of the object falls on the ego." Thus the shadows of those relationships that we would most wish to put behind us pursue us wherever we go. The structure of our narcissistically enclosed relationship with ourselves duplicates and perpetuates the sadomasochistic interactions experienced with the parent. The introjection of that frustrating but actual relationship is preferable to the desolate longing for an ideal parent who never materializes. Given that our traumatic themes are experienced discontinuously— through the roles either of aggressor or victim, with nothing in between—growing up often takes the form of a leapfrogging from an identification with the role of victim to that of aggressor.

From the point of view of the child who is fast becoming an adolescent, it may feel as if one must either keep up and adapt to the necessity of growing up, or be left behind with the helplessness of unfulfilled wishes. Without pausing for a moment of compassion, time marches forward ruthlessly. In order to minimize their vulnerabilities and be sufficiently thick-skinned to cope with whatever hardships reality throws their way, some adolescents may feel they have no recourse other than to reinvent an identity for themselves that is detached from their frustrating parent(s). Rycroft (1965) describes this process as an "ablation of parental images." Under the guise of a self-reliant grandiosity, such adolescents may attempt to foreclose further disappointment and shame at the hands of others.

The chronically disappointed child now becomes the toughened-up adolescent who accommodates to his frustrations by taking them in and identifying with them. Through defensive detachment, he shifts his self's center of gravity from the subjective experience of helpless yearning toward an identification with the negation of those yearnings. This shift of identifications is simi-

lar to the defensive dynamic Anna Freud (1936) described as identification with the aggressor. Such identifications, she noted, are
not with the person of the aggressor, but with the aggressive behavior itself.

In contrast to a more personal identification with a parent that
would enable the child to re-create or "reconstitute the object"
(Loewald 1980a) within, identification with the aggressor more
closely resembles imitation. In an interesting paper, Gaddini (1969)
suggests that unlike identification, which refers to the verb *to have*,
imitation refers to the verb *to be*. By establishing a fusion of self
and object, it is a means of overcoming a sense of separateness.
Imitation thus may be viewed as an attempt to undo the experience of alienation wrought by the traumatic theme.

Like many of us, Todd, a 45-year-old man, was far more eager
to trace his lineage to one parent rather than to the other. He
proudly saw himself as his mother's son, while avoiding and dis-
claiming any meaningful filial links or needs in regard to his father. Todd grew up in a family of six; he was the third of four boys.
He remembers that his father was constantly at his mother's beck
and call. By a stroke of fortune, or so he thought, his mother
anointed him as the favorite of her four sons. She challenged him
to strive hard in school, and he rewarded her, in turn, with maxi-
mum effort and excellent grades. In return, he got out of doing
many chores around the house, for which he incurred the wrath
of his brothers. Todd's strivings and labors in school bore fruit as
he became a successful professional.

In the meantime, Todd never made any headway with his father. Like oil and water, they did not mix well. Whereas his father
expected all his sons to participate in Little League, Todd despised
the whole endeavor. More and more, his father favored his other
three sons with his attentions, while either ignoring or bullying
Todd. Todd recalled one episode with particular indignation. The
whole family was in an uproar because of a missing family heirloom that his father blamed Todd for losing. When the heirloom
finally showed up, Todd never received an apology from his father.

Eventually Todd turned the tables and transformed the insult of being targeted and left out into his own contempt for his father. This was not difficult as his father was a weak man with a bad temper. Todd identified with the aristocratic airs and manners of his mother in this matriarchal family, and looked down on his father's obsequious, slavish attitude to his mother's wants. Her wishes were his father's command. At the same time that Todd was being seduced into being his mother's pet, however, he also pitied his father for his hapless position in the marriage.

In his adult life, Todd has experienced severe marital problems. Significantly, he finds himself overpowered by his wife in decisions about how to spend money and to raise their children. He punctuates his sense of chronic impotence and shame with explosive tantrums that serve only to exacerbate the tensions of the marriage.

Perhaps not coincidentally, Todd has become the father whom he had disowned. His alienation and contempt covered over an underlying pity, even compassion, that Todd had felt for his father's plight in the marriage. The most apt punishment for the crime of turning his back on and betraying a father of whom he was ashamed was to be visited with the same behaviors he most despised. Todd's guilt for being ashamed of his paternal lineage came back to him with boomeranging vengeance: he now incurred the same weakness he despised in his father.

Another patient of mine recounted how distressed she would become whenever her mother blamed herself repeatedly for the ills of the world. In spite of all the daughter's attempts to reassure and cheer up her mother, it was no use; her mother continued to flagellate herself. Like many children of depressed parents, this patient suffered through the cumulative traumatic experience of not having a lasting impact on her mother's mood. This daughter attempted to bridge the alienating gap left by psychic loss by subsequently taking on her mother's stance and behavior of moral masochism in her own adult life. When a parent has not accepted any other gift, sometimes such commiseration seems like the only option left. After all, imitation is the sincerest form of flattery.

Sometimes such imitation seems so uncannily accurate that we sense that the image of the parent has not been adequately "chewed up" and internalized, and a fixed imprint of the frustrating behavior of the parent remains stuck in the craw at the more superficial, behavioral level of imitation. If unpleasure is consistently evicted from a person's most profound psychic depths, as Freud suggests—or perhaps, more accurately, is never internalized to begin with—we might conclude that to the extent the external world is experienced as nongratifying, it will fail to penetrate a person's inner life. But because something, some structure, even the bad, is better than nothing, it is adhered to imitatively. Such persons, as if under the influence of a psychic autoimmune system gone out of control, attempt to gain mastery over the traumatic experience through the use of a hypercritical mental activity. In giving the appearance of complying with and imitating the parental aggressor, however, such individuals may only be playing dead. By perpetually forbidding themselves the awareness of wishes that led only to endless disillusionment, they may be attempting to tuck their wishes away in the protective custody of the unconscious. There, insulated temporarily from further harm, a person's most cherished desires and their accompanying fantasies await their opportunity to be resurrected for another day.

4

The Compulsion to Repeat: Homesickness and to Begin Again as if for the First Time

We shall not cease from exploration
And the end of all our exploring
Will be to arrive where we started
And know the place for the first time.

—T. S. Eliot, "Gerontion"

A magic dwells in each beginning and
Protecting us it tells how to live.

—Hermann Hesse, *Magister Ludi*

PREMATURE LOSS AND HOMESICKNESS

John is a 32-year-old, melancholy looking, soft-spoken Mexican-American man who came for a consultation because of problems he was having with his girlfriend. Early in the first session, in words that were barely audible, he stated that his mother died suddenly of a stroke when he was 12 years old. Ten minutes later, however, he proceeded to describe a recent argument he had with his mother. When I pointed out my confusion, John replied that his biological mother died when he was 12, and that the mother with whom he argued was his stepmother. I then asked if it would be all right with him if for the sake of clarity we refer to his step-mother as his "stepmother" and to his mother as his "mother." With a chuckle, he agreed. Although this request may have seemed presumptuous, I sensed somehow the importance of distinguishing between the memory of his mother and his stepmother.

As it turned out, precious memories were all John had left to him of his mother—memories that he hung on to for dear life. In the chaotic aftermath of his mother's sudden death everything was all a blur. In his pieced-together memory he found himself and his four younger sisters whisked off immediately from his mother's funeral to a plane bound for Mexico. He and his sisters stayed with his grandmother there while his father remained in Chicago. A year later, when John returned to Chicago, he recounts disembarking from the plane and seeing his father, who then introduced him to an unfamiliar woman by his side, saying "This is your new mother."

In the ensuing years, John's memory of his mother was buried under the rubble of everyday life struggles. The "overt yearning" that Bowlby (1979) indicated was necessary for healthy mourning was blanketed over by a series of injunctions: John was not to speak of his mother and he was to refer to his stepmother as "Mom."

Of course, a person cannot be prevented from thinking his own thoughts. During his teenage years, John clashed with his parents and withdrew frequently to his room. Once in his private domain, he opened up his remembered cache of buried treasures: he reminisced about sitting by his mother's side while she knitted, he reminded himself of her warmth and easy laugh, he could still taste her cooking—and then it was over all too soon. John clung to his storeroom of precious images—simultaneously distant and vividly clear—as if they had happened yesterday.

For twenty years, John's passion—what mattered to him most— was saved for his internal love affair with his mother. As far as the external world was concerned, with one profoundly meaningful arm of passion tied behind his back, he drifted through his life, doing what he had to do to get by. He protected the vivid but fading world inside himself from any of the injunctions and restrictions outside; he determined that never the twain would meet. Perhaps even his almost inaudible soft-spokenness reflected his difficulty in modulating the difference between the silent speech of thinking to himself and speaking out loud to others.

As John waited, longing for his mother's return, he lived two parallel lives: his nightmarish motherless existence, and a wished-for life in which he consoled himself constantly with the fantasy of how things would have been different had his mother been there. This what-if life of dissociated fantasy drained the passion John needed to make a deeper commitment to the living.

Like John, many children do what they have to do at the time to cope with their stresses and then fall ill after the fact, as the strain culminates in the residual illness of premature loss . . . homesickness. Usually, we think of homesickness as a form of separation anxiety, such as when a child is dropped off at a sleepaway camp, and can think of nothing else but returning home. Homesick children cannot be distracted or consoled; only the arrival of a desperately awaited mother or father is sufficient to calm the fears of a homesick child. Whereas homesickness appears to be a dis-ease about facing the unknown, I would suggest that it has more to do with an anxiety about maintaining one's connections with what is familiar. This insecurity of the homesick is especially pronounced when there is a feeling that the relationships on which they depend have been cut short before reaching their natural conclusions. A sense of unfinished business, such as not successfully cheering up a depressed mother before leaving her, may especially fuel the restless unease of homesickness. In this regard, separation anxiety may derive not only from worries about what will become of oneself, but also from trepidation about how the significant figures in one's life are faring while one is gone. I am reminded of a scene from the film *The Wizard of Oz* in which a homesick Dorothy pictures a distraught Auntie Em fretting over Dorothy's whereabouts.

When children use defensive detachment to flee their disillusionments, it may compound their sense of homesickness by alienating them from their experiences. This sense of alienation may eventually evoke feelings of derealization, a phenomenon that Freud (1936) described in "A Disturbance of Memory on the Acropolis" as "What I see here is not real" (p. 244).

The problem of realizing our experiences (life is felt as real) or derealizing them (life is felt to be a dream or hallucination) is, I believe, of underappreciated importance. Perhaps the anxiety of facing the unknown in death, for example, derives from the human incapacity to fully realize the meaning from each passing moment. As Emily, a character in Thornton Wilder's *Our Town* (1938) says: "Do humans ever realize life while they live it?—every, every minute?" As a consolation for the incapacity to realize the quality of our experiences, we may seek out quantities of repeated experiences. For example, the continued pursuit of fame through recognition by a large audience may take up the slack for an ever-elusive intensity and depth of quiet intimacy. In this sense, repetition is an attempt to remedy that lack, and resolve the nostalgia of homesickness; it is an antidote intended to make up for our human limitations in realizing the quality of our experiences.

REENACTMENT: TO BEGIN AGAIN AS IF
FOR THE FIRST TIME

Freud (1914) has pointed out that repetition is simultaneously an obliteration of memory and a form of remembering. But it is also an action memory of participatory reenactment, and that is the whole point. In suspending consciousness, the action memory of reenactment annuls the passage of time by collapsing past into present. When the past is thus relived as if it were present, it fosters the constructive illusion—the transference illusion—that a second chance is a first chance to derive the meaningfulness of the real from within one's own life.

Eliade (1971) thus emphasizes that "reality is acquired solely through repetition or participation; everything which lacks an exemplary model is 'meaningless', i.e., it lacks reality" (p. 34). Freud (1925), too, noted this link between repetition and confirmation of the real: "The first and immediate aim, therefore, of reality testing is not to *find* an object in real perception which corresponds to the one presented but to *refind* an object, to convince oneself that it is still there" (pp. 237–238).

The transference may be viewed as a pattern of repetition in which we use each refinding of an object as a confirming mirror to reflect back the reality of our lives. Touching base with the familiar counteracts the derealizing alienation of wandering endlessly through the strange and novel. When a reconnection with a home base makes what is distant vivid and real again, the sanity of personal identity is maintained. In re-establishing a sense of personal continuity, we re-create the present as a new beginning in the image of our re-discovered origins. Van der Leeuw (1957) thus speaks of primordial time as creative. Through the repetition of myth, today is always created anew.

When two people fall in love, they frequently have the sense of being soul mates who have known each other for a long time. This sense of re-finding each other, by providing a secure bond of commonality, enables the two lovers to re-create each other with renewed passion, as if meeting for the first time. What happens to this process of re-finding and re-creating in the wake of trauma?

A family reunites each Christmas with full-hearted participation and good feeling for a loving exchange of gifts and a holiday dinner. Each reunion occurs within an illusion of primordial time of re-finding and re-creating, as if no time at all had passed between the very first celebration and the last one. The past masquerades convincingly as the present, to the good cheer of all. Paradoxically, this illusion of continuity and identity in time, buttressed by the backbone of reunion, lends a reconfirmed sense of the real to the participants.

After fourteen years pass as if they were none, the father in the family dies. In this fifteenth year the family assembles again for the Christmas celebration, but things have changed. The father, ever-reluctant about great expenditures and extravagance, could always be counted on to say, "Aren't we overdoing it a little?" Or after all gifts were exchanged, with dramatic flair, he would retrieve one final surprise out of the closet. But no longer. And without him the family cannot seem to re-find each other in quite the same way. They cannot re-create the illusion of celebrating Christmas as if for the first time in the face of the palpable fact of the father's death. As trauma wrenches the past from its identity with the present, rupturing the illusion of a continual new beginning, an awareness of the passage of time intrudes rudely into the void. The loss of the father is a gaping wound in the continuity of the family's life, irrevocably separating the world before from the nightmare after it.

Without being able to anchor themselves in the familiar, the members of this family are stranded, cut loose from their moorings. They may do their best to adapt to the external realities of this post-traumatic world with some mechanical semblance of habit. They may laugh with friends, they will attend business meetings, they will watch lips move as others are speaking, but something about it all does not add up: There is something ghostlike and unreal about going through the motions of existence after the experience of trauma. Despite all their conscious efforts to keep up with the ongoingness of life, these people remain unconsciously preoccupied with the past, as they wait and search repeatedly to return to the world that was lost.

To the extent that all of us have experienced the disillusionments of our particular traumatic themes, no one is immune to
homesickness. In one way or another, our relationships with our
parents often are disrupted prematurely before being fulfilled.
Detachment defenses, following immediately on the heels of our
disillusionments, further alienate us from the roots of our being.
Our adult characters, constructed on the defensive pillars of self-
reliance, are fraught with repeated symptomatic attempts to turn
back the clock. Repetition aims to make real the home one has
lost sight of, so that one can begin again, as if for the first time.

IDENTIFICATION WITH THE AGGRESSOR:
ON THE OUTSIDE LOOKING IN

When we attempt to take flight from our disillusionments, but
instead remain preoccupied with them, there may appear to be
only two discontinuous choices for identification—victim or aggressor. This discontinuity also parallels the defensive abruptness
with which we detached from our pain. In this sense, the transition from childhood to adulthood, often reflecting a shift from
passive to active, and from victim to aggressor, resembles a dissociative leap rather than a graduated walking into the grown-up
world.

Rather than experience the continuing degradation and shame
of finding her wishes falling on deaf ears, the child may become
the adolescent or adult who forecloses further injury by deflating
her own desires. Her self-criticisms shield her from further disappointment. Thus, Freud (1917) has pointed out that a person's
turning upon herself with harsh rebukes is a way of protecting
herself against the full realization of loss, and Rochlin (1965) has
added that superego attacks on the self may be a means of warding off abandonment.

One might think of the defensive dynamic of the identification with the aggressor, when it is directed against oneself, as an
ongoing superego process that is directly reflective of one's trau-

matic theme. The experience of chronic disillusionment becomes so unbearable that one bridges the chasm between oneself and the psychically lost parent by narcissistically becoming the parental aggressor to oneself. A primary aim of superego formation and its ongoing maintenance may be to placate the powers of the previous generations, through offering oneself as an imitative replica of them, when no other offering seems sufficient. In this way, identification with the aggressor is used pervasively to give defining form and content to a bridge of repetition connecting the present to the previous generation.

A daughter, forever frustrated in her unending attempts to take her mother's mind off her marital unhappiness with her father, may unconsciously inhibit the pleasures of her own life. She may select a man for herself who will treat her no better than her father treated her mother. In this way, she attempts to give the gift of sacrificially joining her mother in her misery, when none of her other offerings seemed to help her mother.

In this sense, identification with the aggressor is not solely an involuntary defensive maneuver designed to protect against a sense of helplessness. It is also a means by which a person embeds herself in a repeated bad relationship instead of no relationship. As the psychic reality of the transference tells us, when the future is perceived, created, and delimited by the images of the past, the uncertain dangers of encountering novelty and solitude can be eliminated.

Inasmuch as negating one's wishes also limits the possibilities of who one can be, identifying with the aggressor is a means of self-definition, of setting one's outlying boundaries oneself before they are set by someone else. In the defensive aim of covering over the soft underbelly of childhood helplessness, as concretized by the traumatic theme, identification with the aggressor defines one's identity from the outside in. By knowing who one cannot possibly be, one defines who one necessarily must be. Moreover, this self-enclosed stance of being on the outside looking in forecloses any genuine interchange with the external world, and thus any new learning.

That is precisely the problem. In the unconscious determination to adhere to imagined ties with one's parents, one rigidly duplicates the sadomasochistic relationship experienced with them. In terms of the traumatic theme, we become acquainted only with the sadistic role of negating wishes, or the masochistic role of yearning indefinitely. Without any other perceived options in between these discontinuous choices, we may remain unconvinced that there are alternate ways of being. Thus, the transference, and for that matter, all subsequent relationships, to a greater or lesser degree, becomes the playing field for the reenactment of the sadomasochistic aspects of our traumatic theme(s).

Sometimes our hatred of the parental victimizer of our traumatic theme is so profound that we may avoid identifying with the aggressor to the extent that we leave ourselves open to exploitation. One patient of mine, Joe, wondered whether he should break up with his girlfriend of two years. Although he said he "loved" her, he had not been attracted to her since the beginning of the relationship; as a result, he slept with numerous other women. In addition, he complained that his girlfriend frequently humiliated him in public. She had corrected his dancing at a wedding and she would not shirk from arguing loudly in public. He complained also about her walking away quickly from tables in restaurants after eating, leaving him feeling alone and abandoned there.

Indeed, this theme of abandonment was a crucial one for Joe. Whenever he threatened to break up with his girlfriend, she would dissolve into tears and beg him for one more chance. Because Joe has also known what it is to be abandoned in his life, he would weaken immediately. His parents were devoted to each other, but they had little time for him. This was especially true because his younger sister had garnered much attention for sickliness in childhood.

In a sense, Joe projected his own resentment and entitlement about being mistreated and abandoned onto his girlfriend. When she complained of her life with Joe, she was also doing his complaining for his life with his parents. By threatening to abandon her, he became, intolerably in his own eyes, the parental aggressor who had abandoned him. At these junctures, his pull to identify with her experiences weakened his resolve and dragged him back into an unwanted relationship once more.

When an adult oppresses his own wishes as ruthlessly as his parents did, he loses an open-ended sense of what is possible in his life. Because these wishes carry with them vital, potentially rejuvenating ideals, he is also inhibiting the generation and conscious pursuit of his passions and pleasures. In so doing, he renders himself a critical observer rather than a wholehearted participant in his own life. He may then have the sense of being on the outside looking in at himself and his significant relationships and, perhaps most importantly, experience a resulting sense of alienation from his own childhood.

Detached from themselves and encapsulated within the remembered image of the parental aggressor, many adults, to a greater or lesser extent, continually miss the emotional richness of the current moment. In bracing characterologically to avoid a repeat of previous disillusionments, such persons are not truly inhabiting themselves. Instead, their lives may take on a derealized, dreamlike quality—as if life had gone by without having been genuinely lived. In subsequent obsessional and compulsive attempts to recapture the ever-elusive quality of times gone by, the stance of defining oneself from the outside looking in perpetuates the compulsion to repeat. Such individuals often find to their chagrin that they have escaped into a future that is dictated by an imperative to master a past they thought they had left behind. Against the relatively circumscribed backdrop of their experiences of helplessness, character development unfolds, to a greater or lesser degree, through a process of reducing the field of potential destinies to one determined by the quest to undo and relive the past, like a dog chasing its own tail. Meanwhile the future is held hostage to repeated attempts to resurrect and perfect the phantoms of times gone by. In this sense, perhaps we can understand Ferenczi's (1927) comment, "Character is from the point of view

of the psycho-analyst a sort of abnormality, a kind of mechaniza-
tion of a particular way of reaction, rather similar to an obsessional
symptom" (p. 66).

When Gary, the Pakistani-American man discussed in the first
chapter, initially came for twice-a-week psychotherapy, he frequently spoke about the parental voice that had guided his life to
law school. Alongside this overt identification with the aggressor,
Gary secretly searched for ways to capture the childhood out of
which he had been cheated. Whenever he would visit with his
parents, he would ride in the back seat and let his brother drive
the car. Without fail, he went on vacations with his parents. When
he was by himself, away from their prying eyes, Gary would sneak
in his own pleasures. Like the rebellious child that he had never
been, he stuffed his face with hot fudge sundaes while listening to
sports radio, and went to female Jello-wrestling contests. With me
as well he pictured himself a child, sitting on my lap and having
me tell him about the ways of the world.

There is a stereotypical truth about the gay man who cruises
bars to share physical intimacy with more than a few men during
a night. Such compulsive behavior is often viewed by mental health
professionals as intentionally and unconsciously self-destructive,
and perhaps in its effects that is true. I think we would be mis-
taken, however, if we were to believe that the aim of such a person
is to harm himself. Instead, we might view his sorting through
myriad lovers as a fruitless search for an ideal that is never found,
and that therefore must be repeated. Perhaps this person is yearning to be held physically by a man as he never had been by his
father. And maybe for a few brief, blissful moments in the dark he
can paint his own desired image on the anonymity of this strange
man with whom he is locked in embrace. He can then foster the
illusion that the accumulation of years has collapsed in a time warp,
and feel that it is his father who is hugging him tightly, only to be
rudely awakened seconds later to the stranger facing him instead.
Once again, it had only been make-believe, so his private quest
for the lasting peace of his father's embrace must continue.

THE INTERGENERATIONAL TRANSMISSION
OF TRAUMATIC THEMES

While many persons are identifying with the most frustrating aspects of a parent through various forms of self-inhibition, they also may be harboring unconscious yearnings to retrieve what they felt robbed of and what they now feel entitled to. Never having acknowledged the inexorable movement of time, they still unconsciously hold out the possibility of returning to their innocence in the flesh. Unaware of their longings, they never have to confront the fact that childhood, for better or worse, comes but once. Instead, for these adults, filled with the self-denial of introjecting hated aspects of their own parents, the unconscious wish to regenerate their lives with an idyllic beginning springs up repeatedly, as if in polarized reaction to the conscious discounting of such hopes.

With the advent of a new generation, these persons now may externalize the introjected sadomasochistic dialectic of their traumatic theme(s) onto the relationship with their children. Here is a new field on which to reclaim a life that has never been lived out—a life of hopes, dreams, and possibilities. With the power of parental role, such people may view their relationships with their children as a tempting opportunity to reenact and undo the traumatic theme, and, through that undoing, to reclaim a childhood felt to be their just due. They may then begrudge the passing on of a better life to children who are unconsciously viewed as rivals for a new beginning. Such parents may say to their children: "If I had to walk two miles to school, why can't you?" When queried about their statement, these parents might respond, without imaginative access to a vision of their own ideal childhood by saying: "Well, that's how I was brought up," or "That's what my parents did with me."

For such individuals, the resentful afterimages of their particular traumatic themes still burn ragefully bright; they are filled with a righteous sense that they are entitled to have redeemed what was taken from them. These persons may externalize their regret for their own lost innocence into an envy of the innocence of their children who such individuals imagine have stolen that innocence illicitly from them. In this sense, the intergenerational cycle of unconscious envy, transmitted through one's identification with the aggressor in one's own parent, reflects a refusal to acknowledge the passing of one's childhood. Sexual abuse may be viewed as the culminating response to these envious and rivalrous impulses. By spoiling a child's innocence, the abuser, trapped in the fantasized limited-goods universe of envy, imagines he can regain that innocence back for himself. The resulting lack of success in this regard only drives him compulsively to repeat the same actions again.

In contrast, some parents, however, in their zealousness to make a virtue of necessity and not wish for something they cannot have anyhow, may take the notion of making way for the next generation too seriously. Mourning the passing of one's childhood, being the imperfect process that it is, may leave a depressive residue that is reflected in the sentiment of "It's too late for me." In adhering too closely to the self-denying dictates of a normalizing socialization process to be a mature, responsible adult, such persons may overdo it. Defining their parental and adult duties too narrowly, these individuals may give up too much by defensively renouncing different possibilities in their own lives.

Although such adults may think it is too late for themselves, it is not too late for their children, who now become the idealized links to the past from which they themselves feel alien. As hope for a rejuvenating new beginning is transmitted from their own future to that of their children, their sons and daughters come to represent the best parts of themselves. After all, in a rapidly changing, technological culture the future is for the young and the old are quickly passé.

Thus, to the extent that it is difficult to mobilize aggression toward those whom we idealize, such parents may find it difficult to set the containing limits needed for the provision of a safe holding environment for their children. It is not unusual for some parents, instead of saying "No" to their children's misbehavior, to say something like: "Well, that's just the way 5-year-olds are." For such parents their children's expressiveness has a precious naturalness that should remain untouched by any barriers of sullying restrictions. Without the meaningful context provided by such delimiting boundaries, however, the self-expressions of children can degenerate into the anxiety of aimless chaos.

The problem of putting children in positions of authority for their own lives in this way can be illustrated through the metaphor of questions and answers. Perhaps a generation or two ago when children asked questions of their parents, they would receive answers, guidance, directions, even rules to live by. Although child-rearing was less encouraging of individual self-expression and more autocratic, parental decisiveness formed a protective umbrella that enabled children to feel less exposed and alone in the world. The advantage was that, as in any dictatorship, parental answers, whether right or wrong, provided a circumscribed structure that allowed children to remain children and not worry about their own welfare.

In today's world, and not unlike the psychotherapeutic situation in which a patient's question is responded to with a question, a child may not receive a firm answer to his question but rather a return question that puts the burden of decision back on him. Although in some instances the democratic offering of choice to one's children can have salutary effects, at other times the posing of questions to children only offers a semblance of freedom. For it is a freedom that cannot be meaningfully actualized without the holding environment provided by some answers. When a parent responds to a question with his own question, what looks like encouragement of freedom of expression may unconsciously be a pressure on the child to be the authority figure who will care for the parent. When both parent and child search for answers from a larger containing authority, we see the common unconscious roots of envy and admiration in the rivalry for a new beginning.

Kenny, a 9-year-old boy, came for his first session with me and said he "couldn't take it anymore. There's too much pressure." Kenny was involved in a number of sports activities and spent three hours doing homework each day. He was in a bilingual school because his mother was French, and his father, although American, was a strong Francophile. Kenny elaborated that what he especially could not take anymore was doing his English homework *and* his French homework; it was "just too much." Being an extremely engaging, verbal young man, Kenny took to therapy very quickly. He gained immediate relief through speaking about his pressures, especially after we talked about his feeling torn between his French-speaking parent and English-speaking parent during their marital squabbles.

It quickly became apparent that a major source of Kenny's problems was traceable to the problems in his parents' marriage, and the unconscious pressures that each parent placed on him. Briefly, the treatment shifted to couple's therapy, until Terry, Kenny's father, sought individual treatment for himself. Terry was a man of thwarted high ambition. To a great extent, he placed the bitter fallout of his life's disappointments on Kenny. As a young man, Terry had traveled to France to study art, and fancied himself as "another Picasso." He also met a young Frenchwoman; they had a torrid romance and married soon after.

When I queried Terry as to why he and his young bride left France to come back to the States, Terry said that his family did not really approve of his being in France. His enmeshed family, which prized loyalty above all the other virtues, looked askance upon their wayward son who was trying to make something special out of himself. Very soon after he got married, the burden of his family's disapproval took its toll: Terry succumbed to the pressures, and returned home to work in his father's business. He gave up his aspirations to artistic fame, had three children, and embarked on an adult life of inhibition and regret. France, a momentary high point of his life, receded behind him like a wonderful dream. From Terry's point of view, it was now too late to start over; from here on in, life would be a prolonged anticlimax.

Many of Terry's frustrations with himself have been transformed into perfectionistic demands that are imposed on Kenny. It is up to Kenny now to realize the ideals that Terry stopped himself from reaching. Perhaps when Kenny locates the source of his troubles in having to do his "*French homework too*," he understands more than he can say. He discerns the intensity in his father's voice when he checks his son's French homework. He understands and resents that he must follow through on his father's own dashed ambitions. In a sense, Kenny is caught in a double bind: he is bound by the pressure of his father's admiration to carry on where his father gave up; yet, if he does succeed, especially in ways that his father never did, he risks incurring his father's envy. This is especially true when Kenny slacks off and engages in mindless fun as his father never could. At these junctures, Terry jumps on Kenny with the moralistic wrath that only an envy born of regret and harsh self-judgment for missing similar opportunities could muster.

UNDOING AND THE MAGIC OF REVENGE

Why would parents repeat the hated behavior of their own parents in interactions with their own children all so frequently? Why would a mother call her children stupid over and over again, knowing how it felt when it was done to her? Why would a father consistently break small promises to his child if he could not tolerate it when his own father did that to him? Much emotional misery—and much of the misery transmitted from one generation to the next—comes from being untrue to the memory of one's own suffering in this way. Put simply, there is a mystery as to why parents transmit to their beloved children the most despised features of their own childhoods.

Perhaps we can discern a subtle form of revenge in these parents' envious perpetuation of the wrongs done to them. Consciously, a person may say that revenge cannot bring back someone or something that has been lost. In the unbounded universe of the unconscious, however, where the timelessness of the circle replaces linear time, all is possible: beginnings are endings and endings are beginnings; one can go backward as easily as forward and that which has been lost can be retrieved.

If we were to say that the unconscious had a purposeful plan, it would be, with time-traveling acrobatics at its disposal, one that would be far more ambitious than the mere quest for mastery. For as profoundly defeated as a person might become, as long as he still is alive his unconscious works feverishly behind the scenes, manipulating the various levers of the psyche to make the impossible come to pass. Indeed, the attempt to gain control over a traumatic experience, as reflected in the shift from passive to active, may have the primary aim of undoing the traumatic wound. At the very same moments that a person suffers a traumatic experience, he may already be attempting to reverse the course of events. In shifting perspectives from body to dissociated mind, a person gains a sense of distance from himself and thus can foster the illusion that he has annulled the flow of time at the site of his wound. This illusory stoppage of time now sets up the possibility of starting over again, as if one were to leap out of a bus heading in one direction and hop on another bus moving in the opposite direction.

It is in this sense that perhaps we can understand the rejuvenating effects of traveling. When people move from one location to another it is not uncommon for them to claim that they are looking for a fresh start. The sense of agency and initiative that a person generates through such physical movement can have an invigorating effect on the burnout feeling of depression. I have seen a number of couples who have described how the tensions of their problematic marriages seem to dissolve when they travel together on vacation. Travel is not only movement through space, but also provides the illusion that one is able to move through time as well, and to undo one's sense of burnout and embark on a new beginning. In this same regard, fantasies of flying or flights of fancy may be a means of traveling through time and space in order to effect a rebirth. The missed opportunities of the long-ago past may become transformed into a potential *Field of Dreams* (as in the movie of that name), where it becomes possible through the acrobatic magic of mental time-travel to redeem old disillusionments in a utopian future.

Using this notion of mental time-travel, we can revisit the

metaphorical meanings of the somersault done by Balint's (1968) young woman patient. She was an attractive, flirtatious girl in her late twenties whose main complaint was her inability to achieve anything. She could not complete a degree nor respond with any substance to men. She had a crippling fear of uncertainty and of taking any risk. On one occasion, Balint recounts:

> Apparently the most important thing for her was to keep her head safely up, with both feet firmly planted on the ground. In response, she mentioned that ever since her earliest childhood she could never do a somersault; although at various periods she tried desperately to do one. I then said: 'What about it now?'— whereupon she got up from the couch and, to her great amazement, did a perfect somersault. (pp. 128–129)

That somersault proved to be a clinical breakthrough. Perhaps we can understand it at once as a symbolic and physical means of standing time on its head. The young woman's completion of the somersault fostered the illusion, in the most concrete sense, of having created a new beginning for herself.

The reversal magic of revenge may play a similar role in the reenacted sadomasochistic interactions of the traumatic theme; here the disillusioned person holds in her own hands the frustrating power of the aggressor. She then can retrace her steps in time to use a wrong (revenge) to undo a wrong (traumatic experience) and to make a right (create), a perfect new beginning. In this shift in perspective from victim to aggressor in the reenactment of the traumatic theme, the magic of revenge derives from the fantasy of turning *time* as well as space inside out. Thus, with the reversal of time the self-imposed exile of dissociative defense can be rendered into the ground of a fresh start.

Revenge seduces with the illusion that it can transform vice into virtue, weakness into strength, and can convert the defeat of disillusionment and self-alienation into the triumph of a new life. Implicit in revenge are the underlying bylaws of envy and of a life-and-death struggle for limited time and space, specifically for the

inside track that fertilizes every rebirth. In turning passively undergone suffering into the active victimization of another, the
vengeful person attempts immediately to regain a sense of agency
and vital participation in life that had been defensively abandoned
because of her disillusionments. By perpetrating on a new victim-
to-be the same experiences she underwent earlier, this individual
attempts to pass on or rid herself of the reality of her sufferings.
     From this point of view, scapegoating—deriving from the bib-
lical practice in which a goat was symbolically loaded up with sins
and sent off into the wilderness—reflects an unconscious quest to
undo trauma. When something goes wrong in any human group-
ing, someone must become the fall guy, whether he is to blame or
not. In the aftermath of plane crashes, government fiascos, or
sports defeats, someone must be to blame. And it is through the
expulsion of the scapegoated party that the larger group attempts
to purge itself of weakness and start over. Scapegoating is an active hunt for culprits who must carry the sin of proof of one's
mortal weakness away with them. The humiliation of one's traumatized history can be rewritten by projecting and then banish-
ing the memory of one's own victimization to oblivion.
Scapegoating, through the reversal magic of revenge, creates the
illusion that a person's real history, hurdling down its one-way track
toward a rendezvous with death, can be undone.
     Becker (1975) has written eloquently on the subject of
scapegoating, seeing it as an ill-fated attempt to deny and kill off
death itself in the embodied, externalized form of another person. Trauma, as a disruptive wound to a person's continuity of
being, is an insult to any pretensions of an invulnerable immortality. Revenge seeks to undo the profound disillusionment of that
insult and to regain the illusion of life flowing smoothly, as if it
never had been stopped. However, because a person necessarily
must confront gnawing reminders of his frailties, scapegoating
ultimately is no more than a fantasied, unsuccessful solution to
the problem of human vulnerability—and therefore it is repeated
over and over again. The countless examples of mass murder
throughout history attest to the repeated fantasied attempts to fend
off death through the sacrificial offering of others.

From Freud's (1920) viewpoint, the aim of the death drive, as reflected in the compulsion to repeat, is to return organismic life to an earlier state of inorganic quietude. Although one may or may not subscribe to Freud's metaphysical explanation of a death drive as a way of accounting for the compulsion to repeat, I have been impressed by how closely longings for regression parallel Freud's notion about repetition. For example, it has been my impression that after individuals have gone through major transitions or have suffered traumatizing disruptions to their lives, they think back nostalgically to the idealized era or moments immediately preceding the disruption. Thus, Lichtenstein (1977) points out that the first phase of repetition is always a return to a previously existing state. The second phase of repetition is then an instant redirection of the developmental process, a starting over as if the trauma had never occurred.

Loewald's (1980a) concept of an active "re-creative" repetition involves using the past as a home base to serve the constructive illusion of a present as a new beginning. Trauma splits past from present, imposing a consciousness of the passage of time that ruptures the rejuvenating illusion of a new beginning. Rather than confidently use the past to "regress in service of the ego" (Kris 1952), the traumatized person must return *in toto* to the point immediately preceding his split, to a time before his ongoing means of reconfirming the roots of his being was broken. Because this fantasied return to an idyllic era always is based on the undoing of traumatic reality, it never quite reaches its destination. The more overwhelming the traumatic experience, the more urgently the person will try to bury his head in thoughts of the way it was and how it could have been. Like Balint's (1968) notion of "malignant regression," this fantasied attempt to undo what has already been experienced is doomed to failure, and will therefore be endlessly repeated. Although Balint sees "gratification" as the ultimate aim of the spirals of malignant regression, perhaps we will not deviate too much from his intent if we view malignant regression also as an insistence on restoring the world to the way one believes it once was, ignoring what has happened since.

Loewald's (1980a) concept of repetition as a "passive reproduction" of an earlier event fits the person who cannot actively digest the overwhelming quality of his traumatic reality, and who instead waits for a magical return to an imagined ground of innocence. Ultimately, the problem with both passive repetition and malignant regression is that an individual is attempting to find the ground of a new beginning from within the defensively insulated safety of his own self-enclosure. In this sense, the ambitious fantasy of undoing reflects the desperate straits of aloneness in which the person finds himself.

It is precisely because of this isolating quality of self-enclosure that each attempt to begin again resembles a false start. To find a grounding in the real and foster the illusion of a new beginning requires the recognition of another person. In this sense, Balint's (1968) concept of "benign regression," with its aim of recognition, implies that it is not through the undoing of trauma that one finds a sense of the real. It is only by securing a credible witness to one's experience that one can acknowledge finally the reality of the trauma and secure a new beginning.

5

The Silent Loyalty Oath: Symptoms as Memorials to One's Lonely Suffering

When a man gets his finger stuck in the door, his whole being goes with it.

— Hasidic saying

The tragedy of this world is that everyone is alone. For a life in the past cannot be shared with the present. Each person who gets stuck in time gets stuck alone.

— Alan Lightman, *Einstein's Dreams*

It is no good casting out devils. They belong to us. We must accept them and be at peace with them.

— D. H. Lawrence

DAN: THE MUTENESS OF
LONELY SUFFERING

Dan is a 41-year-old man who came for psychotherapy five months after his mother died of lung cancer. He said that he missed her quite a bit, and that it would be difficult to go on without her. In addition, he complained of experiencing anxiety and did not know why. Dan is a successful executive in the music business. Two years earlier, after enduring years of struggling with infertility, he and his wife had adopted a baby girl.

It became clear fairly quickly that Dan's relationship with his mother had not been as rosy as he had described it at first. She had been a depressed, anxious woman who rarely had a good word to say about anybody. She spoke enviously of her neighbors, friends, and other family members. She complained frequently about her lot in life, especially with regard to the family's tenuous financial situation. From a very early age, Dan remembered that whenever his mother was present, a pall seemed to hang over the house.

In sharp contrast, Dan described his father as a "very good man." He was cheerful and hard-working, but unambitious. That lack of ambition annoyed Dan's mother no end, a fact she did not try to hide from Dan. His father's cheerfulness seemed sometimes to be a ray of sunshine in Dan's childhood; at other times, it masked an obliviousness to the mother's crankiness.

Whereas Dan's father was a great disappointment to his mother, Dan himself could do no wrong. All of her hopes to be rescued from her unhappiness rode on Dan's shoulders. If he drew a picture, he was to become a great artist. If he wrote a good paper, he would become another Hemingway. The unspoken message came through loud and clear: there is no middle ground; anything short of greatness is the same as failure. It is no wonder then that at each point when Dan embarked on a separation, such as at the beginning of kindergarten or of high school, he suffered from bouts of anxiety.

111

These anxiety attacks have continued into adulthood. Often on the ride into work on Monday mornings, he would be paralyzed with worry, but could not elaborate on what it was about. One of the problematic aspects of treatment has been Dan's tendency to cover over his depression and anxiety behind a determined show of cheeriness. His sad eyes, however, revealed what was not being said. He tears up frequently when he speaks of those close to him, such as his daughter, his wife, or a good friend, and what they mean to him—as if he cannot believe his own good fortune.

I made numerous attempts to gain access to Dan's dark side by suggesting possible reasons he felt it necessary to be positive. Perhaps, I said, he was afraid that his bad side, his underlying depression, would overwhelm the good and so must be kept under wraps. Or maybe he could not stand to think of himself as in any way resembling his mother. Dan listened politely to these interpretations, but would then change the subject. Instead, he would make frequent calls between sessions, requesting a return call because he was having a "difficult time." Many of these calls have come while Dan has been driving in to work.

Very recently, three years after beginning treatment with me, Dan's symptoms of anxiety and panic came to a head. He and his wife decided to scale back their lives and sell their expensive home. They could make a profit of $200,000. More importantly, Dan thought, his lifelong anxiety over money concerns would be greatly diminished. Meanwhile, his business was going through a low period, a periodic occurrence that always filled Dan with catastrophic images of failure and humiliation.

Soon after making this decision to sell his home, Dan woke up at 4:30 in the morning, knowing that he would have to set budgeting limits on his business. He started sweating, felt faint, and had chest pains. His wife called for an ambulance, and he was wheeled out on a stretcher and taken to an emergency room where he received an angiogram. An arrhythmia was diagnosed, and a small inflammation on the wall of the heart was also found. When I returned Dan's emergency phone call, I said I was glad it was not more serious. But Dan and I knew that this involved more than just his heart. He was scared. I added that something important was going on inside of him that had not been put into words.

Dan came to his next session with a sheepish smile as if to say "Now finally, with these life-and-death stakes at hand, maybe I will be taken seriously." He declared he would do anything to be rid of "this elephant on my chest." I asked Dan how his mother would have felt had she known he would make a $200,000 profit on the house, and he replied she would have been envious. I suggested then that he had been placed in the impossible position of being sent out into the world to succeed financially—where his father had failed—but that if he did succeed he would be one of the many objects of his mother's envy. He confirmed that it was plain she had been envious when he moved into his expensive house.

Perhaps this double bind of damned if you do, damned if you don't had something to do with the weighty elephant on his chest. Dan nodded, but then he wished out loud that he could experience a suddenly resonating "Aha," or be able to break down and sob. Here, too, anything short of a *great* melodramatic expression of underlying feeling was a failure. We tried to talk about the roots and history of the anxiety and depression we had never really explicated. Dan recalled his mother telling him on a number of occasions how she wanted to die. When he was about 5 years old, he remembers vividly that she threatened herself with a knife. Dan shook while he spoke, his eyes welled up with tears, but he said it felt good to share his secret. Another time, she got into an argument with a neighbor and said to Dan, "Let's go, we're going to go away from here." He remembers the terror he felt upon hearing his mother's declaration, and wished he could make life better for her. At the same time, however, Dan admitted dramatically that he hated his mother, wished her dead, and did not feel bad about saying so. We concluded the session, and Dan said it had been very helpful.

Nevertheless, I think we came closer to arriving at something meaningful in Dan's experience when at one point I suggested that Dan felt trapped inside with unspeakable sadness and anxiety, and that he did not know how to get at those feelings and convey it to someone else, like me. In a sense, his muteness was a wish that someone could just discern his desperation and rescue him from his predicament. Perhaps the incommunicado quality of Dan's sense of isolation is itself symptomatic of his story and subsequent journey of lonely suffering. By showing rather than telling, Dan may be attempting to communicate how enclosed and entrapped he felt with his mother, and that there was nowhere to go for help. He could only hang onto his father's cheeriness as a life raft to escape drowning in the deadness of his mother's life. In the following I will explore how this loneliness and incommunicado quality of suffering in childhood may become encoded and memorialized in the shown quality of psychological symptomatology.

THE UNCERTAINTY OF BEING ONE'S OWN WITNESS

Throughout my tenure as a father, I have had ample opportunity to observe my two sons endure assorted accidents as they negoti-ated their respective ways through the obstacles of everyday toddlerhood. On those occasions, for example, when one of my sons would scrape his knee or bump his head, I noticed that there was usually a short time delay before he would break into tears and seek me out for comfort. What kinds of meanings were being imposed on the injury as soon as it occurred? What sort of impact does the realization of injury have on the search for a restorative solace?

In a commentary on a paper of mine (Shabad 1993b), Paul Russell (1993) recounted the following autobiographical incident:

Some years ago when the Dutch elm disease was taking its toll, I was driving on a windy day, when a huge dead tree was sud-denly blown over just as I, a bit too speedily, was approaching it. It crashed, with a mighty thunderous thud, across the road just in front of me. . . . I managed just barely to slow down enough so that bumping into the trunk of the tree did not do much damage to the car or myself. I had to back up and find a detour. As I did so, I thought, ever so briefly, about what would have happened had I been just a fraction of a second farther along. Twenty minutes later, having finally arrived at my destination, I was describing to a friend what had just happened. I found myself, for the first time, feeling faint, dizzy, and sweaty. I had to sit down. [p. 517]

It is significant that Russell's near accident occurred when he was alone. It is only twenty minutes later, when in the presence of a friend, that Russell displayed his symptomatology of feeling "faint, dizzy, and sweaty." When my son injured his knee he was more fortunate in that there was someone he could turn to for solace and recognition of what had happened to him *at the time* it happened. Someone who could bear witness to the reality of his suffering.

Perhaps it is this very transformation of experienced suffering into a witnessed reality at the moment it occurs that inoculates that experience against traumatization. For if, as Russell proposes, trauma can be known only after the fact, through its residual trail of post-traumatic communication, it suggests that the isolation of not being able to convey one's experience immediately is intrinsic to the transformation of suffering into trauma. Similarly, Stolorow and Atwood (1992) have said that "painful or frightening affect becomes traumatic when the requisite attuned responsiveness that the child needs from the surround . . . is absent" (p. 53). As Russell suggests, a person may need a sense of connectedness in order to have the freedom to feel. In Dan's case, he was not able to convey the anxieties and burdens he had experienced in the enclosed space with his mother to someone who would understand. As a result, he turned away from those feelings and any hopes of ever communicating them.

When we suffer as children, we are often not aware of what is triggering our emotional pain, let alone able to convey it in words to someone else. This is especially true of the insidiously cumulative frustrations of the traumatic theme, when we are progressively disillusioned by a parent who continues to be physically present but otherwise unavailable. When no one is there to offer comfort to us, we adapt by learning how to go it alone and rely on our own resources, a stoic self-reliance that all too often seems to be one of the residual effects of growing up. Without another person to validate the event of our suffering, we are forced into the awkward, involuted position of bearing witness to our own experience. This places the child who is suffering alone in the proverbial situation of the falling tree— "If there is no one to hear a tree falling in the forest, then did it make noise?" Unlike trees, however, we as human beings may enlist our minds as homegrown witnesses to our own experience.

At the same time that we take dissociative flight from the trauma endured passively within our bodies, we use involuted mental activity to watch over ourselves, to bear witness to our own experiences. Thus, we not only have an experience of suffering, but also a self-consciousness of our predicament, a self-consciousness charged with the caretaking responsibility of taking up the slack for the witness who was supposed to be there but was not. Now, like a lioness fiercely protective of her injured cub, we may, through the filter of self-consciousness, feel sorry for ourselves, becoming indignant on our own behalf.

There are problems, however, in this makeshift attempt to become witness to our own suffering. Self-consciousness, when born of disillusionment and the flight of dissociative defense, is not grounded in the substantive reality of the body. To the extent that we are not inhabiting ourselves and life is not being lived from within, we do not have a corpus of lived experience to fall back on for a sense of certainty. We know and do not know what should be there, we therefore both know and do not know what is not there, and finally we know and do not know that we have actually experienced a trauma. When Gary emphasizes his incompetence as a lawyer, or his loser status with women, or his nerdy, bespectacled looks, there is a self-conscious quality in his display of pathos. On one occasion, he boasted that he was so desperate to be well-liked in college that he would go to frat parties, get "plastered," and then get on the dance floor and wave and smile to imaginary friends—all to feign a wished-for popularity to anyone who might glance at him. Gary's determination to wear his shame on his sleeve proudly and self-consciously alerted me to the possibility that he may have been attempting to convey the experiences of degradation he had endured for which he had no words.

Russell (1993) uses the metaphor of a camera attempting to photograph its own injury to describe our attempt to bear witness to our own experience. He suggests that because "the photographic perceiving and recording apparatus itself is damaged while it is being built . . . a camera cannot photograph its own injury" (p. 518). In this sense, bearing witness has to do with bearing the responsibility of remembering and testifying to the actuality of one's suffering. Pervaded with doubts, the mind is an uncertain witness to itself. Stolorow and Atwood (1992) suggest that these tormenting doubts about the actuality of one's experience are "an inevitable consequence of the absence of validating attunement" (p. 55). The burdensome tension of being a vigilant watchdog of our own experience so as to prove its real existence eventually becomes too wearing for one person to carry.

THINKING-IN AND ACTING-OUT

Aloneness is a subtle destroyer of the sense of the real. Within our self-enclosed solitude we can become caught up in involuted spirals of *thinking-in*. Through our mind's eye, doubt is sown and cultivated as we become less certain that what happened "out there" actually did happen. The derealizing process of thinking-in works against our quest to prove that our suffering was not just a figment of our imagination, but a real event. Within the enclosed isolation of our own minds, we chase the tail of the real, but we can never quite catch up because we are looking for something that can only be found outside of ourselves. Our lack of success in extricating ourselves from doubt keeps us on a merry-go-round of obsessional thinking that may be perpetuated indefinitely. One of Freud's early disciples, Wilhelm Stekel (1949) put it this way: "The more the patient loses himself in his world of fantasies, the stronger becomes his doubt which always compares fantasy with reality and is unable to obtain congruity" (p. 259).

Take, for example, the abrupt ending of a passionate love affair. Each lover is left to gather up the real pieces of the breakup
that occurred so much more rapidly than they could realize. To
hold onto the elusively real story, the lovers' minds may work
overtime as they attempt feverishly to catch up to the facts that
have passed them by. They think back to their first encounter, to
their growing attraction to each other—as if to confirm for themselves that they were drawn together by irresistible excitement.
They remind themselves of how they became intimate and declared
"I love you" while staring into each other's eyes. Or did they? She
seemed to mean what she said, or did she? With hesitant step and
delicate feeling, he then begins to tread down the memory path
of the breakup. He painstakingly retraces the steps of how good
turned to bad, and reenacts scenes of how the full bloom of passion gave way to complaints about her need for space. His mind
then drifts off, for the burden of bearing witness to his own suffering is too much to bear. No matter how much he goes over it, it
does not make sense. He still cannot believe what happened. And
so he tries to catch the sequence of events one more time . . .

To return to the metaphor of the camera attempting to photograph its own injury, I would suggest that although the photographic apparatus is damaged, we nevertheless, through the use
of self-consciousness, attempt to photograph our own injuries.
However, because of the nature of the involuted mental equipment, when the photograph is developed it is dreamlike and blurry.
In a desperate attempt to develop a clear picture of a real injury,
we snap the picture again and again, typically with the same faulty
equipment, typically to no avail, and therefore repeatedly. With
regard to the uncertainty conveyed by the Winnicottian (1951)
paradox, "Did you conceive of this or was it presented to you from
without?" (pp. 239–240) or "Did I do this or was this done to me?"
we remain mired in doubt. Perhaps it is for this reason that many
psychotherapy patients are uncertain about the accuracy of their
memory when they complain about their parents' actions. They
may wonder, for example, whether they are exaggerating how
much they were ridiculed by their father or ignored by their

mother. If they are just making it up, then certainly they are being unfair by complaining to a therapist about being victimized many years later.

Our aim of objectifying our experience is made difficult by the fact that we have placed our own narrative stamp of memory on our suffering as soon as it occurs. To secure a witness to our experience and transform it into an objective event, we attempt continually to reenact the original scene of the trauma. For the traumatized person embroiled in the repetition compulsion, it may not be easy to discern the differences between trauma as our intended, omnipotently created experience and trauma as an objective event that is independent of our omnipotence. Just as thinking-in has a derealizing effect on a person's experience of lonely suffering, so the countervailing urge to resolve doubt and achieve the objective clarity of realization fuels the various forms of acting-out of the repetition compulsion.

Corresponding to this fundamental inability to determine the cause of trauma ("Did I create my own suffering or did I find it?") is a dark cloud of recrimination that makes it impossible to determine who or what is to blame ("Do I blame myself for my suffering or do I blame another for doing this to me?"). To the extent that we continue to re-create this traumatic scene as a means of securing a validating witness, we may begin to hate ourselves for reproducing our own torment. Locked in our self-enclosed solitude, we may feel that we must answer to ourselves for not fulfilling our own wishes narcissistically, and for continuing to maintain them in the face of an overwhelmingly frustrating reality. We blame our predicament on our desire for something better that cannot be, and attempt to dissociate from wishes that only lead nowhere.

These wishes, however, are also a bridge back to the imagined idealized scenarios, when others should have been there as witness to our experience. Therefore, they are also a disillusioning reminder of the reality of the lonely suffering that we endured instead. By prohibiting the imaginative elaboration and expression of these wishes for a better alternative, we risk further derealizing our pain of lonely suffering into something that may or may not have happened. The more we become burdened with the conviction that we have created our own suffering and are disconnected from the reality of being victimized by another, the more urgently we attempt to convey proof of our victimization.

Where there is impulse, self-recriminations and prohibitions are sure not to be far behind. Addictions are a prime example of how we become bound up in cycles of prohibitive thinking-in and impulsive acting-out. In the aftermath of overeating or engaging in impersonal sex, we frequently aim ruthless criticism toward ourselves. Although with great shame and self-hatred we may declare "mea culpa," it may only be a week later when we find ourselves secretly heading for the refrigerator, the prostitute, the gay bar—as if attempting to remain unknown to ourselves. In a sense, the impulsive acting-out of addiction is a desperately defiant attempt to bring the dignity and meaning of reenacted reality to experiences that have been rendered unreal.

Maybe it is not coincidental that when we are isolated from social reality, the primitive quality of a one-person psychology drive theory of wish and discharge indeed seems to apply. When the delicately intangible interchange of social discourse is not available, we urgently and intensely attempt to maintain ourselves by falling back on the tangible solidity of our biological needs. The spirals of this primitive sort of malignant regression with the aim of gratification (Balint 1968) continue endlessly precisely because we remain self-enclosed. As long as we do not find the realization of experience that can only be discovered through the eyes of another, inner battles to maintain a sane grip on the real will linger, unseen by any outside observer.

THE SELF-BETRAYAL OF FORGETTING ONE'S SUFFERING

Russell (1993) concludes his paper by saying, "The repetition compulsion is an illness of loneliness . . . It is also the individual's only means of reattachment and emotional growth" (p. 521). I would add that an individual's unique constellation of psychological symptomatology reflects the solitary, unspoken journey of the repetition compulsion in its effort to carry the message of the person's lonely sufferings.

Symptoms are thus not only compromise formations between drive derivatives and their inhibitions, as Freud (1926) contended; they are also a means of combating the paralyzingly derealizing effects of thinking-in on the testimony of memory. When patients massively repress their childhood sufferings, when they make their minds a blank in order to survive, they often give a voice of dignity to their muteness through their symptomatology. Behind every person lies a yet-to-be unraveled and spoken story of lonely suffering. In this light, Greenspan (1992) has described the symptoms of Holocaust survivors as an attempt to recount or make a story from what is not a story.

Arthur is a 42-year-old man who presented with symptoms of depression and anhedonia. Although he reported having a successful house-painting business, a good marriage, and three college-age children whom he loved dearly, much to his mystified chagrin he could not seem to derive much joy from his life or significant relationships. And although he was tormented by obsessional concerns of the "other shoe dropping" on the peaceful stability of his family life, of something catastrophic occurring to one of his close family members, he spoke with seeming indifference about his own death, "whenever it happens, it happens."

As Arthur continued to tell his story, it became apparent that his attainment of some measure of success in love and work was a testament to human fortitude and resilience. He came from a broken home that was emotionally and financially impoverished. His father was an unreliable, infrequent visitor to a household in which Arthur lived with his alcoholic mother and younger sister. On numerous occasions, he watched his inebriated mother engage in sexual intercourse with assorted men—some of whom would slap him around. He saw it as his responsibility to take care of his sister, for they were two orphans against the storm. He reported that more than once he would walk miles with his sister to more well-to-do neighborhoods and knock on doors, asking people to feed his sister. Often he would then receive a meal for himself as well.

He recounted that his depression might have something to do
with an incident that occurred when he was 13 years old. He had
gone away to visit his grandmother for three weeks in another state,
only to find that there were strangers living in his house when he
returned home. His mother had left no forwarding address, and
his stamp and model collections were gone forever. He slept on a
nearby park bench for a few days until he was picked up by the
police. Although he finally located his mother soon after this
episode, some friends of the family took him in as unofficial guard-
ians for the duration of his high school years. Without looking
back, Arthur then proceeded on to adult life.

To survive his childhood sufferings psychically intact, Arthur
did his best to put his experiences behind him. He became one of
the numerous secure, well-to-do suburbanites with nice houses and
stable families whom long ago he had resented and envied. In
attempting to take the money and run without so much as a glance
backward, however, Arthur betrayed a silent loyalty oath he had
taken with himself never to forsake his early hardships. Like the
Holocaust survivor who was charged with the responsibility of
insuring that the world bear witness and *never forget*, Arthur, too,
had sworn to himself to bring out the message of his own private
holocaust.

Arthur's dilemma was one not unlike that of an obese person
who undergoes rapid weight loss and then feels alien and fraudulent in his newly attained body, yet is still unable to look at photo-
graphs of his previously heavy self. Arthur, never having caught
up with himself, was trapped in limbo between two unintegrated
identities, between the desire for a better life and his loyalty to a
more unhappy one.

It is in this light then that we can understand Arthur's symptoms of anhedonic depression as a not-so-gentle reminder to heed
his unfortunate beginnings. As possessively envious parents might
begrudge their child a better life, Arthur, through his anhedonia,
spoiled and enviously robbed himself of his own pleasures as atonement for the transgression of forgetting his lonely suffering. It thus
is not coincidental that Arthur's symptoms led him to seek psy-

chotherapy, and to retrieve in words those experiences of suffering that had for so long remained unspoken.

I bore witness to Arthur's experience. We constructed a dialogue between past and present, between a deprived, envious child drowning in misfortune and a more fortunate adult who got out when the going was good. I would take the role of Arthur as a child and declare indignantly, "Who do you think you are, getting so big for your britches? You became one of all those rich people we used to hate. You swore a blood oath that you would never forget and you would remain loyal to me forever. Now you've joined the enemy and betrayed me." Arthur smiled, clearly relishing the game in which we were engaged. He replied, "I didn't desert you. I had to get out. I haven't forgotten where I came from. I'm trying to help both of us."

For people who as children have endured psychological hardship in isolation, it is almost incomprehensible when good fortune knocks on the door many years later. If such individuals were to embrace a contented life, then who would carry the baton of remembering what occurred long ago? If Arthur were to live happily ever after, then no one would ever know the travails he had to get through to live securely. These experiences, never relayed to another person, would sink into the meaninglessness of unrealized obscurity. If so, then toward what end did he suffer? For what? What was the point of it all if his experiences never were to be memorialized through the validating eyes of a witness?

It is similar to a boxing match in which one boxer pummels the other one mercilessly, until finally knocking him into submission. The victorious boxer stands over the prone figure for a moment, and then leaves the ring with hands raised in triumphant pride. Slowly, the humiliated, defeated boxer struggles to his feet. Now, finally, ready to fight again and win back his self-respect, he begins to shadowbox, all the while saying to himself: "I'll show him, he won't get away with that." The problem is that now there are nothing but shadows left to fight, for the winner has long since departed from battle and gone on to new challenges. Thirty years may go by, but haunting afterimages of his humiliation will not let him forget. He never did get satisfaction for his wounded sense of dignity.

The indignity of such victimizations is made infinitely worse if there is no one to witness the event and offer consolation. Another person's compassion implicitly demonstrates to the sufferer that the witness not only has seen what occurred, but also has some feeling for what he has endured and shares his suffering in spirit. The sufferer knows he is not alone, and does not have to go to any great lengths to prove that what happened really happened.

For persons who never have secured a witness to validate their experience, it is both too early and too late to encounter an empathic, generous lover or a comfortable, secure life many years after the fact. Too early, because they are not ready to relinquish the memory of their lonely suffering until it has seen the realized light of day. Too late, because their good fortunes have arrived at the scene of the crime only belatedly, after the damage has been done.

There are, however, those few individuals who seem to have a sixth sense of knowing what is good for them. Such persons often are able to use their lonely suffering as a starkly contrasting reminder from which to appreciate with immense gratefulness the new life in which they find themselves. Although their degree of gratitude may still indicate that it is all too good to be true, a certain practical streak seems to keep them headed in the right direction. Many others, however, cannot easily give up the resentment and indignation of their lonely suffering until their experience of victimization has been recognized to their satisfaction. If it is too late to take newly discovered witnesses back in time to the scene of their suffering, it is not too late to bring reenacted proof of that experience into the present.

However, rather than embrace the ready-made solution provided by a newly found empathic witness, such persons often are compulsively drawn to individuals who will enable them to reenact the original problem as a way of trying to solve it. Some women who had unreliable, alcoholic fathers, for example, even though they may profess a desire to settle down, may frequently be attracted to unreliable, restless men who will not commit to them.

If a stable, generous man does enter the life of such a woman, she may find him boring—almost as if his stability does not fit who she is and who she has been. In this sense, romantic attraction may be a vehicle by which problems of the past are reidentified and reenacted to ensure that they are not forgotten. Sometimes, however, this sort of reenactment as memory is manifested primarily as part of a person's character. As we have seen in the case of Arthur, the story of lonely suffering is maintained and memorialized in symbolically encapsulated form through the repeated symptom of anhedonic depression.

SYMPTOMS AS SELF-ENCLOSED ATTEMPTS AT COMMUNICATION

External events do not just happen to us; they do not just stamp a fixed impact on our receptive inertia. We immediately elaborate on the givens of life, creating what we find as we go along. Rather than exist only as passive objects prompted by Freudian drives or narcissistic needs (or what Mitchell [1988] speaks of in terms of the metaphors of the "beast" or "damage," respectively), we ultimately fashion meaning out of the internal and external imperatives of our lives. With the first glimmerings of self-reflection, an overseeing or narrative function insures that meaning will be imposed on a continuous flow of experiences so as to make a coherent and meaningful story. Romanyshyn (1982) speaks of psychological life deepening the empirical world so profoundly that what is, is inseparable from how it is perceived.

The multitude of meanings that can be retroactively imposed on prior experience, however, is so malleably dependent on the shifting actions, moods, purposes, and will of the person in the present that it is easy to second-guess the real existence of that experience. Because it is at the beck and call of such impermanence, where only doubt is certain, the meaningful continuity of our life stories may degenerate into the meaninglessness of randomness, where one interpretation of meaning is as good as another. We may then wish to have less interpretive power over our experience, and instead hunger for something that has its own real existence independent of our subjectivity. In this regard, we seek not so much the freedom to deconstruct objective events into so many relative elements and differently experienced perspectives, but to elaborate our experience into the memorable status of something real and objective. Our task entails discovering a reality beyond our creative control in order to confirm that our experience is not merely a dreamlike figment of our imagination. Through the validation offered by another person outside the area of our omnipotence, we can emerge from our inner worlds to make the unconscious conscious and the created real, thereby arriving at a sense of realization.

Symptoms may thus be viewed as self-created communicative actions intended once and for all to build a lasting monument to one's experiences of suffering. This self-revelatory urge to transform one's forgotten experience into the objectivity of a memorable reality strikingly resembles the impetus animating the artistic process. If the artistic process consists in creatively elevating one's experience through its dramatization into an objective event, then the neurotic could be said to create his illness of symptoms in a dramatic attempt to objectify his unwitnessed experience of suffering. Because this illness is an involuted work of art with a very private language, however, its artistic aim of objectification through self-disclosure remains ever-elusive. For this reason Rank (1936) described the neurotic as an *artiste manquée* (a missed or failed artist). In effect, the neurotic misses as an artist because his self-enclosed communicative attempts are so indirect that they never find their sought-for audience.

Perhaps the more unheeded the symptomatic message, and the more doubt-laden the memory of our suffering, the more we must raise the decibel level of our choked-off communications. Thus, the self-enclosing pressures of thinking-in may become so isolating that a person's character structure may disintegrate or break down. Extreme obsessional defenses are frequently the last bastion of character maintenance before a nervous collapse. In breaking down or collapsing, we seek desperately to come out of the circular fixity of chasing our own tail and to find an opening to others. In this sense, an acute psychotic episode may be viewed as a radical attempt to cure ourselves by breaking open our self-enclosed prison and initiating an otherwise prohibited overture toward others. Perhaps this is what the German poet Rilke (1934) has in mind when he writes: "If there is anything morbid in your processes, just remember that sickness is the means by which an organism frees itself of foreign matter; so one must just help it to be sick, to have its whole sickness and break out with it, for that is its progress" (p. 70).

SYMPTOMS AS ONE'S INTIMATE CREATIONS AND THE RESISTANCE TO CHANGE

During the Middle Ages deviant behavior was attributed to possession by the devil, and a person's evil or dissenting spirits were removed by exorcism or burning at the stake. In modern-day psychology, we have become more sophisticated and perhaps more humane in our attempts to disentangle people from their unwanted demons. Whereas in earlier times whole human lives that were thought to be possessed by sin were eliminated, now internal parts of the self or internal selves may be cast away with the aid of various treatments. Many behavioral psychologists detach problematic behavior from the whole person of a patient as if to say, "I may not like your behavior, but I like you." Some mental health professionals probably cope with much of their countertransference hatred in this fashion. They attribute their dislike of the patient to the patient's psychopathology or illness rather than viewing it as an inherent part of the person. In so doing, however, clinicians rob their patients of their personal dignity as adults, people who are responsible, to a great degree, for earning like or dislike from others.

When patients come to psychotherapy with urgent pleas for the therapist to alleviate their suffering by helping them get rid of their most troublesome symptoms, they are, in a certain sense, betraying the integrity of their full selves. Often, patients count on the treatment and the eradication of their symptom pathology as something that will allow them to emerge from therapy as brand-new, changed persons. And when the desires of patients to change align with the therapist's hope for the patient's future, we are said to have built a therapeutic alliance. The idealizing transference then could be described as an intensification of the trust patients put in therapists to deliver them from their suffering—and, to some extent, from themselves. From this viewpoint, the therapeutic alliance is a collaboration to transform patients with their unacceptable symptomatology into the symptom-free persons they have not yet become. Often, if things are to proceed well in treatment, everyone—therapist and patient alike—is all too happy to be rid of such troublemaking symptoms as depression, or bad choices in relationships, or work inhibitions. However, patients may view their symptoms as something akin to a very personal secret friend of whom they are publicly ashamed, but privately proud. Although symptoms may be experienced as unwelcome alien intruders, they also are among the most intimate of one's creations. This view of psychological symptoms as self-created for the purpose of conveying and memorializing one's suffering has fundamental implications for the concept of resistance in clinical work. Thus, alongside a patient's initial hope to change into the better person she will become, there is also from the onset of any treatment an underlying dignity of the intact self that resists the unspoken coerciveness of therapeutic change, and that clutches the unwanted suffering child of the symptom tightly to its breast.

This becomes clearer if we imagine the self as an extended family to which even the wayward and deviant belong. Any attempts to extract or eliminate only the problem-child member call forth fiercely protective reactions from the rest of the family. Although an older brother may beat up his younger brother as a matter of habit, he may also be the first one to rise to his brother's defense if an outsider were to bully his younger brother in the same way. It is one thing to target one's own symptoms for ridicule and vicious criticism, but let someone else try it, and it is then, and only then, that patients may discover an invisible loyalty to an aspect of themselves that previously they had considered a foreign body.

Symptoms are often retained as one's intimate creations until the reasons for their coming into being have been fully acknowledged and witnessed by the therapist. Some patients may entertain fantasies of their parents at long last bearing witness to their suffering and begging for forgiveness. Soon after Gary began psychotherapy and joined Alcoholics Anonymous, he expressed the following fantasy: he imagines himself telling his tale of self-sacrifice and loneliness to his A.A. group with his parents also sitting in attendance. They would hear how he turned to drink to escape the demons of his isolation. Upon listening to his story, his parents, aghast and shocked at the revelation of this darker side of their son they had never known, would break into tears, approach Gary after the group, and beg him for forgiveness. This fantasy helped Gary and me understand that a powerful motive animating his embrace of suffering and victimization was to alert his parents to his plight.

To the extent that the unwritten contract between patient and therapist to effect change does not take into account patients' ambivalences about leaving old parts of themselves behind, these ambivalences may set up a resistance against any singleminded pursuit of cure. For example, a perfectionistic, bulimic patient, who habitually complied with the high achievement standards of her parents, one day emerged from a hair salon feeling very happy about her new hairstyle. She was also relatively satisfied with her weight at the time and felt more attractive than usual. On her way home she received many looks that confirmed her feelings. When she arrived home, her roommate complimented her on the new hairdo. Yet a few minutes later, when she was alone in her room, the patient found herself feeling extremely annoyed and irritable. When all goes well, sometimes it goes too well.

Unheard voices, locked away in the dark oblivion of the unconscious, strive at the most inopportune times for the dignity of realized expression. Through guerrilla-like ambushes of repeated symptomatology, patients rebel against the tyranny of their own repression, imposed in the name of compliantly getting along. It is precisely because everyone else would be rid of these subversive symptoms that patients hold on all the more tenaciously to their personal "black-sheep children," as if in sentimentalized embrace to protect them against all those who would do them harm.

One married man reported having unwanted homosexual liaisons with anonymous men. It was not readily apparent what the patient's sexual orientation was; what was significant, however, was that because of the patient's ruthless self-condemnation, he defiantly sentimentalized his homoerotic feelings, as if shielding them from imagined global enemies. As a parent might compensate her children for neglecting them by showering the children with reparative gifts, so this patient indulged his disavowed wishes with compulsively expressed actions. These symptomatic reenactments implicitly expressed an urgent demand for the unconditional acceptance of those yearnings that he perceived everyone (and most importantly himself) had vilified.

It is not unusual for patients to come to their sessions and recount sheepishly, as if apologizing to the therapist, how they "screwed up" again, by manifesting their own particular type of symptomatology once more. At these junctures in treatment, I sometimes suspect that patients secretly take a perverse pride in not betraying an earlier edition of themselves in the face of being seduced into changing for the better, with me as therapist posing as the serpent. When therapeutic movement comes too quickly, some patients may be tempted to break a silent loyalty oath they took with themselves during the loneliest of times, an oath never to forget.

Freud's genius lay in his recognition that, no matter how much one would will it to be so, there can be no volitional killing off of a part of the self without doing an injustice to the self as an integral whole. After all, a patient's particular constellation of symptoms is also his creation, his offspring. Perhaps the same gifts the child offers that are not accepted by and unwanted by parents are taken back to curdle bitterly into symptoms that are then presented to the world, as the unreceived tears of a weeping child become the stuck sadness of an adult's depression. Or perhaps old, unheeded voices, split off from any say over the self's actions, may literally return from the repressed in the form of auditory hallucinations. Just as each branch reaches back to the trunk of a tree, the untold stories underlying each symptom cry out for recognition of a whole self.

BOB: FROM SYMPTOM TO WHOLE PERSON

Bob is a 28-year-old man who came for psychotherapy because of what he called a sex addiction. He said he had been participating in a sex addiction support group for the last year, but the problem had persisted nevertheless. He had a serious relationship with a girlfriend and he was distressed that his problem might interfere with and ruin that relationship. Bob said that in his job as a software salesman he traveled a great deal. During those trips, when he was alone in his hotel room, he would engage in phone sex or have a call girl come to his room and dance for him.

Bob hated himself for these compulsive dalliances that he saw as betrayals of his girlfriend. He was desperate to be rid of his symptoms. His support group colluded with Bob's self-recriminations, viewing his addiction as a destructive, anomalous behavior that should be killed off through sexual abstinence.

In Bob's twice-weekly psychotherapy with me, our approach to the problem was quite different. I made it clear that because I did not view his sex addiction to be physiologically based, it probably would be more helpful to understand it rather than to eliminate his behavior immediately. I emphasized that his sense of shame and the group's encouragement of abstinence only served to strengthen the behavior's persistence. Despite the potential risk of Bob's feeling blamed for his addiction, perhaps paradoxically, he seemed visibly relieved when I placed responsibility for his symptom back in his control.

With this ethic of understanding guiding our work, we sought out the reasons this particular symptom was created at this particular time. As Bob's story unfolded, he recounted that he grew up on an isolated farm in Wisconsin as an only child. His father was a long-distance truck driver and he described his mother as cold, unaffectionate, and noncommunicative. As he spoke about his mother's emotional withdrawal from him, tears of indignation and self-pity frequently welled up in his eyes.

Bob was an exceptionally bright boy and excelled in school. He used his academic prowess to escape the desolation he felt in an empty house and to go away to college. Soon after he graduated, he met his girlfriend.

For many persons who have felt emotionally abandoned at an earlier time in their lives and who then later meet the perfect answer to their yearnings, it all may seem like a dream that is too good to be true. Bob, too, felt that meeting his girlfriend was the best thing to ever happen to him. Yet it was precisely her warmth, her buoyancy, and most of all, her loving acceptance of him that did not fit the bleak emptiness of his previous life. She was so good and so precious to him, in fact, that Bob did not feel that he could afford to expose the dark side of his early experiences for fear of alienating her—experiences that he was all to eager to put behind him anyway.

Rather than risk sullying his girlfriend's goodness, Bob nursed his old wounds in private. The problem was, however, that to the extent he could not trust his girlfriend enough to convey to her his experiences of his early isolation and his concomitant resentments, he remained isolated in his insulated, unarticulated world. His girlfriend could then only remain a dream idealized from afar, someone who could not be let in too deeply. Consequently, Bob lived the life of a charlatan: he was in constant fear of being found out and abandoned.

A potentially tragic scenario thus began to emerge, one in which Bob held on tenaciously to his sense of emotional bereftness, determined to memorialize what no one else knew about or would remember. In the meantime, he did not accept the soothing love he always fantasized about as a salvation because it did not seem as real to him as the memories he kept alive in secret. In a sense, his girlfriend's offerings of love went by the wayside because they came too late to save him from his isolation.

Although Bob's bitterness had to be expressed in some way, even if through the nonverbal actions of his symptomatology, he tried to shield his girlfriend from these deepest of shames. Bob and I came to understand that the loneliness he felt in far-flung hotel rooms conjured up the feelings of homelessness, displacement, and emptiness he had felt in the physical presence of his withholding mother. His phone calls for sex were both a way to keep himself company and to express his resentments toward his mother via displacement through the sexual objectification of women. Bob determined to protect his girlfriend from these split-off sentiments because, although he envied her fundamental optimism, he also needed her hopefulness.

Bob endured many tears of indignation and sadness as he worked through much of what had previously been disowned, and that had then manifested in an unwanted addiction. As he began to confide more in his girlfriend about his private vices and the history behind them, he was able gradually to reintegrate what he had split off. A few months later he accepted a promising career opportunity in another state and asked his girlfriend to marry him. She agreed.

Although patients may express tremendous disgust and shame regarding their presenting problems, I believe it is of fundamental importance that we, as clinical practitioners, maintain a consistent ethic of understanding the whole person and the reasons for the symptoms coming into being. The witnessing of the patient's prior experiences depoliticizes the question of the appropriateness or inappropriateness of the symptom and paves the way for it to be welcomed back into the mainstream of the self. In this way, the power of the symptom, derived largely from its status as a dissident with respect to the political correctness of the rest of the personality, is largely diffused. As both therapist and patient together unravel the tale of suffering underlying the symptom's existence, patients gain a needed voice to articulate that what happened to them really happened, thus saving them from having to prove it through repeated symptomatic actions.

If these patients' symptoms were to be killed off, the stories that they contain would not be told, and the patients' experiences of suffering, starved of a life-giving witness, would shrivel up into the meaninglessness of a hallucinatory episode. Symptoms thus are pregnant with constructive meaning, created as they are with the purpose of bringing the dignity of recognition, sometimes many years later, to a person's experiences of lonely suffering. As those experiences are finally revealed in the presence of a credibly empathic witness, they are infused with the meaningful breath of real life, if only for a moment.

6

On the outside Looking in: "Waiting at the End of the Block" and the Sense of Entitlement

Love must be spontaneous to be a spiritual bond in the beginning, and it must remain spontaneous if it is to remain spiritual . . . and those of us who do not believe in the possibility of free love ought to declare frankly that we do not, at bottom, believe in the possibility of freedom.

—George Santayana

The love of liberty is the love of others; the love of power is the love of ourselves.

—William Hazlitt

WOUNDED DIGNITY AND WAITING
TO BE DISCOVERED

An 8-year-old boy has just gotten into an argument with his 4-year-old brother. Tempers flare, voices are raised, until finally the older one pushes the younger one down. The younger boy, in turn, breaks into tears and calls out for his mother. She races in to see what is going on, sees that her younger son is on the ground, and gives her older son a tongue-lashing. Since this scene has now been repeated for the umpteenth time, the 8-year-old has had enough of his mother's favoritism toward his brother. On this occasion, he declares loudly "I'm running away" and races out of the house. Every few steps, he turns around to see if his mother will come after him. He makes it to the end of the block, stops, and waits to see if his mother will chase him down, ask for forgiveness, and bring him back into the fold. At the same time that he awaits her apology, however, he holds onto himself tightly with arms folded, curling up in a self-protective ball to shoo away any would-be comforters. With injured dignity and huddled in self-induced isolation, this boy licks his wounds, all the while waiting for the consolation he cannot accept.

What if, at this point, the mother, perhaps inundated with the psychobabble of "manipulative behavior," "power struggles," and the like, decides not to reinforce her son's behavior, and does not attempt to retrieve him and make up? Or perhaps she may have habitual difficulty in being the first to reach out to reconcile; after all, she thinks, her parents never extended themselves generously toward her. Why should she reinforce her son's temper tantrums? Let him learn a lesson . . . In the meantime, her son remains alone at the end of the block waiting . . . and waiting . . . sometimes many years for the mother who never followed.

When a child reaches out toward a parent repeatedly and gets no response, he may become ashamed for not being able to keep up with the ruthlessly indifferent exigencies of the real world. Embarrassed by the exposed truth and humbling implications of his dependence on others for a sense of significance, and following the lead of his unresponsive elders, he pretends not to be acquainted with many of his deep-seated wishes for relationships. Just as his mother left him to his own devices in his lonely corner at the end of the block, the son now duplicates his experience of maternal neglect in his attitude toward his own desires. As long as his wishes to receive parental concern go unheeded, they are a source of humiliating vulnerability that he attempts to hide under a veil of indifference.

Occasionally, I have asked various adolescents with whom I work at an inpatient unit how they feel about the chronic absences of their fathers. Frequently, they respond sullenly, "I don't care about him. He didn't care about me. Why should I care about him?"—as if deeply held longings could be eliminated so easily.

"Waiting at the end of the block" could have been a passing moment of childish defiance and self-pity had the mother attended to her older son's hurt. If left unheeded, however, his indefinite waiting may eventually become entrenched in his adult character as a chronic pout. In this sense, a pout, reflected in a defiantly protruding lower lip, exaggeratedly embodies the ambivalent tug-of-war between fervent desires to be attended to and a stubborn defensiveness about acknowledging those desires to oneself, let alone to anyone else.

In an attempt to forestall further injury from the outside, we re-create that very same injury within and become the chief culprit in oppressing our own wishes for acceptance and recognition—not unlike the way collaboration with an invading enemy hounds the true representatives of the host nation into exile. In thus being excluded from having any consciously expressive voice in the governance of our life, such disillusioned wishes become the black sheep in our internal family. Yet these very same wishes lie at the core of our being, carrying with them a yet-to-be-attended message of lonely suffering for a not-yet-located witness. Disavowing them leaves them without the overt championing of an active benefactor, making their communication still more roundabout and difficult.

Like a parent who walks many arms-lengths away from a child who is a cause of embarrassment, we may pretend that our desires do not belong to us, but this pretense leads to a problematic passivity. Indeed, our search to reveal and convey our experience to a validating witness often becomes so circuitous because the source of the longing is disavowed, that it may instead be more accurate to describe this passive form of searching as a waiting to be discovered. In relinquishing the active pursuit of our own aims, and abdicating control of the direction of our life to others, we allow reactivity to supplant proactivity. When we are unguided by the personal truth of our desires, life loses its sense of destiny and meaning. Everything now seems beside the point and a sense of emptiness may pervade relationships and activities. The meaningless mutterings of small talk may fill a life in which far more important matters go unmentioned. Alongside this sense of alienation is an underlying restlessness and a determination to be taken seriously. As the direct expression of wishes gives way to the passive indirectness that informs psychological symptomatology, there is a risk that no one will get the message of lonely suffering. Thus, the message must be repeated again and again, ever more emphatically.

Debra is a 50-year-old single nurse, the oldest of five children. She has a depressed 76-year-old mother who both is dependent on and critical of her. Nevertheless, Debra still feels obligated to keep her mother company on weekends. Much of her childhood was spent sacrificing her own needs in exchange for her mother's approval. Debra resents the time and energy she spent ignoring herself, as well as the blind faith that she placed in the fantasied payoff she would receive for her good deeds. From her viewpoint, life owes her a lot, and after years of laborious caretaking, she should not have to lift a finger to receive her just desserts. Instead, she entertains fantasies of the day that an anonymous man would hear her give a public speech regarding patient care and be so moved by her presentation that he would come toward her, discovering her specialness in a crowd.

Gary, too, had fantasies that professional success would mean that women would be clamoring to be part of his life. In effect, he was promised as much by his parents, who indicated that he would be rewarded in the adult future for the hard work he put in as a child. To Gary, that meant receiving the love and softness of a woman that he missed from his mother. He expected that a bevy of women would be so dazzled by his works that they would approach him first. Thus, waiting for his day of promised deliverance to arrive, he never took the first step toward dating any women. That was not part of the unwritten contract imprinted in his head. Throughout his years of treatment, Gary has fantasized many times of being desired very desperately by the woman of his dreams. In his more rageful moments, he imagines her having to grovel toward him as he did toward his mother. He and I have come to understand how his prior experiences of being humiliated on numerous occasions have led him to avoid taking any initiative toward meeting a woman. *This* time, she will have to come toward him.

And so it went with other issues for Gary—in a pattern of compliance, resentment, and entitlement. When he changed professions and his income decreased significantly, he would not negotiate a lowered fee on his own behalf. Although I offered to adjust the fee, he insisted on paying the previous amount. Only in later months and years did a more entitled Gary emerge, visible in his periodic delays in paying. Later on, it turned out that Gary thought that I should have insisted on lowering his fee because he was a good, loyal client. Gary's determination never to be humiliated again meant that he could not expose his wants and vulnerabilities more directly to possible rejection. Rather than go to bat for himself, he waited for me to anoint him with my financial favors. I have been struck continually by the extent to which Gary's determination to cover over his shame and protect himself from further disappointment has disabled his sense of initiative.

THE TRANSFORMATION OF IGNORED WISH
INTO ENTITLED NEED

Behind our humbly compliant masks, disowned wishes lie in wait for their turn at a moment in the sun. In dim realization of their voiceless plight, we protectively embrace those disavowed wishes against everyone—including ourselves—who has done and would continue to harm them. We may view our feelings as if they were little children who have been mistreated for too long and are now owed some reparative indulgences. With a sense of resentment and indignation, we retrieve them from their exiled silence with a vengeance—by providing them a sort of rebirth as entitled needs. Looked at another way, our wishes, having been denied access through the front door of our house, are permitted to break in the back window, now in the form of needs.

Thus, we elaborate on our disillusionments defensively and then oppress ourselves to preempt a greater hurt from the outside world. In this light, the experience of deficit is a product of disillusionments and subsequent defenses that are intended to foreclose further injury. Our characterological self-oppression may then lead to a righteous indignation on behalf of the wishes that have been rendered mute, and to a sense of needful entitlement. In this way an intrapsychic polarization between shifting identifications is set up between our prohibitions—our ruthlessly inhibiting attitude toward our own wishes—and the boomeranging return of those wishes from an internal exile, now embellished in the form of needs. The experience of being needy is a sort of private exclamation of indignation against the frustrations first initiated by others, and then perpetrated as our own cruelty to ourselves.

The language of need, expressive as it is of the biological mandate to survive, bypasses freedom of choice: the response to a need is already predetermined by the life-or-death imperative of filling the need. There is an interpersonal pressure to fill needs, but a choice of whether or not to grant wishes. The constraint that our needs place on the way others are to respond to us can serve subtly to cover over the criticism we fear we would be subjected to for merely wishing to receive care. In this sense, through the expression of needs and the automatic no-choice mandate to fill them, we look to be rescued by others from our harsh attitudes toward our own desires. For example, the rigid playing out of need as somatic symptomatology can mask internal battles that otherwise would take place between desire and self-denial. It is as if a patient who is basking secretly in the attentive ministrations of a therapist were compelled to justify to a phantom accuser why she *must* receive the pleasurable attention: "Don't blame me. I can't help it. I have no choice in the matter. It's just that I am so empty that I need to be filled."

Unfortunately, various techniques of psychoanalytic psychotherapy frequently collude with the stringent dictates of patients who would deny themselves the luxury of wishing. A therapist must empathize with the needs of patients with character disorders, but may not gratify the wishes of the Freudian neurotic. Mitchell (1991) notes pointedly about psychotherapy that when a patient's diagnosis is more serious, her experience of the treatment may be more gratifying.

Whereas the psychic pain resulting from disillusioned wishes may be viewed as an inevitable lesson of hardship to be learned on the road to maturity, the emptiness stemming from need deprivation requires urgent attention. The proliferation of these different attitudes toward wishes and needs makes it necessary to justify our wants by other more desperate means. When a culture is too indulgent of needs and not kind enough to its citizens' wishes, it sets up an impetus to transform wish into need.

Due to the oppressive harshness turned against wishes, or maybe because, as a popular song puts it, one can't always get what one wants, we have become a culture in which desires are communicated by the word *need*. I remember when I was a child it was still typical to hear people say: "I would like to speak to you later" or "I want to go downtown today." In modern parlance, one is apt to hear instead: "I need to speak to you later" or "I need to go downtown today."

Perhaps it is not surprising then that today various groups and individuals seem to vie jealously for their piece of the victimization pie, as if experiences of insult and injury were to be displayed proudly as a heroic badge of honor. Must people go to the extreme lengths of displaying and proving their victimizations, of exhibiting their wounds on talk shows and referring to themselves as "survivors" (when their lives are not at stake), before eliciting the compassion of the community in which they live? Can we not be more understanding and empathic to the everyday disappointments and disillusionments that people live through?

NEED AND DEMAND: COERCIVE VIOLENCE IN GIVING AND RECEIVING

Having a sense of self-righteous entitlement following an experience of victimization may be preferable to the sense of guilty indebtedness we may experience after actively pursuing our wants. Consequently, we may be tempted to sacrifice or give of ourselves first, so that afterward we can anticipate the payback of need fulfillment to which we feel entitled. We look to others to redeem our suffering, to be compensated for our travails, and to be rescued from our sense of exile.

In such circumstances, there often is no compromising and no neutral ground in interpersonal relations when there are competing interests. If we do not act assertively on behalf of our desires, we are likely to feel resentful; on the other hand, if we do take initiative and do what we wish, we often feel guilty. What to do? My own bias is that, perhaps paradoxically, it is more constructive for our culture and less sociopathic for us to assert ourselves freely and then feel the brunt of our guilt. In guilt we feel the pressure of reparative urges to make it up to others, to do good by them. This contrasts sharply with the entitlements that we may feel are owed us when we have selflessly put our own wants to the side.

Unlike wishes, which implicitly convey a request to receive from another person, needs, with their implications of requirement and demand, may do violence to the free discourse of giving and receiving. After all, experiences of disillusionment regarding one's wishes have brought bitter shadows of resentment, indignation, and entitlement in their wake.

What needful persons may idealize at a distance and have always considered so urgently necessary to their lives may be viewed quite differently when the ideal comes down to earth and is actually engaged at close proximity. Thus, for example, a man may seek to win back the estranged girlfriend who had rejected him, and who he now feels he needs. While he pursues her single-mindedly, he is intent on changing her mind about him. It is only after he succeeds in wooing her back that the humiliation of her rejecting him and his desperate neediness of her may surface in their relationship. When the most spiteful and malevolent of resentments have not been fleshed out and verbalized, we may see a form of "malignant regression" (Balint 1968)—an endless spiral of need and demand, in which the repetitiveness of the cycle derives from the perpetual sabotaging and refusal of precisely what is needfully sought.

We are always active participants in the process of receiving the offerings of others. In various ways, we may guard against the influences of others, spoiling the compliments that we receive or not internalizing the kind words of others. This view of receiving as an actively dynamic process has important implications for the understanding of emotional emptiness. When we are desperately thirsty, for example, it does not matter to us from which cup we drink to quench our thirst. It has been my experience in working with certain emotionally empty patients, however, that such patients are tremendously selective about those from whom they receive their gifts. As one patient remarked wryly about his wife, "If she were dying of thirst in a desert, she would want a lemonade." This selectivity concerning who will be one's benefactor, as well as what the gift should be, may reflect a sense of entitlement more than it does an experience of emptiness.

Mary has many good friends who treat her with kindness and

respect, but she perceives her mother to be harsh and rejecting. She struggles with severe depression as she waits, grieving and aggrieved, to receive what she has not received from her mother. It seems she cannot—or perhaps, will not—let herself receive anything good from her friends, thereby not letting her mother off the hook of being the mother the patient feels she should have been. To receive from her friends would imply that she is capable of going on with her life, and leaving the sufferings experienced at the hands of her mother behind.

When we have been embittered by years of emotional starvation, the consensual mutuality of giving and receiving does not do justice to our sense of being entitled to some recompense. The calm of a belated reciprocity does not undo the failures, insults, and shames of the traumatic theme. Rather than receive and accept graciously the gifts that are offered in one hand, we prefer to grab what has not been offered freely from the other hand. Withheld love or objects that have not been offered voluntarily take on a forbidden, idealized quality. If we are fueled by resentment and a sense of neediness, we transgress the boundaries of a free give-and-take by coercing or grabbing the gift that has been held back. Intent on biting the hand that feeds us, we may discover to our chagrin that we cannot use the treasures we have stolen for ourselves anyway.

As can be seen when a temperamental child swipes a toy from another child only to be bored with it moments later, perhaps the point of entitlement lies in pursuit and conquest. Only by coercing another person into surrender may the indignities of not being heeded by one's parents be reversed. The relationships of entitled persons often have a seesaw quality in which the partners chase the hard-to-get, and lose interest after the other person has been gotten. The compulsive tendency to win and to prove their worth over and over again lends a gamelike quality to the relationships of such individuals.

Jeannie is a 48-year-old woman who came to see a female supervisee of mine for therapy because of feelings of loneliness and depression. She is very overweight, sports a little-girl hairdo with barrettes, and wears Mickey Mouse and baby animal T-shirts. She is the fourth youngest of five children, for whom her parents never had enough time. She remembers her father, narcissistic and childlike, telling her repeatedly that she should not expect much from or bother other people, or they would think she was a nuisance. Jeannie often left her aloof, withdrawn mother alone because of her father's admonitions. Indeed, in making herself inconspicuous throughout her life, Jeannie has shown how seriously she has taken her father's words to heart.

At her high school prom, she offered to clean up the kitchen, while others danced the night away. Later on, she would visit women friends with families and would tell them she was just happy to sit on their couch even if they did not interact with her, saying, "Just let me blend into the furniture."

At the end of the fourth therapy session, Jeannie approached her therapist with open arms and declared, "I need a hug." Taken aback, my supervisee embraced half-heartedly. At the next session, Jeannie became annoyed when the therapist broached the subject. Two months later, and two days after Jeannie lost her job, she came to her session tearfully and said, "I want you to hold me" with a sad–angry look.

When a person's resentments are not worked through openly but remain hidden within the fabric of entitled expression, a form of coercive violence may limit the freedom of others to give willingly. Problems may ensue when some therapists, already burdened with indebted feelings of countertransference guilt, collude with the pressures exerted by entitled patients. This is because, in doing so, such therapists may allow themselves to be viewed as an object created by the patient, with little or no autonomous existence of their own. When one attempts to kidnap other persons from their own subjective orbit so as to hold them hostage to one's own demands, the violence of coercion is depersonalizing in its effects. Rather than a two-person psychology, this more resembles a one-and-a-half person psychology of a person and his created object.

In this involuted, narcissistic sense, entitled patients may use the therapist as a vehicle by which to circuitously "give" to themselves, thus subverting the unpredictability of opening up to the real person of the therapist. The therapist's ministrations may be viewed then as omnipotently coerced by the same pity that patients feel for their own plight. I am reminded of a remark that Gary made early in treatment; he said that he was convinced that when others said "I love you" to him they did so because they felt sorry for him. When offerings of love are perceived to be disingenuous or interpreted as pity, patients may respond with indignant rage for being patronized. Sometimes the interpersonal field of give-and-take may become so constrained by the coercive effects of obligatory giving and entitled needfulness that human relations are emptied of any spontaneous desire or genuine caring. There is no real love that I know of that can be given on demand.

ABANDONED TO A SENSE OF ENTRAPMENT

Often it is the same person who takes care of and involuntarily gives to others out of obligation habitually who then feels entitled to demand his or her just due from someone else. Such caretakers often bend over backwards for people they perceive to be weak and helpless and therefore incapable of giving back in a mutual relationship. They have learned to be good martyrs and not ask for favors from someone who already is depleted, downtrodden, and victimized. Instead they may turn to someone else they perceive to be more capable of filling their needs. In this arrangement, caregivers who are weighed down by years of worrying about and giving compulsively to a weaker person may seek to relieve themselves of their burden by leaning on a third person who is perceived to be stronger.

A despair of attaining a reciprocating mutuality, of freely and spontaneously giving and receiving within the same relationship, may, already early in life, give way to a split between relationships that are designated as either compulsive caretaking of the weak or entitled receiving from the strong. Here we see how an unwritten social contract governing the interchange of giving and receiving can become a coercive means of ensuring that what goes around, comes around.

In my view, such a sharp demarcation between relationships that are either giving or receiving ones often originates in the child's triangular relationship with her parents. When a father is either physically or emotionally absent, or both, it is left to the son or daughter to worry about and care for a mother who is perceived to be needy, helpless, and/or depressed.

Typically, we think of persons as helpless when they are unable to help themselves. But none of us are born able to care for ourselves. Infants are helpless precisely because they have not yet had the opportunities to receive help from their caretakers. In this sense, I believe it most useful to view helplessness relationally—not as a self-contained inability to help oneself, but as a not-receiving and not-retaining the help of another person.

For every learned, aided step of developmental competence that children take, whether learning how to eat or how to walk, they pay an incremental price of relinquishing their dependence on those who had taught or helped them in their initial endeavors. Individuals who are more dependent may attempt to bypass paying this price of losing the company of others, finding it too great a cost in exchange for being able to do for oneself. For these persons, to remain helpless, or without help (by *not* internalizing the offerings of others), ensures that dependence on the competence of others will continue, and that they will not be abandoned. In this sense, adult helplessness can be viewed symptomatically as an anxiety-motivated attempt to enforce dependence and to retreat from transitions to relative independence within the developmental process.

There are many mothers, for example, whose self-esteem has been constructed primarily around being of special value to their children. As such, they are dependent on their children's need of them. By not taking compliments well, or by not accepting and internalizing the loving meanings inherent in the offerings of their children, such mothers continue to remain helpless, or without help, thereby binding their loyal children to them. If these mothers were to use their children's offerings to construct an autonomous sense of competence and self-esteem and a sense of their own subjectivity (Benjamin 1988), they would free their children to separate with good conscience. Sometimes the ultimate gift that parents can give to their children is simply to accept their love with grace.

When a mother habitually frustrates her children's attempts to cheer or calm her, they may learn to keep their sure-to-be-thwarted wishes to themselves. But children do not have to offer anything tangible for them to feel that they are laboring on behalf of a parent. Indeed, a child's desire to be of use, inhibited by the mother's inability to receive those entreaties, may become stillborn at its inception. The resulting false start attempts of the child to give of herself may then be reflected in the dead-end ruminations of obsessional worrying. The arduous mental work of worrying about a mother's well-being may be so consuming that it alone may constitute a feeling in the child of busy caregiving. Thus, Winnicott (1960b) has described the process by which parentified children construct a caretaker False Self that has the purpose of propping up the mother's emotional life as primarily mental. Moreover, the fruitless effort involved in the covert work of worry about a parent may not be apparent to any outside onlookers. In this regard, children often have the experience of being abandoned to a self-enclosed isolation in which they are burdened with caretaking pressures. And because they may feel that there is no one else to help watch over a mother who is perceived to be helpless, such children may feel solely responsible for her well-being, with little choice but to take care of her.

I believe that this early sense of being trapped in isolation with another who is perceived as needy and yet who is not able to be helped is a primary reason many adults dread being alone. For in being alone, they are not only responsible for themselves, but also carry within the heavy burden of obligation to care for the now-introjected mother who would not take in anything good for herself. In solitude, then, such individuals may have a vague sense of panic about being simultaneously entrapped with and abandoned to someone who is without help or helpless.

Such a sense of abandoned entrapment, in addition to engendering a pressured sense of indebtedness toward the remembered image of a mother who cannot do for herself, also stimulates a desperate, entitled urgency to be rescued from this predicament. The developmental prototype for this sense of entitlement often derives from the father who should have been there to take care of his wife but was absent, leaving that task to his children in his stead. Weighed down by their burden of obligation, these children thus may become entitled adults who turn to the third party of the outside world to lighten their load. Indeed, the greater the pressure of obligation (and of the accompanying sense of inadequacy of not doing enough for the parent), the more urgently will such persons search for a stronger other to take over the burden of their lives. The continuing quest for a powerful, omniscient figure who will do their thinking, worrying, and deciding becomes a central aspect of the transferences of these individuals.

PSYCHOTHERAPY AND THE FREEDOM
TO BE CREDIBLE

How then should a psychoanalytic therapy approach the sense of indebtedness and inadequacy of such patients, as well as their accompanying resentment and entitlement? Questions of "How are we to link up with each other?" and "How are we to love each other?" constitute the intangible essence of how we are to communicate the stories of our lives. It is this ambiguousness in the potential space of cultural life that explains why human relations depend so much on value systems and ideologies for guiding norms. Whether we are speaking of the wider culture or of a culture of two, as in psychotherapy, we cannot evade the implicit ideologies and values that frame the ways people reveal the characterological residue of their untold and unmourned stories of lonely suffering to each other.

The psychotherapy relationship is not an isolated research enterprise into experiences of patients at a remove from their society, but rather it vitally reflects and influentially contributes to the social contract governing the cultural surround. The respective visions of various psychoanalytic practitioners as to what constitutes an analytic cure, as well as their consequent use of the therapeutic relationship to effect that cure, carry implicit, unarticulated assumptions concerning what one person can appropriately expect to receive from another person. In this sense, the particular way we choose to participate in the treatment relationship reflects, perpetuates, and creates—with all the hypnotic power of the transference—an influential link in the interpersonal chain of giving and receiving. I believe it is not too far-fetched to suggest that the relationship between analyst and patient, largely because of imperfectly resolved transferences, has a pervasive impact on the cultural norms of how human relationships are constituted. Due to the residual power of unresolved transferences, the structure of the analytic relationship may become an influential template for the proliferation of the patient's other relationships in the cultural surround.

Psychoanalytic psychotherapy has an interest not only in the disclosure of the unconscious contents of the mind, but also in the conscious, evaluative attitudes that patients take toward the new discoveries about themselves. By expanding this potential space of attitude, we can begin to cope with the various givens of their lives, and even have the constructive illusion of modifying them. The way therapists encounter patients when they present themselves for treatment intensely flavors the emotional valence of acceptance or condemnation with which the bits and pieces of analyzed experience are to be viewed. The prisms through which we understand ourselves are closely linked to the ways our revealed stories are received by others.

For patients who have long been fixed in their self-enclosed isolation, the experience of being understood by someone *outside* of their omnipotence is indispensable before they can become convinced that they no longer have to be solo travelers in their lives. This sense of company in patients' lives helps, in turn, to soften the self-demeaning pressures of inadequacy stemming from earlier feelings that their gifts have not been good enough. Paradoxically, it is these very same self-recriminations that may push patients to solicit a credible witness to their lonely suffering in the first place.

The therapist's freedom of choice and freedom in retaining her own subjectivity in responding to patients are fundamental to her credibility as a witness to the patient's story. The credibility of the therapist, lying beyond the controlling reach of the patient, facilitates the patient's task of objectifying his experiences, thus enabling him to come out of his involuted spirals of thinking-in and symptom enactment. Need and the coercive expressions of entitlement may curtail this freedom of response between patient and therapist. Thus, entitled patients may attempt to ensure that they are responded to as they feel they should be, rather than risk encountering the spontaneity of a person-to-person process.

Patients sometimes are diagnosed with narcissistic personality disorders because of the therapist's feeling of being depersonalized in this way; the therapist may say, "I felt like I was part of the furniture," or "When he was speaking, I felt like I might as well have not been in the room." Some therapists then believe that by immersing themselves empathically in the patient's experience and by offering themselves as a selfobject for the patient's use, they can help fill the void left in the wake of early deficits. The implication here, conveyed by the patient's need to make the person of the therapist into his object, is that the growth of the patient's true self is facilitated best when there is only one person in the room at a time. I find it strange, however, that such a diagnosis, made by means of the therapist's countertransference feeling of depersonalization, should then become the pathway chosen for its treatment.

The depersonalizing effects of coercing care from a therapist transform the possibility of receiving a freely given love into a demanded, for pity that the patient already feels for his own plight. Winnicott (1969) says that a patient who cannot place the analyst outside the area of the patient's omnipotence "can never do more than experience a kind of self-analysis, using the analyst as a projection of a part of the self" (p. 91). The emptiness that results from such a pseudo-personal interchange reinforces the patient's underlying despair about ever securing a credible witness who is independent of his imprint. This attempt to rigidify the treatment relationship by holding the therapist as a captive audience belies the patient's mistrust that the therapist would be a willing participant in the relationship, if given the choice. After years of waiting at the end of the block, the patient may have become too despairing and resentful to trust the free choices of other persons to deliver the empathic attentions that he craves. Yet leaving it up to the therapist to be caring or not caring may be the only chance the patient has of finding finally a credibly empathic witness to his story of lonely suffering.

Instead of negating their individuality in order to prepare themselves for the role of the patient's created object, therapists can best lend an objectivity to the patient's experience by retaining their own personhood. The patient, because of his history of defensive isolation, must be able to find the grounding of the therapist's personal center of gravity in order to use it creatively. Winnicott (1969) thus says: "The object, if it is to be used, must necessarily be real in the sense of being part of shared reality, not a bundle of projections" (p. 88).

Because it is precisely the freedom to say "No" that lends meaning to a "Yes," it is the therapist's freedom to hate that lends a necessary believability to any loving affirmation that is received by the patient. As Winnicott (1947) notes, "The analyst's hate is actually sought by the patient, and what is then needed is hate that is objective. If the patient seeks objective or justified hate he must be able to reach it, else he cannot feel he can reach objective love" (p. 199).

If one were not to smile back at a smiling baby, the baby will not die. However, if that baby is not smiled upon by her parents for a prolonged period of time, eventually she may become an embittered adult. Nevertheless it is precisely because of my concern that a mutually respectful and loving quality be retained in adult human relations, that I believe people must be free both to smile and not smile at each other.

THE QUEST FOR DUPLICATE EXPERIENCES AND THE DESPAIR OF WORDS

For many patients, the credibility of the therapist as a witness is something that cannot be conveyed by words alone. For the patient who has huddled in self-enclosed isolation, waiting for someone to retrieve him, words are insufficient to make up for the lonely times he has endured. It is too easy for the therapist to discharge her therapeutic tasks oh so correctly: to nod her head empathically, to make clarifying interpretations to show she understands. She will go home that night and enjoy her family, her patients' tales of woe blending in with the other stories of the day that have been left behind. If she is an experienced therapist, she has learned to disentangle her patients' stories of suffering from her private life, so much so that she may take a secret satisfaction that she has been spared the misfortunes that befall her patients.

For patients who have had their fill of waiting alone in the silences between self and other, there sometimes is a resounding emptiness to such lip service. It is too late for all talk and no action; the desolation of nonbeing has wormed its way too deeply into the blood. These patients have been too much on the periphery of their lives to entrust the therapist's words with the task of incorporating them into the human community.

The very necessity of building a bridge of communication implies a separateness between self and other. In civilized life, the use of language reflects a trade-off in which we relinquish a precise identification of personal experience in exchange for a communicable but more approximate articulation. This tacit compromise allows for a chance to meet on the common ground of an intermediate social space. For some, this transitional verbal area of social life in which we find only the linguistic representations of each other's subjective realities does not do justice to the experiences of private suffering that have been endured. As there is no stopping a starving person once he begins to eat, patients who have lived in their own company for too long will have no part of any separateness once they have caught the therapist's attention. The differences in the experiences of patient and therapist seem too wide a gulf to bridge through words alone. From the point of view of many patients, only the *communion* of actions through the engendering of parallel duplicate experiences will convince the therapist of what they have suffered.

Such questions as "How will you as a white person understand me as a black man?" or "How can you understand how it feels to be a woman?" reflect not only a conviction that racial or gender differences prevent true understanding, but also a despair that words alone could be sufficient to bridge the gap of difference and separateness. Yet to categorize experiential differences along ethnic, racial, or gender lines obscures the tragic element of the fundamental separateness between any individual's experience and another's, as well as our shared identity as human beings. The mistrust of words reflects a fear on the part of patients that the limited imprecision with which private experience can be conveyed verbally will prevent one from ever emerging from one's existential isolation as an individual.

The quest for communion—or duplicate experiences—may intensify, especially in the wake of trauma, when self-enclosing defenses accentuate one's sense of isolation. The therapeutic value of self-help support groups, for example, is predicated on the sharing of like experiences. Experiences that were perceived as shameful within the inward churnings of one's own lonely counsel may now be transformed by group support into a prideful badge of honor. The narcissistic and incestuous desire to find a mirror of oneself through sameness and familiarity thus may transform shame-inducing experiences of trauma and victimization into the foundation of a proud new identity.

I fear, however, that when one ties one's identity to a group based on duplicate experiences, it may only reflect one's disbelief

that true understanding and compassion can be found in someone who has had a markedly different life path than oneself. When
a sameness of experience is ensured, it reinforces a belief that
words may not convey one's unique experiences satisfactorily. As
efforts to articulate one's experiences into words degenerate into
the passivity of sharing parallel lives, civilized life is at risk of becoming fragmented into categories of persons who share like
experiences of suffering and victimization.

Patients often seek help in individual psychotherapy precisely
because they presume difference; therapists are thought to have
something to offer because they are wiser or stronger, or more
emotionally balanced and better able to cope. Although these sorts
of initial idealization are probably fundamental in explaining why
patients come to rely on therapists, they may also leave distressed
patients ashamed of their relative inferiority and envious of the
therapist's equanimity.

For patients who have devoted much mental work to worrying
about the care of others, the effort required to bridge the gulf of
this difference in words may be more than they are willing to make.
Let the burden fall on the therapist to prove to the patient that
she *really* understands. Many therapists may feel that while they
have paid their respects to the patient's experiences of lonely
suffering, it still did not seem to be enough. From the point of
the view of such patients, verbal exchanges between two talking
heads will not suffice. It is too easy for people to speak and not
mean what they say. No, the therapist must convince by giving of
herself with the emotional blood and guts of embodied experience.

Once in therapy, patients who have resented being left indefinitely to their own devices may now, with entitled indignation, feel
justified in exacting a price for being abandoned. In this light,
projective identification may be viewed as a means by which a
patient attempts to reveal his story of helplessness and lonely suffering without words; to show it rather than to tell about it. In a
dark, reversed version of the Golden Rule, the patient may identify with the aggressor and do unto the therapist the evils that were

done unto him. By engendering a duplication of their experience of helplessness in the therapist, patients are saying, in effect, "Now you know how I feel." Nevertheless, although projective identification may be the patient's desperate attempt to be understood, it also has an envious, vengeful quality that reflects the patient's long-standing experience of being on the outside looking in. The phrase "Now see how *you* like it," at once reflects an attempt to communicate one's experiences as well as the bitter aftertaste of lonely suffering. Here the vindictiveness of envy seeks to collapse difference and level the playing field by coercing the more fortunate, strong therapist to share the envious patient's fate.

In my view, these are critical clinical junctures in which the therapist's ideology and values come into clear focus. As clinicians, what are our opinions of how love can or should be conveyed? What are our values concerning togetherness versus individuation? Must love be proved through a loyal sharing of misery with the sufferer? Or is that too much of a placating of the less fortunate one's envy? Perhaps a nonmerging compassion can be sufficient in becoming a credible witness to another's suffering. Certainly patients have their own implicit opinions and expectations about these matters, but it is also important to ask, What are ours?

7

The Evil Eye: Envy and Begrudging the Passion of a New Beginning

As for Envy, that emitteth some Malign and Poisonous Spirits, which take hold of the Spirit of another, and it is likewise of greatest force when the cast of the Eye is Oblique. It hath been noted also, that it is most dangerous, where the Envious Eye is cast upon Persons in Glory and Triumph and Joy.

—Sir Francis Bacon

Grievous is the burden of excessive praise, for from the eyes of Zeus is cast the thunder-bolt.

—Homer

ENVY AND THE IMMOBILIZATION
OF PASSION

At the end of Chapter 1, I discussed the separation guilt that children may experience in the process of growing up. When parents accept and make use of their children's offerings, it may help repair the breach caused by an increasing realization of separateness. In this chapter, I will explore the other side of this generational tension—parental envy. I will use the metaphor of the evil eye to examine how parents, and mothers specifically, attempt to freeze and take possession of the child's development. I consider this significant because, as the result of self-denying defenses designed to ward off the evil eye, the child who is envied often then becomes the parent who envies.

Whereas fate seems to smile on a chosen few whom she visits with good fortune, others are left only to watch with a "lean and hungry look." Perhaps, however, it is not the smile of fate but the smile of a mother upon discovering her newborn for the first time that sets a child on course to fulfill its destiny. A destiny unfolds not only by way of the child finding the mother he creates, but also through being the found child that the mother has created. A baby's squeals of delight when playing peek-a-boo, or a toddler's peals of laughter when playing hide-and-seek, testify to this fundamental excitement in being discovered—as if confirming to the child that he was meant to make an appearance in this world.

Harold Boris (1994) has suggested that it is precisely this feeling of "meant to be" that envious persons lack. Envious individuals covet what other persons take for granted: a sense of validity that lends meaning to further development. Preoccupied with securing the foundations of a real identity that is meant to be, they neglect the process of becoming. Since life is never static, however, it is tragically ironic that in their desperate attempt to hold on to their security they lose it. They wall themselves off from the give-and-take with others that is the source of psychological growth.

It is often very late before such persons realize in their own fashion that securing a reason for being cannot be separated out from the process of becoming whoever they would become.

By disavowing and concealing wishes that have been chronically disappointed by parents, these persons lose access to the building blocks of their particular truth, without which they have no guideposts by which to live. In waging war against their own desires, envious individuals empty themselves of the passion that could move them forward and toward others with an element of hopefulness. Passion thrives where there is a certainty of conviction and a destined sense of purpose. People who are divided against themselves and closed to the life-giving replenishment flowing between themselves and others risk drying up their wellspring of passion. Passive and adrift, they alienate themselves from their own unique flow of life.

When we stifle our own passion in attempting to fulfill our destiny, we trap ourselves in a web woven of self-envy. If we should become aware of a best friend getting married or getting a promotion, we are forced momentarily to confront ourselves for not getting on with our own lives. Unable to find a way to jump-start ourselves out of our self-made morass, we cast an envious eye on the unfolding destinies of others, attempting to immobilize, swallow up, and take possession of their passions; we begrudge other persons their passionate movement to become whoever they are destined to become. By thus attempting to make the lives of others the stagnated equal of our own, we are able to find justification for our own inhibitions. Thus, Scheler (1912) views envy as deriving from the despair of being impotent to affect the course of one's destiny.

Because envy has so much to do with the passion that is essential to mobilize or inhibit psychic growth, it hovers over the comings and goings that mediate the developmental process. To the extent that parents may inhibit some of their own individual pursuits to give birth, care for, and stand by their children, they may not always find it easy to sit by and watch those children move on with their lives. The intergenerational transfer of the flow of life from parents to children may not come without a feeling on the parents' part that some sort of toll must be paid by their children before they are permitted to become independent. When children attempt to separate and ignore the thank-you's of reconciliation, parents may look on the procession of their children's developmental changes with a covetous evil eye—an eye intent on holding still and capturing for themselves the youthful passion that moves their children forward. The self-envier who begrudges others their inner peace and freedom to become does not spring from nowhere. When children do not work through their disillusionments and are intent on covering up their vulnerabilities and shames, they may become embittered adults who are alienated from their own desires. For such adults, consumed with regret and envy, the new beginnings and fresh opportunities available to the young may be too tempting a target to pass up. Thus, just as the "evil eye" was once widely believed to be spread by contagion, so envy is passed contagiously from one generation to the next.

DAVID AND THE EVIL EYE

The tremendous power attributed to the envious evil eye was highlighted for me during a three-year-long psychotherapy with a 6-year-old child whom I will refer to as David. When I initially met with David's parents to gather information, they noted that their son reportedly picked on his 3-year-old sister. They mentioned also that David had trouble relating to his peers because he would get very upset when he lost at competitive games. David's mother was quite reserved, even somewhat cold, and often avoided eye contact. She seemed torn between telling me about her son's problems and keeping them hidden behind a defensive front. In marked contrast, David's father was agreeable, and seemed eager to ingratiate himself with me, as if he were attempting to make up for his wife's rough edges.

On the day of my first meeting with David, I heard him before I actually encountered him. His voice, clearly louder than is typical for polite society, carried well beyond the waiting room. When I went out to meet him, he clung to his mother's arm for a few minutes, and refused to let go. With a little coaxing, he took a chance and went with me to the playroom. David's sense of emptiness became apparent when he immediately began to dig a deep hole in the clinic sandbox. When I asked him what he was doing, he replied that he was digging a hole to China to get some food. To facilitate the building of our relationship, we then made a habit at the beginning of each session to go to the hospital cafeteria, where typically he would buy a bag of corn chips.

During these visits to the cafeteria, he would require that I not watch while he inserted the coin into the vending machine. Afterward, whenever I glanced casually at his newly acquired possession, he became very angry and hid the bag from my view. On our way back from the cafeteria, we usually stopped at a wishing fountain in the hospital where he would silently make a wish to himself. Again David became irritated if I did not avert my eyes from him while he was making his wish, as if the malevolent potency of my evil eye could reach inside of him and steal his private pleasures.

David's exquisite sensitivity to the fragile boundary between the presence and absence of valued objects emerged as a major theme in his play. A continuing thread tying our sessions together was his recurring attempt to master his acute sense of helplessness through a magical process of reversal and undoing. Session after session, David spontaneously created an ongoing script in which he identified with the aggressor and I was to express an anticipatory fear of undergoing all sorts of tortures and torments—most of which revolved around the experience of being abandoned. At these times, he appeared to derive a special delight in seeing me "cry" plaintively at being left all alone. This clued me in not only to his sadism, but to the sadism to which he himself had been exposed.

Initially, I complied with my assigned role of sufferer. Gradually, however, I began to play with the script that David had laid out for me. Occasionally, he would become upset and annoyed at my not following his instructions. At other times, however, he would adjust to my improvisations and play along with me, as I adjusted then to his improvisations as well. With this newly shared spontaneity—and my modeling of self-protectiveness—David began to gain a new confidence and flexibility in recognizing the free agency of others without undue anxiety. This, in turn, enabled him eventually to make friends with his peers more easily.

David's sense of emptiness stemmed from his difficulty in internalizing and retaining good things for himself. At the age of 6, he was already begrudging himself the pleasures and passions of life. Because of his difficulty in establishing emotional object constancy, or what Adler and Buie (1979) have called "recall evocative memory," David had little sense of his personal past or feeling of an individual identity. Without the stabilizing anchor of an internal center of gravity, he felt a tremendous sense of vulnerability and exposure to the arbitrary whim of forces beyond his control. Much of David's anxiety derived from his helpless sense that his fate depended on the purposes of others and their envious designs upon his cherished possessions.

Four months before the psychotherapy ended, David and I began to reclaim some of our therapeutic heritage. David, fascinated with the then-recent discovery of the lost episodes from the classic TV series *The Honeymooners*, began spontaneously to discuss our own lost episodes—our past sessions. We took turns reminiscing and recreating bygone sessions in which we were, of course, the celebrity stars. As the stars, we answered questions from an imaginary studio audience on the Donahue show about the different episodes of our shared history—all the while giving credit generously to each other for the success of a particular episode in true show-biz style. In this way, piece by piece, we reconstructed our therapeutic roots together which, in turn, helped generate and establish for David an internalized memory of our relationship.

"YOUR EYES ARE BIGGER THAN YOUR STOMACH"

It seemed to me that David was struggling with the loss or abandonment of treasured objects and good introjects, memories, and images to a sadistic and envious evil eye set on depriving him of them. Using the metaphor of the evil eye to understand David's anxiety thus reveals a vivid, meaningful underlayer of primary process thinking and imagery. A rich and substantive literature in mythology and anthropology lends credence to David's experience. In the myths of the Medusa, Orpheus, and Narcissus, a stare, a glance, or even a brief glimpse has a petrifying or fatal effect upon its victim. Among people in many primitive cultures there is a widespread fear of being photographed for fear of being robbed of their souls. In clinical work, paranoid patients may sometimes ask defensively, "Why are you staring at me like that?" Virtually all languages, ancient and modern, contain a word or expression for the evil eye or its equivalent (Ellworthy 1895). Although many educated people of the modern world view belief in the evil eye as superstition, I would suggest that even today, vestiges of this belief are visible in the inordinate power we ascribe to the envy of others.

What is the envious evil eye after? Whenever as a child I would complain of being extremely hungry, and my mother would respond by saying, "your eyes are bigger than your stomach," she was pointing out the obvious fact that I would always aspire to eat more than I could ever hope to consume. This saying alludes also to a deeper, tragic fact about the human condition: the fulfillment of our desires and ambitions will be always frustrated by the limitations of living within one mortal body. For the eye does not seek so much what it possesses already, but what it does not have. The eye seeks to transcend the limitations of stomach and body; it aspires to more. It is the expressive vehicle of desire, greed, and ambition.

Dundes (1981) states "Man is born with only so much life force and he is therefore ever anxious to replenish it" (p. 267). This is especially true of an unrealized life. When something does not go well, we all would wish for another opportunity to correct it. The future is potentially an inexhaustible wellspring of renewal through which the past can be undone and perfected.

Yet while time may be thought of as an ever-flowing river, a human lifespan can only go so far. For us, the human order of a shifting cycle of generations, conforming to the dictates of mortality, marks off the ascending and descending transitions of our biological clocks. As the harbingers of aging approach and the illusion of an indefinitely extending future erodes, reverberating pangs of regret threaten to consume us in despair.

The missed and now dead opportunities of an idealized past can be revived, however, if they are imagined as living opportunities that have been stolen and fulfilled in the now idealized lives of other people. This sense of being robbed of the life to which we feel entitled helps us justify our coveting of the futures of others. When greed for an eternal flow of life encounters the roadblock of death, it finds an alternate route to salvage the past through envy.

In his cross-cultural study of the evil eye, Dundes (1981) views the continuum of wet-dry as a primary metaphor by which to understand the evil eye's envious quest for a fountain of eternal youth. Because life is born in and depends on liquid, and loss of liquid means death, he suggests that wet and dry correspond to life and death. Whereas the drying process increases as we age, as in "dried up like a prune," until finally culminating in death where one "bites the dust," liquidity, whether in the form of breast milk or semen, supplies the ever-rejuvenating flow of life. For example, Dundes notes that in some societies if a baby returns to the breast after having been weaned, it is said to cause the baby to have the evil eye. Perhaps we could say then that those persons who possess the evil eye have an overweening desire to turn the unidirectional course of human time, as delimited by the cycle of generations, on its head and grab more than their allotted share.

The evil eye is characteristic of those who have had a turn at one or another stage of life, but who crave more. Like the mythological vampire who feeds off the blood of the living to sustain itself, envy fights the constant dying of the light by capturing and drinking from budding life that is in the process of becoming. In his study of the evil eye, Schoeck (1955) suggests its main targets are "everything that is vital yet incomplete in the process of becoming; everything that is beautiful and precious yet easily harmed"

(p. 196). Thus, women in childbirth and very young children and those with a tenderness of constitution are most vulnerable to the envy of the evil eye.

SEPARATION ENVY: MATERNAL POSSESSIVENESS AND CASTING THE EVIL EYE

Many adults who have devoted their early years to the fruitless labor of worrying about and caring for their parents' emotional lives have the sense of growing up too quickly. From the time such persons are evicted prematurely from their innocence, they already begin to harbor unconscious yearnings to retrieve what they felt robbed of and what they now feel entitled to. As adults they may externalize their regret for their own lost innocence into an envy of children who, they imagine, are living out what they missed.

When such individuals become parents, the advent of a new generation may stir up powerful ambivalences. For such parents, it is not a simple matter to accommodate themselves consistently to the unpredictable fits and starts of their children's growth. However, one constructive way in which parents can resolve these ambivalences is through identification. As long as parents can bind the invigorating freshness of their children's innocence to themselves via identification, they will not have a great urgency to grab or spoil it enviously. Identification neutralizes envy by enabling parents to take sufficient possession of their children's growth so that they feel they are really participating in their children's lives. Through their empathic identification with the new beginning of their children, parents can cultivate the illusion of reliving their own childhood in a better way. Conversely, in allowing their parents to take identificatory participation in their accomplishments, children can placate the parental appetite for a new beginning. In this regard, parenthood, and perhaps motherhood more intensely, becomes a natural therapeutic means by which parents can heal the wounds of their own childhood by partaking in the better life that they are generating for their children. Through this parental identification with the young, there is an illusion of continuity in which, to a greater or lesser degree, the distinction between past and present is obliterated.

When children grow further away from their parents' sphere of influence, however, the parents' illusion of identification and continuity with their own childhood is ruptured because now the generational difference between parent and child is exposed. The promise of renewal evaporates as the dream of identity of past and present gives way to the reality of time and history. It is at this point that parents, desperately grasping at the straws of eternal youth, may find envy raising its covetous head and attempt to grab, hold back, and take possession of their children's growth. Here, we may recognize a parent's separation envy of the developing child who is involved so centrally in the process of becoming. Mothers, in particular, have the profoundly intimate experience of carrying their children within their own bodies for nine months, a tie so intimate that nature has seen to it that the baby's birth does not rupture the bond, but merely punctuates it with the mutually binding give-and-take of suckling and being suckled. This intensity of attachment often is surrendered only grudgingly to ever-greater spaces of separateness.

For certain narcissistically fragile women who feel worn down from giving of themselves unilaterally all their lives, the fullness of pregnancy may bring with it a wonderful sense of creative majesty and compensatory renewal. However, for such women giving birth may come to signify that, yet again, they are being deprived of a supremely significant possession. As a child empties the mother of life-sustaining milk, using her up and then leaving her, the mother may feel that her primary access to a new beginning is being removed. If we view castration as the annihilating, denuding loss of a person's particular source of procreative power, from the mother's viewpoint such a loss may be felt especially in the separation and growing independence of the child from her sphere of creative influence.

Although from Klein's (1957) viewpoint it is the infant who, full of greed, envies the mother the contents of her breast, it is also plausible to say that the mother envies the infant its opportunity to nurse from her breast—especially if she feels forgotten and unappreciated. Of course, both explanations can be true. As Klein herself noted, a mother's real withholding actions may stimulate the infant's greed and envy.

When a mother withholds provision for the infant's growth and increasing separateness, she also is expressing an urge to grab back and to regain what she feels is hers, and thereby make herself a bearer of new life again. In this light, it is interesting to note that the root meaning of evil eye derives from the Latin *fascinatio*, to fasten one's eye on, or to bind one substance to another. To the extent that the newborn's physical separateness and individual life are narcissistic insults to the mother's temporary glory of being the creative source of a new beginning, the primary manifestation of her envious evil eye is to begrudge the child its independent life by binding it to herself. Just as we find in primitive mythology that ancestral spirits rise up to devour children, we could say the ancestral spirits of the mother—the ghosts of her own missed childhood—may be tempted to reincorporate, by means of the envious evil eye, the budding life of her own child.

These ideas lend the necessary human dimension and motive force that make it possible to understand Rheingold's (1967) important concept of unconscious maternal destructiveness. For Rheingold, maternal destructiveness reflects the mother's unconscious urge to reincorporate the life to which she gave birth. Roheim (1955) has stated that "to possess the evil eye means to have oral aggression or a desire to eat the child" (p. 7). A baby's impulse to put a brightly colored object in its mouth exemplifies the close primal connection between visual stimulation and oral incorporation, as in the French expression "to devour with your eyes." Muensterberger (1969) also notes that "the belief in devouring demons is a projective manifestation of ideas which are clearly preoedipal and are very often connected with food sacrifices to deceased ancestors" (p. 209).

When a mother fastens her eyes adoringly on her child, these fantasies of maternal incorporation are reflected in phrases such as "you are the apple of my eye," "you are so sweet I could eat you up," or "you are so beautiful I can't take my eyes off you." And for those maternal appetites that cannot tolerate any delay of gratification, it is interesting to note that the closest equivalent for the evil eye in the Philippines is *bati* or "hot mouth" (Flores-Meiser 1976).

THE WITCH IN SHEEP'S CLOTHING: THE DANGERS OF MATERNAL ADMIRATION

It is not an accident that in the literature on the evil eye, doting words, compliments, and praise—especially of young children— are viewed as particularly threatening to the well-being of the child. Behind the veil of praise and admiration, lurk envy and the desire to possess.

Farber (1966) observes insightfully: "Whereas true admiration keeps its distance, respecting the discrepancy between the admirer and the admired one, envy's assault upon its object with a barrage of compliments serves not only its need to assert itself in the costume of admiration, but also the lust of the envier to possess the very quality that initially incited his envy" (p. 122).

Parental admiration and idealization of children thus may be viewed as a reaction formation to parental envy, its flip side. Because the parent's coveting of the child's new beginning may be disguised by doting involvement, the fear of the envious evil eye may be manifested in a diffuse anxiety concerning a hidden evil instead of a more focused fear of a tangible danger. In this sense, the persecutory anxiety of paranoia, too, has more to do with the enemy that is shrouded in darkness than the threat that is apparent for all to see.

These persecutory anxieties can be accentuated by a mother's angelic, overprotective solicitousness, which the child may perceive unconsciously to be a mask for her hidden destructiveness. Because there is little opportunity to alleviate or work through these anxieties by overtly directing aggression and consequent acts of reparation toward a seemingly saintlike mother, a child may be hard-pressed to resolve his ambivalence toward this imagined witch in sheep's clothing. Instead, he may split his image of the mother into the good, overly angelic, doting mother who is present, and the hidden mother who is imagined to be voraciously possessive and witchlike. In the fairy tale "Hansel and Gretel," the witch tempts and entraps the two children with the sweetness of her home in order to make them prisoners for her next meal.

Muensterberger (1969) thus states: "The common belief in witches tells us something about the mother's quite open ambivalence toward her children and shows a predominantly orally oriented mechanism of defense, which splits the mother image into the good, devoted mother and the dangerous, treacherous witch" (p. 209).

In this regard, envy, especially of young women, is a central motive animating the malevolence of witches. In "Snow White and the Seven Dwarfs," the evil stepmother/witch begrudges her stepdaughter her beauty. In the renowned film version of *The Wizard of Oz*, the Wicked Witch of the West (colored green with envy) wishes to possess Dorothy's ruby-red slippers that will eventually return Dorothy to her home. Here the Wicked Witch, locked out of her own inner space in the cold (water eventually melts this witchlike block of ice), seeks to take the symbolic slippers that ultimately will deliver Dorothy to a home and childhood from which the witch herself feels exiled.

The rivalry for the possession of a new beginning is based on what Foster (1965) calls the "image of the limited good." Whether it be a life-giving manna, regenerative youth, or food, there is only so much life to go around. Thus, Boris (1994) suggests that envy has its roots in the rivalry of natural selection. If one lives, then the other dies. The notion that there is only so much good to go around forms the basis for an antagonistic zero-sum principle of social interaction where others' success means we must go down to defeat. When we are happy, then others must be unhappy, and if we are unhappy it must mean that others are doing well. When others belong to the communal procession of life, participating busily in its becoming, then we are on the outside, looking in, watchful, with an envious evil eye.

This sort of envious, antagonistic view of others does spiteful violence to the social discourse of giving and receiving. Where antagonism rules, we may be inclined to spoil a received gift in order to begrudge a triumph to the other. Or if we feel completely left out of the process of psychic growth and becoming with no prospects of inclusion, we may be inclined to present the other with a spiteful gift of misfortune. Such spiteful gifts, for example, may take the form of spells cast by witches on the blooming of young life. Significantly, a primary meaning of casting the evil eye on children has to do with the act of bewitching. For example, in "Sleeping Beauty," the evil fairy, when not invited to the baptism of the newborn princess, casts a spell that will cut short the princess's future, and in some versions of "Hansel and Gretel," the witch's house is made up of children who have been frozen in place. It is only after the witch dies that her spell is broken and the children come to life again.

When the envious evil eye targets a developing child, it petrifies the child's ability to move. Similarly, when a mother is threatened with the growing independence of her children and thus the exposure of her own mortal vulnerability, she may bind her children to herself by halting their separation from her. By usurping the desires of her children as if they were hers, and absorbing their life-sustaining fluid of passion, a mother can transform a freely willing child into a captured object of her territorial domain. The envious evil eye thus may be viewed as a metaphor to describe the narcissism of maternal possessiveness. The depersonalizing effects of the narcissistic exploitation of children, of transforming the independent person of a child into a mother's possessed self-object, may be viewed as a modern-day version of the mythological motif of suffering under a spell cast by a witch's envy.

SELF-CONCEALMENT AND THE IMITATIVE MAGIC OF MASKS

No wonder compliments are trusted so rarely, and so few people handle them with grace. A suspiciousness of the motives of the giver of compliments runs very deep. We may look upon praise and admiration warily because we suspect that the envious evil eye with its unquenchable desire to possess is hidden underneath.

The fresh blood of raw innocence exposes a tempting target of vulnerability to the envious evil eye. Whenever some cherished form of new life is created and is in the process of becoming revealed, whether it be a child about to be born or a newly conceived idea about to be spoken, that revelation of passionate life must be concealed from danger. In order to retain a physical and psychological sense of integrity, children learn to ward off the possessive gaze of antagonistic others. Thus, defensive strategies to protect against too much kindness, such as concealment and the use of masks, are evident in belief systems throughout the world.

One primary form of defense that has been used against the envious evil eye is the mask. The word *mask* is a corruption of the older Greek meaning of amulet, the purpose of which was thought to be to attract and neutralize the malevolent influence of the evil eye. Various charms and brightly colored stones have been employed as magical amulets in this way. Similarly, when a person is charming enough to divert and hold the gaze of the evil eye, he is able to serve as a protective buffer for the exposed and vulnerable. Taken further, a charismatic person, having the capacity to impart passionate life to a large audience, may be viewed as an effective counterforce to the enviously absorbing or drying influences of the evil eye.

The representation of the phallus, worn around the neck, also has been employed as a protective amulet against the evil eye. In this regard it is interesting to note that the word *mask* derives from the Latin *masculus*, or "virile male" (Thass-Thienemann 1973). In ancient Rome, there were "societies of masks" or male secret societies whose function was to terrify women.

Perhaps it is only the charming, if not charismatic, male who is attractive enough to divert a mother's evil eye from her vulnerable daughter, hence his appeal. In many fairy tales it is the kiss of Prince Charming that finally breaks the spell cast by the stepmother or witch on her stepdaughter. Similarly, the father may have a primary protective function of diverting a mother's enviously possessive gaze away from her separating and individuating children.

In New Guinea, masks are worn to safeguard the birth of new
life. Napier (1986) points out that masks, worn during various
transitional rites and rituals, have the purpose of concealing and
overseeing the authentic passion of developmental changes and
transformations as they occur. Masks are designed to preserve life-
in-process from annihilation at all costs. In nature, too, camouflage, like that of the chameleon, frequently serves as a protective
shield against predators.

This use of a mask or "double face" to preserve a core self is
reminiscent of Winnicott's (1960b) distinction between the False
Self and the True Self. Children construct a False Self to protect
the True Self from the exploitations of the outside world. In this
sense we might view the False Self as a mask of compliance designed to placate the voracious, narcissistically exploitative appetite of the parent's evil eye.

The strange or contorted features of the mask may be viewed
as a means of reproducing an imaginal representation of that
which is most feared so as to co-opt its power. In Greece, it was the
mask of Medusa, with her shining eyes; in Egypt the eye of Horus,
attached to necklaces, has been used as a protective amulet against
the evil eye. Although the Old Testament expression "an eye for
an eye" has come to signify the equalizing justice of revenge, we
can also discern in it an attempt to neutralize or undo the evil
influence of threat through imitative magic. I am reminded here
of a 17-year-old Korean-American schizophrenic boy I saw a few
years ago. He was hospitalized after reporting he heard voices telling him to kill people. He also spoke in a very high voice and had
let his fingernails grow very long. When I questioned him about
his voices, he said they sounded like "shrieking cats." With his own
high voice and long fingernails, this boy may have been trying to
combat his antagonistic voices with his own form of feline power.

When one puts on the mask of the enemy and merges with
the source of one's fear in this way, the power of a parent's antagonistic evil eye can be neutralized by imitative or sympathetic

magic. The imitative reproductions involved in the compulsion to repeat a dreaded experience, for example, may be understood as a vehicle by which children can inoculate themselves magically with the representation of threat so as not to be overwhelmed by its actuality. This is consistent with Freud's (1920) view that active mastery of trauma is a primary aim of the repetition compulsion.

Spitting on a baby also has been employed as a defense against the evil eye. By placing their saliva as a sort of territorial stamp on the newborn and thus bringing it into their area of omnipotence, parents can imagine they immunize the infant magically against the larger threat of oral incorporative encroachments. Such traditions as baptizing babies by immersing them in water, or circumcising infants by cutting off a piece of penile foreskin, by exposing the newborn only briefly and representationally to the specific danger that is feared, may also be viewed as ways of inoculating a baby against other greater dangers. Baptism thus safeguards against the fear of being reincorporated in the mother's watery womb, as circumcision protects against the threat of castration.

INCEST: THE CROSS-GENERATIONAL TRANSFER OF DESIRE AND ENVY

Although parents may warn their children against the dangers of the outside world, at the same time that they are doing so they may also be claiming their children as their own possessions. Inoculating children against the evil eye by means of spitting, baptizing, or circumcising may all be ways that parents put a territorial stamp on their children. In this same way, members of enmeshed families may use the mistrust of strangers as a pretext to huddle together indefinitely.

It is for good reason that developing children shield themselves from the parents' evil eye. For within the cauldron of possessive desire and envy lie the messy entanglements of physical and emotional incest. Nowhere is it more obvious how parents bind their children to themselves than through the narcissism of incest. In subtle and sometimes not-so-subtle ways, parents play out their desires for a new beginning by grabbing at their children's innocence.

When children are idealized, admired, and envied, and thus elevated unconsciously to positions of higher authority, the transfer of passions is apt to cross generational boundaries. In family after family, whether in broken homes or intact families with faulty marriages, children are used as hidden consorts for opposite-sex parents and as loyal duplicates of same-sex parents.

At the very same time that a husband and wife are grounding themselves in a life of security with each other, the husband's transfer of possessive passion may leapfrog over the generations from his mother to his daughter and the wife's from her father to her son. The pervasiveness of such hidden oedipal victories, gained through cross-generational favoritism, indicates that this intergenerational transfer of passion is a primary means by which children are evicted prematurely from their innocence and moved into an impinged-upon world of knowledge and responsibility for the significant adults in their lives.

In soliciting her father's protection against her mother's evil eye, a daughter may, ironically, fall prey to the father's narcissistic sphere of influence, and thus to his womb envy. Men who have felt that their mothers withheld a life-giving sustenance may be prone especially to acting out their womb envy with their daughters. Such fathers may attempt to bind their daughters very closely to themselves and, in some cases, molest them physically.

Similarly, mothers who seek to retain some sense of their girlhood may elevate their sons into the position of the protective father who was not there when the mother was a little girl and needed him most. Far too quickly her son then becomes the father to the man in himself. This pattern of de facto oedipal victories is evident especially in a culture of broken homes in which fathers leave their families, and leave their sons to fill the void left in their wake.

This same son, attempting effortfully to meet his mother's needs but feeling overwhelmed and inadequate to the task of satisfying a full-bodied adult woman, becomes the man seeking to regain a little boy's confidence. He may take his tender-aged daughter from her relatively compliant mother and bring her prematurely into his paternal sphere to shore up his fragile sense of narcissism and authority. In so doing, he attempts to undo the sense of inadequacy he feels about being unable to meet his mother's erotic needs by reenacting the same passions with his daughter. Now *he* has the grown-up body and regained sense of being a powerful little boy.

Even if the boundaries of her bodily integrity are not crossed, this little girl, flattered by the narcissistic charms and attentions received from her daddy, may become drawn via emotional incest into his sphere of influence. Perhaps beginning with puberty and later as a grown woman, she, having felt too alienated from her mother, may turn on her early loving experiences with her father and renounce her girlhood complicity in them. She longs, instead, to return to the slow rhythms and idealized restfulness of a mother–daughter relationship free of the possessive influences of male intrusion.

From the daughter's standpoint, the father as outsider has introduced an alien reality into her life with her mother before she was ready. If only her father had not been so overzealous in his involvement, she fantasizes, she would have received what she needed from her more reticent mother. In the daughter's mind, the voluntary unfolding of the separation-individuation process was unnecessarily and unfairly preempted by her father's involuntary kidnapping of her away from her rightful place next to her mother. Perhaps sexual abuse has caught the public imagination because, in addition to its real exploitative features, it has become a metaphor for this sort of premature phallic intrusion by fathers into the womb of the mother–daughter relationship.

The incestuous desire of parents to take possession of their children's developmental souls dovetails closely with the admiration and envy that are central to the power of the evil eye. In incest, the aim of the evil eye—to freeze the ongoing development of children—is enacted when a child is rendered a sexually or emotionally possessed prisoner of the parent's narcissism. Like narcissism, incest is antidevelopmental in that it is a means of holding on to the familial and foreclosing the novel.

SELF-CONSCIOUSNESS: CHARACTER DEFENSE AND BECOMING THE EVIL EYE TO ONESELF

It is apparent that the exposed and vulnerable child cannot simply depend on the parent for protection from the envious evil eye. To protect his endangered integrity, the child learns to curl in on himself to conceal his essence from the prying eyes of possessive envy. Oscar Lewis (1951) succinctly summarizes the virtues of such self-enclosing concealment: "The man who speaks little, keeps his affairs to himself and maintains some distance between himself and others has little chance of creating enemies or of being criticized or envied" (p. 297).

Winnicott (1949, 1960b) notes that the infant spontaneously uses a reflexive mental activity to defend against the territorial impingements and encroachments of the outside world. Along these same lines, in Chapter 3 I suggested that mental activity is the primary vehicle children use to merge with what is most feared. Already early in life, children may attempt to immunize themselves against threat by inoculating themselves with the guise of the enemy.

Perhaps not coincidentally, curling in on oneself self-consciously, like the petrifying spell cast by the evil eye, tends to freeze or inhibit the spontaneous movement and expressiveness of the body. Whether it be a teenager stuttering while speaking with a person to whom he is attracted, or a basketball player who misses an easy basket because he had too much time to think, self-consciousness paralyzes, distorts, and casts doubts on whatever it sets its eyes on. Like the petrifying spell Narcissus cast on himself by staring at his own image, the narcissism of a self-preoccupied consciousness slowly drains the body of its animating passion. Inasmuch as narcissism and hypnosis have similar root meanings that relate to causing sleep, perhaps we could say that narcissistic self-preoccupation has the hypnotic-like effect of casting a spell on one's own growth.

Perhaps it was because of a fear of introducing these inhibiting effects of self-consciousness prematurely that in ancient Greece mirrors were removed from women at the time of childbirth. And although later in childhood mirrors have often been used as protective amulets to divert the attention of the evil eye, in Romania years ago it was considered dangerous for children to glance at mirrors before their first birthday for fear of casting the evil eye on themselves. Mirrors were removed from the baby's room or they were covered up (Murgoci 1923).

As defenses that once were concrete and external—such as masks, charms, and amulets—have been brought inward into the omnipotent sphere of mental activity, they have become entrenched ritualistically as part of the repetitious process of character. The repeated incantation of certain words, for example, used originally to ward off the evil eye, has now become the repetition of rules, habits, and traits that lend character its stability.

These ritualistic aspects of character, reflecting different pathways of reconciling with the past, enable us to maintain our integrity in the face of threat. By reproducing imitative replicas of the way things were, we placate the possessive envy of parental ancestors. In so doing, we assuage our sense of separation guilt by giving away a semblance of ourselves before our whole self is taken. In this sense the replication and maintenance of ritual and tradition may be a means of lending a representation of ourselves to possessively envious parents and ancestors before going on with life again.

Sometimes, however, we go too far in offering pacifying gifts to the envious. In wearing a mask of complicity, we sometimes give ourselves away to such a degree that we can no longer retrieve ourselves. When we not only take on but also take in or inoculate ourselves too deeply with the countenance of the enemy, the masks of narcissistic defense become entangled and confused with the narcissistic attacks they were designed to diffuse. The enemy now lies within. Through an identification with the aggressor, we may inhibit and renounce the very same desires that the envious evil eye would begrudge.

Sam is a 34-year-old married man who initially came for psychotherapy because he had a crush on a male co-worker. He said that he had been attracted to men for most of his life, but always had tried to suppress his feelings.

Sam's history was replete with loss and abandonment. When he was 3 years old his mother was hospitalized with severe back problems. When his father was not able to care for him because of traveling for work, Sam was sent to live with his aunt and uncle during the week. Although they were good to him, he remembers waiting intently for Friday nights to come, when his father would pick him up for the weekend. His mother returned home after six months, but again was hospitalized for a prolonged period of time because of a herniated disc.

When Sam's mother was home, life was not much better. She was an unstable woman given to unpredictable bouts of temper. She required full attention from her son, frequently inserting herself in the middle of his activities to demand that he make her a meal. Often, after he had settled down to bed, she would call out from her bedroom for one more favor. Sam remembers bitterly how during his junior high school years he was not allowed to go out with friends after school because his mother didn't want to be left alone.

When Sam did succeed in making his mother feel irreplaceable, she could be quite sympathetic to him. He got into the habit of bringing her his troubles, and she, gratified over being needed, helped him with his problems. But it was all too much and too close. Once while imagining what kinds of reactions he would get if he were to reveal his homosexuality, Sam remarked wryly that his mother probably would prefer it if he were with a man anyway. To break away from her, Sam finally moved to the Midwest from his hometown on the East Coast.

Given his mother's possessiveness, and the lengthy separation that he endured from her when he was 3 years old—during the rapprochement phase of separation-individuation (Mahler et al. 1975)—Sam may have viewed her leaving him as a punishment for his separation and betrayal of her in the normal course of development. From Sam's vantage point there were but two extremes: to reexperience maternal abandonment and with it the terror of annihilating nothingness, or to remain forever loyal to a possessive mother. No matter where he makes his home, or how far away he travels from her, there she always seems to be.

Sam's dilemma of incompatible extremes surfaces whenever he attempts to advance his career by taking promotions at new companies. Rather than be excited about the prospects of his new position, Sam becomes pessimistic and anxious about all the things that could go wrong in his new job. He torments himself, constantly questioning and second-guessing whether he should have left the security of his old job. Sam's pessimism may be a way of taking on one anxiety so as not to experience a greater dread. His attempts to improve himself professionally and to develop a better life independent of his mother's gaze fill him with terror over her retaliation. Both his dampening-down of his own spirits and his overt expression of anxiety squash the excitement of separation that always had been forbidden to him. This pessimism enables him to placate the evil eye of envy that now dwells within him and to evade its imagined wrath.

Sam has come a long way in his twice-weekly treatment. After eight years of grueling work, he has gotten divorced, come out as a gay man, and has now settled down in a stable, intimate relationship. He has continued to make advances in his career despite his anxieties.

NEGATIVE SUPERSTITION: SELF-RENUNCIATION AND FOOLING THE EVIL EYE

It is because Sam's relationship with his mother's envy is antagonistic that he must use the reversal magic of a pessimistic dampening-down of his excitement to fool her. Such reversal magic is rooted in negative superstition. Unlike the positive superstition of hallucinatory wish-fulfillment, which is based in the belief that fate is in benignly gratifying synchrony with one's wishes, negative superstition reflects the conviction that an antagonistic other is out to thwart one's hopes.

Charles Odier (1956) describes these phenomena in the moral masochist: "In his eyes all that goes well goes too well and becomes suspect and a source of worry. In short, things go well when they go wrong. A healthy and complete happiness is not considered as such but as being a course of unhappiness. On this point the modality of the masochist joins that of the superstitious person" (p. 273, footnote).

The jinx phenomenon is another example of negative superstition. By revealing a hopeful thought or fervent wish, or by exposing one's happiness, one has jinxed or ruined the possibility of good fortune. For example, when birthday children blow out their celebratory candles, they are urged to keep their wishes private lest they not come true if they are revealed. If one does err in pronouncing one's good luck, then it is imperative to knock on wood to undo the mistake of revelation.

In different societies throughout the world, a newborn is sometimes referred to as "ugly thing" to shield it from the evil eye. In the traditions of the Masai tribe, when a child is born, they declare openly that the child is bad, but to themselves, they say the child is good; for to avoid praise, they say in the nation of Mali, is to avoid the evil eye. In our own language, we may say "break a leg" when we wish someone good fortune. Perhaps even the gruffness with which many adults, often of peasant stock, speak to children, reflects the superstitious need to disguise their affections from the evil eye.

The Stoic philosopher Epictetus (quoted in McCartney 1981) speaks tellingly of this need to detach stoically from the source of one's affections:

Whenever you grow attached to something, do not act as though it were one of those things that cannot be taken away; but as though it were something like a jar or a crystal goblet, so that when it breaks you will remember what it was like and not be troubled. So too in life, if you kiss your child, your brother, your friend, never allow your fancy free rein nor your exuberant spirits to go as far as they like, but hold them back, stop them, just like those who stand behind generals when they ride in triumph, and keep reminding them that they are mortal. [p. 21]

It is significant that in numerous fairy tales the spell cast by the witch resembles more the temporariness of sleep than the permanence of death. Perhaps, too, the self-induced spell of character defense, of inhibition and self-renunciation, is intended to be short-lived. Like the possum who plays dead in order to avoid an actual death, a person operating by the magical laws of negative superstition renounces or kills off his wishes by relegating them to the unconscious, so that the envious evil eye may be deceived and the stuff of dreams may live for another day. In this way, the characterological mask of repeating self-renouncing incantations enables us to preserve and renew our lives continually for each emergent moment.

Our efforts at self-preservation, however, come at the cost of sacrificing the expressive and revelatory quality of our lives. By insulating ourselves behind the self-deflating masks of our character, we gain a compromised security without a revitalizing passion. Our capacity to hold protective illusions provides us a safe harbor for the unselfconscious pursuit of fulfillment of our wishes and free engagement in creative play. By knowing too much, the introjected evil eye self-consciously punctures these illusions with gleeful relish.

Recently Gary decided to apply to graduate school in the helping professions. Although he wanted an advanced degree, the primary reason he went back to school was to meet people and make friends. He admitted that he especially would like to meet a woman there. For a little while, Gary struggled with whether these social aims were reason enough to go to graduate school.

He was admitted to an excellent school, and found out that a woman with whom he had worked five years earlier was going to be in his graduate section. He was quite distressed about the news, and wondered how he could proceed with his plans to be a more confident social being. When I asked him to elaborate, he explained that this woman had known him in less happy times. She had seen him when he was more socially awkward and isolated. What would she think of him if she saw him stride assertively toward a woman after class and start speaking with her? He thought he might become so paralyzed with self-consciousness over being watched that he was not sure what he would be able to do. I asked Gary whether he was afraid whether this woman, like his mother, upon witnessing his newly found confidence would be tempted to mock him and say, "Big man, eh?" Although Gary did not always agree with allusions I made to his mother, on this occasion he smiled and said, "I think you may have something there, Shabad." For Gary, the evil eye of his mother's envy and his humiliating memories of being deflated have a transferential omnipresence; wherever he would take initiative toward pleasure or assert his independence, in his mind's eye one of her surrogates would be sure to raise her watchful eyes.

Segal (1981) has described the tendency of certain individuals to spoil, inhibit, and paralyze their progressive creative capacities. This sort of self-envy may eventuate in such adults secretly idealizing those unassimilated aspects of childhood that have been left behind and continue not to be realized. Such individuals sometimes find, to their envious chagrin, these missed, idealized aspects of themselves in the lives of others, often children, as if the young had stolen their innocence illicitly. With their masks of character defense in tow, envied children thus become the self-envying adults who begrudge others what they do not allow for themselves.

RAINY-DAY FRIENDS AND THE COLLECTIVE MASK OF NARCISSISM

The character defenses that children construct to shield themselves from the envy of their parents overlap with the adult masks that later in life are intended to protect them from the envy of their fellow citizens. And with good reason: as the original open face of a child's innocence is replaced by the mask of self-renouncing character defenses, she encounters a community of self-denying brothers and sisters who, like her, envy others for what they have begrudged to themselves.

Gradually, such individuals learn to conceal their animating passions behind the cool attitude of a social False-Self mask. Indeed, to the extent that it is socially inappropriate for adolescents or adults to wear their hearts on their sleeves, the False Self may be viewed as a culturally sanctioned protective amulet designed to conceal one's true nature from the envious evil eye. Far from being fair-weather friends, the relations between rivalrous siblings of a given culture become governed by the misery loves company motto of rainy-day friendships.

Lewis (1951) illustrates how such rainy-day relations operate in a small Mexican village: "There is a greater readiness to commiserate in another's misfortune than to take joy in his success, resulting in a more widespread sharing of bad news than good. There is an almost secretive attitude toward good fortune and boasting is at a minimum" (p. 297).

Bound together by the mutual jeopardy people take on to stay out of harm's way, culture ties the interests of its disparate members together through the lowest common denominator of shared commiseration. Kierkegaard (1846) notes that: "In an age which is very reflective and passionless *envy is the negative unifying principle*" (p. 47); and "The envy which establishes itself is the process of leveling and while a passionate age storms ahead setting up new things and tearing down old, raising and demolishing as it goes, a reflective and passionless age does exactly the contrary: it hinders and stifles all action; it levels" (p. 51).

The passionate pursuit of each individual to become who he or she is destined to become is based on having a sense of freedom to create and find, to leave and return, to separate from and reconcile with loved ones. Leveling, in contrast, is a collective means, operating by way of cultural homogenization and individual self-renunciation, of equalizing the fortunes of all, and thus pla-

cating the covetous appetite of the envious evil eye with reassurances that no one has anything worth envying. As in a large enmeshed family, the mutual possessiveness of one for all and all for
one becomes a cultural mandate that narrows each individual's
field of vision of what is possible.

When children conceal their exposed face of True-Self innocence behind a ritual mask of persona, they reinvent themselves
around a new False-Self face that provides them entrée into the
wider socialized community as a person. By repeatedly donning
the normalized mask of self-envying character defenses that inhibit
and cover over individual differences of passionate becoming,
children begin to resemble each other more and more as they grow
older. In this way, each person's self-esteem and narcissism gradually become intertwined with every other person's self-esteem on
the paradoxical basis of wearing the mask of self-inhibiting character defenses.

Siebers (1983) describes this social construction of narcissism
as a "frightening mask that may be placed over the face of any
member of the community. . . . It portrays the stupefying look
[of Narcissus] turned upon itself" (p. 85). By means of a tacit
consensual agreement to mirror and validate each other's self-
concealing masks, the collective construction of narcissism protects against an underlying mutual envy.

To provide the stability of social cohesiveness, and lend a
meaning to the masks of narcissism, standards must be constructed
to differentiate one person's worth from that of another person.
Thus, an adolescent's self-esteem may become dependent on living up to the invisible social standard of coolness or an adult may
be guided by the convention of what constitutes normality.
Kierkegaard (1846) strips the emperor of his clothes to reveal the
illusory nature of these hierearchical cultural constructions: "In
order that everything should be reduced to the same level, it is
first of all necessary to procure a phantom, its spirit, a monstrous
abstraction, an all-embracing something which is nothing, a mirage—and that phantom is the Public" (p. 59). The pervasive
imitative processes of conformity and fashion are ways of cultivat-

ing sameness, and of evading the underlying omnipresence of the envious evil eye by not giving it an exposed target of individual difference. Eugene Ionesco's (1960) play *Rhinoceros* depicts the absurd degree to which human beings will conform blindly to meaningless social norms.

The social mask of the False Self mediates a leveling off, a pressure to fit in and not stick out. No one individual should stray too far from the pack for fear of incurring the wrathful envy of the others. Individual self-denial has become institutionalized pervasively as a cultural norm, whether manifested in the Protestant work ethic or the asceticism of virtually all religions, or even via inhibiting obsessions around food. On the Pacific island of Tonga, for example, there is a tradition in which the king requires all those who are present while he is eating to turn their backs on him. In our own culture, too, if one of us goes to a restaurant with a friend, it may be discomfiting to eat while the friend just looks on. If the diner should savor a hot fudge sundae, she may be stared at with a mixture of envy, admiration, and embarrassment—How can one person take in that much pleasure at one sitting so shamelessly and defy the envious evil eye? It is no wonder, then, as evidenced by the growing prevalence of eating disorders, that the unbridled joy of eating with gusto and then gaining weight—a sign all too visible to the envious evil eye that one has internalized pleasure and sustenance for oneself—may give way to obsessional ruminations and ambivalences about eating.

SELF-ENVY AND THE PROBLEM OF CONSCIOUS INTERNALIZATION

Psychotherapy, being a transformative process with the aim of giving birth to new life, heightens the patient's sense of vulnerability to the envious evil eye. Because the attachment to the therapist as a good mother may incur the jealous rage of an introjected possessive mother, patients may make efforts to distance themselves from what is enviable—the benevolent ministrations of the therapist. Thus, self-envying persons may have trouble consciously receiving and taking in the offerings of the therapist. The ever-vigilant, introjected evil eye of such patients may attempt to poison, deprive, and inhibit whatever good is derived knowingly from the therapeutic process. A transference of antagonism, constructed upon the animus of envious spite and manifested in a resistance to change, is from the very beginning of treatment wedded to the contrasting wish to grow.

Alongside the transference of antagonism exists a positive or idealizing transference that may be based in a faith in the protective, amulet-like power of the therapist's charisma. It is precisely because patients seek desperately to be liberated from their internal prison of self-envy that they may project a larger-than-life illusory power onto the therapist that transforms him into a charismatic savior. Because all receiving, changing, and individuating must be done unconsciously, out of the field of vision of the inhibiting eye of self-consciousness, patients often place responsibility for their growth in the charismatic therapist's passion to heal.

The vulnerability of patients to their own self-punitiveness prompts an urge to eat in secret, that is, to receive from the therapist without knowing it. This mental passivity and dependence on the therapist's charismatic capacity to transform is also manifested in patients' tendencies to take in blindly whatever is offered. Thus patients may express a desire to be hypnotized, or to receive behavioral prescriptions, as if it were better to become an unknowing automaton acting out the commands of the therapist in charge. They may accept the therapist's interpretations uncritically, or imitate the therapist's manner, jargon, or tone of voice to obscure their own individual participation and responsibility in the process of change.

Such unconscious internalization of the therapist sidesteps the problem of self-envy. By taking in without knowing it, patients remain locked in their self-enclosed prisons, hoping only to sneak something transforming past the sentry of the introjected evil eye. The primary therapeutic task thus becomes one of healing the split between the unconscious and conscious, of helping patients not be afraid to know about their animating passions to change. In a sense, patients must relearn the natural tendency to pursue wants as they once did—without overthinking—when they were much younger.

Gradually the internalization of a trusted relationship with the therapist becomes a real corrective to patients' persecutory anxieties concerning an uncontrollable, antagonistic fate. As patients learn gradually to distinguish between the inhibiting, self-depriving use of consciousness and the potentially liberating effects of self-tolerance, self-knowledge becomes less frightening. When understanding becomes a primary aim, the envious evil eye of self-consciousness may be transformed into a more benevolent, accepting self-awareness.

The acquisition of a newly found courage, at first based in a power borrowed from the relationship with the therapist, enables patients to ally themselves with the previously confidential wishes, pleasures, and passions that form their personal truths. Ultimately, it is the life task and responsibility of each one of us to affirm our personal truth courageously in open defiance of the envious evil eye and its various surrogates of misfortune.

8

Giving the Devil His Due: Spite and the Struggle for Individual Dignity

The eye of him who sees me will behold me no more. . . .
Therefore I will not restrain my mouth:
I will speak in the anguish of my spirit,
I will complain in the bitterness of my soul.

—Book of Job (7:8–11)

Man may consciously, purposely desire what is injurious to himself, what is stupid, very stupid—simply in order to have the right to desire for himself even what is very stupid and not to be bound by an obligation to desire only what is sensible.

—Dostoevsky, *Notes from the Underground*

THE PARENTAL EXPLOITATION OF THE CHILD'S WISH TO BE OF USE

In Chapter 2, I suggested that parental recognition and acceptance of a child's unique offerings engenders a sense of worth or personal dignity, and of having a special part to play within the human community. In the following, I will discuss the ramifications that occur when this sense of personal dignity is not acknowledged. When parents exploit their children's wish to be of use, they turn their children into humiliated outsiders. This sense of humiliation may paralyze developmental initiative and bind children ever more closely to their parents as compliant objects. Such individuals then may feel that the only recourse they have to win their freedom of autonomy back is to spite the ideals and dictates of their parents.

I use spite here to refer to those occasions in which individuals do harm to themselves intentionally, although not always consciously, to punish those on whom they depend. On the surface of it, the self-destructiveness of such cutting off one's nose to spite one's face seems to defy common sense. But for those persons who feel themselves to be playthings at the disposal of others, there is a perverse logic to injuring themselves as toy-objects. In removing themselves as objects, such individuals deprive the tyrannizer of the opportunity for further exploitation. In this sense, spite may be an attempt to destroy oneself as an object so as to give birth to oneself as a human subject with dignity.

At some point, a child's increasing separateness and autonomy may rupture the parents' illusion of an everlasting togetherness. This separateness confronts the child with the need to emerge as an individual while maintaining an appreciative tie to the parent left behind. It is a delicate balance that can be upended easily by the parent's perception that the separating child is betraying him and leaving him for dead. Indeed, those narcissistically vulnerable parents whose sensibilities are possessively envious may exert an unconscious pressure on the child to adhere to a uniformity and togetherness at all costs. Rather than recognize the burgeoning personhood of their children, such parents lay colonizing claim to them as territorial possessions. They recognize the child only as a created extension of themselves, while not acknowledging the child who has a mind and will of his own. By attending only to the child of whom they conceive, parents cast out the child who exists outside of their omnipotent control. Through this sort of unconscious but purposeful exclusion from their field of perception, parents banish their children to a sense of lonely exile.

Thus, when parents demand that their children conform too closely to the created objects of their imaginings, children may feel themselves to be a misfit with the parents' conceptions. Not being accepted readily as gifts into their parents' good graces leaves such children in a crisis of meaninglessness, of having nothing to live for beyond their own individual existence. Until a sense of belonging and worthwhileness is secured, there is no reason to sustain their own lives. The parents' nonrecognition of their children precipitates a sense of incompleteness that, in turn, precludes the child's developing a sense of worthiness to receive what is necessary to individual growth.

Dreading the obliterating experience of being cut off, these children may attempt repeatedly to sell themselves into their parents' good graces by shaping themselves according to their parents' specifications. Their reason for being, devoted to the aim of "earning their keep," becomes a labored effort to make themselves available solely for their parents' use. When children offer themselves to be used and disposed of according to the whims of parents, they become vulnerable to the "soul murder" (Shengold 1991) of depersonalization. Rather than be viewed as an individual person with a will of her own, such a child may be gobbled up as a means to serve the parents' ends. Then, when such parents have finished using them, these children may be disposed of temporarily until needed again. These youngsters remain on the outside looking in, and ever more desperate to come in from the cold.

Eventually such children grow up to feel their lives are not their own but instead the playthings of powers far greater than themselves. As the active initiative of developing their own lives gives way to the despair of a reactive passivity, such individuals are unable to liberate themselves from the bondage on which they feel their life depends. They perceive themselves as having no freedom of choice to say yes or no or to love or hate, much less the freedom of movement to come and go as they please. Without the luxury to make healthy use of objects for their own sustenance and growth, they are compelled by their sense of exclusion to remain compliantly under the possessive yoke of others. With nowhere to go, and without real hope of any prospects of improving their lot, such individuals are left with the acute sense of being helplessly exploited and imprisoned.

THE SPITEFUL RETURN OF THE INSULTED, INJURED, AND IGNORED

Dostoevsky's (1864) short novel, *Notes from the Underground*, is an uncannily insightful portrait of a man struggling to reclaim his self-respect from humiliations suffered at the hands of others. Rather than remain a plaything that is retrieved and disposed of at the whim of those on whom he depends, the Underground Man rebels. He seeks out a recognizable individual face for himself among the collective mass of interchangeable faceless parts. The Underground Man proclaims of the human endeavor:

> Just his fantastic dreams, his vulgar folly that he will desire to retain, simply in order to prove to himself . . . that men are still men and not the keys of a piano . . . for the whole work of man really seems to consist in nothing but proving to himself every minute that he is a man and not a piano key! [Dostoevsky 1864a, p. 21]

When Lucifer, in John Milton's (1667) *Paradise Lost*, is excommunicated from heaven and "hurled headlong from the ethereal

sky," he remains ever the proud rebel and declares, upon survey-
ing his underworld exile, "here at least we shall be free." The
Underground Man, too, attempts to fashion a virtue of freedom
from the defeat of expulsion and disposal. Instead of letting himself be scapegoated, he makes his escape by removing himself
voluntarily to his underground world of self-enclosed isolation. At
least here within the shut-up privacy of the underground, he can
claim the freedom so intrinsic to his individual dignity. Again, in
the words of the Underground Man: "Man everywhere and at all
times, whoever he may be, has preferred to act as he chose and
not in the least as his reason and advantage dictated and one may
choose what is contrary to one's own interests . . . what man wants
is simply *independent* choice, whatever that independence may cost
and wherever it may lead" (Dostoevsky 1864a, pp. 17–18).

But there is no freedom to be found in escape. No matter how
much we would will it to be so, the lot of the human condition
prevents us from finding the freedom we crave in isolation from
one another. Even in the deepest recesses of our being, we remain
chained in love and in hate to others in our imaginings. No matter how much distance we attempt to put between ourselves and
our perceived oppressors, the humiliation of our expulsion pursues us unrelentingly. As one of Sartre's (1946) characters says in
his play *No Exit,* "Hell is other people." Once the experience of
being overlooked and depersonalized is in the blood, there is
nowhere to hide.

When the problematic tensions of domination and submission
enter into the human equation, there is nothing left for the sub-
jugated to do but fight back. Someone has to pay for the Underground Man immersing himself in a "conscious burying oneself
alive for grief in the underworld for forty years . . . in that hell of
unsatisfied desires turned inward" (p. 271). Within this internal
dungeon the residue of unexpressed rage over the various indignities that have been endured settles into the involuted churning
of resentments nourished, bitternesses cultivated, and vengeances
plotted. There is now a reflexive response of vindictive spite, as

the price levied for having been humiliated and sent out into the wilderness. By way of defiance against the status quo—whether in the form of the rationality of self-interest, conformity to social conventions, or parental dictates that are transformed into internalized commands—spite cries out its displeasure at being overlooked, its dignity unrecognized. Spite is the lonely, exiled voice of the lost cause that, by reflex, goes against the grain of all expectations. As the Underground Man states his case,

> I don't expect I shall be able to explain to you who it is I am actually trying to annoy in this case by my spite. I realize full well that I can't "hurt" the doctors by refusing to be treated by them; I realize better than anyone that by all this I am only hurting myself and no one else. Still the fact remains that if I'd refuse to be medically treated, it is only out of spite. My liver hurts me— well, let it damn well hurt—the more it hurts the better. [Dostoevsky 1864b, p. 263]

When disposed of like human refuse, expelled individuals lack the confident wherewithal to move directly toward the freedom of autonomy for which they yearn. Instead, such persons may feel compelled to partake in spiteful guerrilla attacks of passive-aggressiveness against those they perceive to be their puppeteers. When one feels impotent to break the chains that bind by any other means, spite offers an attempt to liberate by destroying the corrupted relationship of exploiter and exploited.

MARTY: LEADING WITH ONE'S WORST FOOT

Not long ago Marty came to his therapy session, sat down on the sofa, and began fidgeting from side to side. He looked up at me with a sheepish, slightly mischievous grin and announced that he was having "hemorrhoid problems." I asked him whether he had told other people about his ailment as well, and he said he had. I

remarked that it was an unusual topic to use in greeting, mention-
ing that typically people keep their affairs of the underside well
hidden. We then began to explore the different meanings of leading with his worst foot instead of his best.

I suggested that the playful devilishness of his smile seemed to
reflect a perverse enjoyment, even pride, in telling others first thing
about his hemorrhoids. We then began discussing his encopresis
in grade school, and I wondered if perhaps speaking to others
about his hemorrhoids today was the grown-up version of "shitting
in his pants" back then. Despite the ostracism he had suffered at
the time, perhaps even then, he was announcing his presence with
a backsided smile.

The theme of welcomes, greetings, and hellos had been a
problem for this 32-year-old man from the beginning of his life.
He had been conceived immediately following the sudden death
of his older infant brother, a death that was never completely
mourned by his parents. The image of his brother remained frozen and idealized in his parents' memory. Marty never was able to
emerge from the shadows of being a second-team substitute and
be accepted as a first-teamer in his own right. When he first told
me about his encopresis, I asked him if he could remember how
he used to feel when he went to the bathroom and sat on the toilet.
He reminisced about how he had pretended that when he was on
the toilet he was a spy and that he was supposed to check in at
headquarters for further instructions. Perhaps, I suggested, he had
to report back to the invisible central controls held by his lost
brother whose life he felt he had stolen.

It is strange how the vagaries of fate link the downfall of one
family member to the good fortune of another. If his brother had
lived, Marty would not have been born. Because he owed his life
to his brother's death, he never attained the secure sense that he
was meant to be in and of himself. He made his appearance in
the world because of an unforeseen tragedy.

Without a sense of a secure place for himself, he could not
risk expressing aggression overtly and directly toward his caretakers. Because, from its inception, his life had come about at the

expense of his brother's, he lacked the fundamental feeling of rightfulness that he needed to take active initiative. Instead, his acceptability came to be based exclusively on fulfilling stringent "conditions of worth" (Rogers 1961) that were reactive to his parents' desires. His healthy creative inclination to offer himself as a usable gift to his parents was exploited so that he came to view himself more as an extension of their needs and less as a person in his own right. With his personhood usurped and possessed by his parents, his sense of fraudulence became more pronounced.

He described his parents' selfish concern with their image in the community at the expense of their children's dignity. He remembered many parties hosted by his parents in which he and his sisters were exhibited as valued objects for the parents' friends. He recalled that on one occasion his mother announced, "Marty just loves green peas" to an assemblage of company, when, in fact, Marty hated green peas. For Marty, this example demonstrated that his mother did not really know who he was. Indeed, in private when there were no guests to impress, his parents would be absorbed with each other and leave their children alone, even to the point of neglecting them. Not only did he have to labor to please his parents, but he also offered his good works to his three sisters who rewarded him with the designation of "honorary sister." All the while, Marty, feeling he had sneaked into life illicitly and anxious that his "crime" would be discovered, drifted into a furtive, secret existence. He reacted to others and kept his wish to be accepted and celebrated as a "boy" in his own right buried.

Marty's grade-school encopresis was his way of saying "enough is enough"; attention must be paid, his dignity as a person to be taken seriously must be heeded. Rather than feel obliged to report back to his brother's ghost while sitting on the toilet at "central headquarters," he held back and delayed the inevitable in order to make a declaration of independence against all those who owned his life. So that he would no longer be put on exhibit, he ruined the exhibit. He displaced his wish to soil his parents' gatherings by having "accidents" at school. He thereby stripped away his guise of falsehood to reveal, perhaps not coincidentally, the humiliated outsider he felt himself to be.

BEING OVERLOOKED AND FALSE
COMPLIANCE WITH PARENTAL IDEALS

On more than one occasion I have been frustrated, as have many others, by having to wait in long lines at grocery stores. It seems (perhaps only in my mind's eye), that it is precisely because the clerk at the cash register knows that I am in a hurry that she dawdles, spitefully withholding from me the seconds and minutes I deem precious. Perhaps from the clerk's point of view, however, she feels she is being passed over in a cursory fashion exactly because I am in a hurry, as if she were only a trivial way station to some more important destination. Her spiteful passive-aggressiveness of withholding compliance with my expectation of hurry is her determination to stand up and be counted for more than just a means to my end. Through her resistance, I am forced finally to take notice of the real person who is willfully impeding me in my aims.

We are well acquainted with children who, even when momentarily ignored, do something naughty or mischievous. At such times, we may declare matter-of-factly that such children are seeking negative attention with the understanding that some attention is better than none at all. I have wondered on these occasions why these children do not seek positive attention more directly, especially when it is clear that the parents would be more forthcoming in giving it. It is as if children, upon their return into the fold from momentary isolation, must spit out a certain bile before proceeding to more peaceful means of reconnecting. Since giving and receiving make up the essence of human relating and interchange, children cannot help but fashion a gift of themselves to bring back to their parents. These gifts, fundamentally self-relevatory in nature, are also communicative. By spitefully fomenting diabolical mischief for those who have overlooked them, children attempt to tell their tale of expulsion.

One particular way in which children may feel overlooked occurs when parents do not see the actual child in front of their face, but instead zero in on the person they would like the child to become. Children often exact their petty vengeances for being insulted, injured, and ignored in this way. As socialization increasingly imposes its narrowing, normalizing constraints, they find more secretive or passive-aggressive means of undermining parental and social expectations to fall into line, even if to their own detriment. The parental pressure on children to prepare for achievement in the future can become an especially sensitive target for the passive-aggressive attacks of spite. When children strive too long and too hard toward the fulfillment of parental ambitions, they hunger as adults for the nonconstructive aimlessness of playing around and just wasting time. Whereas once braininess was their greatest ally in service of their parents' ambitions, now their minds become their greatest foe. With goal-directed activity dissipating into the circularities of mental inertia, such individuals make a fervent plea of incompetence. Through their protestations of "I don't know how to do this," they are begging finally to be allowed to abstain from the rat-race focus on success. Many patients exact a belated passive-aggressive revenge against their parents by devoting their lives self-destructively to the spiting of parental ideals that they could never truly make their own.

One patient, Marv, speaks of his "unbearable misery" in being a doctor. He did not understand how he had come to choose a career in medicine. Somehow, he said, it seemed to have chosen him; after all, throughout his life he had operated under the mandate to care for others. He underachieved consistently as he moved from one unchallenging position to another in which he .was a small cog in a large wheel. By making his professional life as self-defeatingly unpleasant as possible, he attempts to alert others to his unfortunate tale of compulsive caretaking. Maybe then someone will take pity and rescue him from a fate he cannot find the strength with which to extract himself.

Gary felt pushed throughout his childhood to think about, to work toward, and to prepare for his future. He was a good boy who did his homework diligently, helped his immigrant parents entertain their American guests for dinner parties, and woke up especially early to save his mother from doing the dishes—all to keep the family's anhedonic somberness and depressed mood at bay. In the meantime, Gary's own developmental requirements as a child went unheeded. He was discouraged from having his own friends and from watching TV, or what his mother labeled "the idiot box."

Gary fulfilled his parents' ambitions admirably. He went to a top-level law school and became a corporate lawyer. Perhaps fittingly, although his personal views were pro-labor, he found himself advocating in the courtroom against the side with which he felt secretly allied. For fear of injuring his already downtrodden, "pathetic" parents even further, Gary never even allowed himself a glimpse of a personal truth that would run counter to his parents' goals for him. He was so desperate to lift his parents' spirits that he never untangled his own wants from the wished-for child of their imagination. Instead, he frequently buried his frustrations in the oblivion of drunken stupors.

Soon after beginning treatment with me, Gary began to look for a way out of the illusory prison that he had constructed with his parents. He stopped drinking and attended A.A. meetings. But he had trouble disengaging himself from his previous identity, because that would have meant an irreparable act of aggression toward his parents and their lofty image of him, to which he, too, was now attached.

Instead, I noticed how he exaggerated his deficiencies, created pathos from his solitariness of having no friends, and claimed incompetence rather than admitting distaste for the law work he did that went against his personal beliefs. With acute self-consciousness, Gary wore his cloak of being pathetic proudly, like a badge of honor. On one occasion (he was now 32), Gary drove home 300 miles so he could help paint the basement in his parents' home. They, however, had a party to attend that Saturday night so Gary painted alone. And painted . . . and painted, so that when his parents returned they would discover him painting and ask incredulously, "Why are you still painting?" Maybe then, pushed to the edge of compassion, they would take pity on him finally and instruct him to stop.

In Gary's prostrating of himself and making a dramatic example of a humiliated life with which to flagellate his parents, we see the perverse logic of cutting off one's nose to spite one's face. Perhaps the logic is not so perverse, however, since from Gary's point of view the face is not his. It is the false face of compliance with the powers that be. By exaggerating his humiliations, bathing in pathos, and exhibiting his downfall to all onlookers, Gary attempts to demonstrate, in no uncertain terms, the extent of his victimization.

RESENTFUL CLINGING AND PUNISHING THE CONSCIENCE OF THE OTHER

In "The Uncanny," Freud (1919a) speaks of hidden but eerily familiar elements that attempt to return from the repressed. Through the compulsion to repeat, such unaccepted, exiled bits of experience struggle to gain a needed voice of dignity within the collective chorus of the person's psyche. The exile's perpetual struggle for reconciliation or for inclusion within the collective gives these demonic elements their hovering, haunting quality. I believe Freud's description of the return of the repressed from an intrapsychic netherworld has applicability to interpersonal situations as well.

From this point of view, scapegoats, as embodiments of projected, repressed aspects of ourselves, return spitefully to haunt the conscience of those who have forsaken them. Using the seeming perversity of their masochistically self-defeating actions, scapegoated individuals disturb the peace of mind of the complacent, reminding them that their sense of uniform well-being was gained at the scapegoat's expense. These are the unwilling martyrs who are not noble and who do not disappear easily. They cling resentfully to those who would gladly be rid of them, and they go where they are not wanted. They make their suffering plain to all those who would prefer to avert their gaze. They remain in situations precisely because they suspect they are not welcome, or they arrive early at appointments, parties, or meetings because that is just the time for which they have not been invited.

In Part I of Dostoevsky's (1864) *Notes from the Underground*, the Underground Man seeks to recoup a certain dignity in his isolation, as he speaks philosophically about the freedom that spite affords him. In so doing, he attempts to break the stranglehold that his own unmet need for human companionship has placed on his life. Part II then fills out the human picture, revealing a far more vulnerable side of the Underground Man in which his sense of worthiness is bound slavishly to the way others view him. The humiliating quality of the Underground Man's desperate, resentful clinging is the other side of the coin of his involuted spiteful ramblings.

As a spokesman for the return of the insulted, injured, and ignored to the concrete world of human relations, the Underground Man invites himself to a dinner among acquaintances who barely tolerate him. He then lets the reader in on his thoughts: "You'd be pleased if I went away, gentlemen, wouldn't you? But I shan't go. Oh, no. Not for anything in the world. I'll go on sitting here on purpose" (p. 300). The Underground Man seems indifferent to his own humiliation, but perhaps he would say the better to haunt his companions with his downtroddenness. In this sense, the spiteful, haunting quality of resentful clinging derives from the wish to arouse and punish the conscience of the powerful other.

As the expert on these matters, the Underground Man expounds:

> If you have toothache, you don't lose your temper in silence. You groan. But these groans of yours are not sincere groans. They are groans mixed with malice. And it is the malice here that matters. . . . He knows perfectly well that he is doing no good with his groaning, he knows better than anyone that he is merely irritating; he knows that the audience before whom he is performing with such zeal and all his family are listening to him with disgust, that they don't believe him in the least, and that

in their hearts they know that, if he wished, he could have groaned differently and more naturally, without such trills and flourishes, and that he is only amusing himself out of spite and malice.... "I'm worrying you, am I?" he seems to say. "I'm breaking your hearts, I'm not letting anyone in the house sleep, am I? All right, don't sleep. I want you, too, to feel every minute that I have toothache." [Dostoevsky, 1864b, p. 274)

Sometimes, persons go to great lengths of self-destructiveness to disturb the "sleep" of their perceived oppressors. I have seen patients who have become so caught up in the tunnel-vision of spiting parental ideals that they lose sight of the fact that the intended audience for their vindictively self-injurious actions has long since disappeared. Perhaps a father has been buried for twenty years in the cemetery, or a mother has Alzheimer's disease and is in a nursing home. Or worse—their parents couldn't care less. In their twilight years, many such parents have gone on to the pursuit of their own happiness and are oblivious to the relative success or failure of their children's lives. For those patients who have sabotaged their own lives as they indulge their vengeful fantasies of spite, it is sometimes a wake-up call to realize that no one is paying attention and that their self-defeat has been for naught.

Individuals who have long been wedded to their spite may attempt to put off the day in which they would have to confront these painful truths with their accompanying regrets for wasted time. When faced with the prospect of change, such patients may continue to embrace a sense of fatalism ever more tenaciously, as if to justify why they were helpless in the first place.

These are patients who may exhibit what Freud (1923) called a "negative therapeutic reaction." Freud describes such patients this way: "When one speaks to them or expresses satisfaction with the progress of the treatment, they show signs of discontent and their condition invariably becomes worse . . . one becomes convinced, not only that such people cannot endure any praise or appreciation, but that they react inversely to the progress of the treatment" (p. 39).

When the symptomatic "groans" of patients are not heeded and their stories of being exploited and overlooked remain untold, they may feel that they are betraying their histories. Patients may then be tempted to raise the spiteful noisiness of their symptoms a decibel louder so as to disturb the conscienceless stupor of the introjected dictates of parental voices. Soon after entering Alcoholics Anonymous, Gary said, "If my parents say one word of praise about this, I will be in the nearest bar the same day." Here we might even see angry ruminations of suicidal ideations: "I'll show you. After I'm dead, you'll be sorry. You'll all be crying at my funeral."

FROM OBLIGATION THROUGH
RESENTMENT TO THE FREEDOM TO LOVE

Many spiteful individuals feel trapped in prisons of helplessness and hopelessness—often of their own making. Experiences of being exploited and ignored are taken in from the past and spewed out as invisible chains of bitterness and constraint on their future. This passivity of self-confinement then becomes the breeding ground for a life in which they react spitefully rather than act creatively.

Although such spiteful persons struggle mightily to assert their individual dignity by exercising at least some form of freedom of choice, their strivings often are tragically misbegotten and incomplete. Because their sense of worthiness and meaning depends so fundamentally on those whom they would spite, their passively vindictive attempts to liberate themselves are akin to spitting in the wind. They remain imprisoned, forever bound to their jailers as their loyal opposition. Indeed, indoctrination and opposition may be viewed as two sides of the same coin—a coin on which we attempt to imprint a sense of certainty where there is none.

From the standpoint of the process described in Freud's (1911) notion of hallucinatory wish-fulfillment, we can see why the omnipotence of positive superstition holds that if you wish for something desperately enough, it will come true. Individuals who subscribe to positive superstitions use a narrowing field of perception to hold on very tightly to what they consider the objective truth of their illusions, for such truths will survive only as long as there is a closed fundamentalism or totalitarian uniformity of thought. Such persons may go through the ritualized motions of unquestioning devotion to a God, to a mother, or to any other system of beliefs or norms because they fear the angst of opening up to free inquiry would be like opening a Pandora's box of uncertainty—too great. They seek indoctrination into an inviolable body of truths—of family, religion, nation, and even of analytic training. Where there are questions, and it becomes possible to imagine alternatives to a given dogma, then the illusion of that dogma being the absolute, uniform truth is ruptured. Better not to have the choice.

As much as the fundamentalist adheres to the truth of his positive illusions, the spiteful rebel strikes out against the totalitarian pressure toward uniformity wherever it is found. As Dostoevsky's Underground Man says, "I admit that twice two makes four is an excellent thing, but if we are to give everything its due, twice two makes five is sometimes a very charming thing, too" (Dostoevsky 1864a, p. 23). Like the child who points out the illusion of the emperor's clothes, dissidents in exile spitefully strip away the dreams of others when they can no longer muster dreams for themselves.

For these persons, often proud of their anarchistic fearlessness, no truth is too harsh to bear. In fact, the more disillusioning the better, for then the more courageous and honest they can feel themselves to be. Filled with a mixture of envy and contempt for what they see as the happy cattle who chase their comforting fictions in conforming droves, these individuals comfort themselves with the thought that at least they are living in the grounded world of the real. As pessimists who claim sole interpretive dominion over reality, they relegate optimism to the fantasies of naive dreamers.

What these spiteful, anarchistic rebels do not see is that their own would-be encounter with the truthful world of disillusionment is also an illusion, one based in negative superstition. The omnipotence of negative superstition, hardened into a learned helplessness through numerous disenchantments, is counterphobic in nature; here, if one wishes for something it will not come true precisely because one wished for it. Thus, equipped with their defense of anticipating the worst, chronic skeptics bravely confront disillusionment as inevitable truth. The tenacity of their embrace of the "No," however, belies their fear of succumbing to the seductiveness of wish and illusion—and being disillusioned all over again. Where indoctrination ruled in the first stage, here in the second stage individuals declare their reflexive opposition to all given doctrine.

A third stage in which individuals move toward a tolerance of uncertainty and genuine freedom requires some active mobilization of aggression. In order to disentangle the meaning of their lives from the dictates of rules imposed by significant others, such persons must accept their own intrinsic worth sufficiently to risk making an assertive stand against the powers that be, whether they are the ideals and norms of parents, peers, or culture. Only then will they be free of the spiteful prison of resentful attachment sufficiently to affirm life again.

Take the example of a middle-aged woman who has cared for her mother's needs all her life. Now, at 53, she continues as if by rote to escort her elderly mother to lunch, to the doctor, to the park, and anywhere else her mother desires. As they walk along, her arm interlocking dutifully with her mother's, she asks herself whether she really loves the elderly woman by her side. It is her mother, after all, and look how devoted a daughter she is. But she is not so sure. This woman reacts so ritualistically to her mother's wishes that she cannot tell where obligatory compliance ends and love begins.

What this woman does know, however, is that somewhere inside she harbors a deep resentment toward her mother for always having ignored her needs so blithely. When will enough be enough? When will she finally get her turn at the good things in life as just reward for her generous deeds?

So often we tend to think that ideas or feelings we hold privately are truer and more authentic than those we show more openly. Perhaps we believe there is a touch of the false and disingenuous about our public expressions, as if they were constructed for social consumption. Thus, this woman of 53, keeping her resentments to herself, suspects that secretly she really despises her mother—her actions notwithstanding. She fears that if her truth be known, a verbal stream of vitriol would come pouring out with no end to it. All the more reason to keep the nasty person she senses herself to be under lock and key. And so she exists from day to day, a compliant "yes" on the outside, and resentful fantasies of how to say "no" on the inside.

This woman has deceived herself into thinking she is nothing but the bitter, vindictive human being of her private fantasies. I say deceived, because if she were to transform her hidden bile into spoken words, her resentment perhaps would begin to evaporate as other emotions and thoughts would begin to stir inside of her. Spontaneously, she would desire to make reparations for her words, to engender good feelings in her mother again. To her relief, she might discover a long dormant love that she never knew existed, a love that could only become tangible once hating became an available part of her emotive repertoire.

Part III

Psychotherapy:
The Quest for
Self-Acceptance

9

Bringing Heaven Down to Earth: The Idealizing Transference and the Search for a Powerful Other

There is only one real deprivation, I decided this morning, and that is not to be able to give one's gift to those one loves most. . . . The gift turned inward, unable to be given, becomes a heavy burden, even sometimes a kind of poison. It is as though the flow of life were backed up.

—May Sarton

Ah, *mon cher*, for anyone who is alone, without God, and without a master, the weight of days is dreadful. Hence one must choose a master, God being out of style."

—Albert Camus

UNDERSTANDING AND CARING

When I was a child, my mother would talk sometimes about her father dying in a Nazi concentration camp. I remember vividly how tears would well up in her eyes whenever she spoke about him. On those occasions, I felt tremendous compassion for my mother and an inarticulate helplessness to make her feel better. During my growing-up years, the Nazis and their death-dealing concentration camps came to personify the ultimate, incomprehensible evil.

As an adult I have become intensely curious about the psychology of the Nazi–Jewish relationship. What are the underlying meanings and fantasies of Nazi ideology? How do Jews and what they represent fit into that ideology? I have sublimated my rage and indignation about who hurt my mother and killed my grandfather into an inquiry into the whys and wherefores of Nazi genocide. I have attempted intellectually to destroy the integrity of the hated or unacceptable behavior presented to me by analyzing it into its constituent, rear-guard parts of motives and reasons. The psychoanalytic quest for knowledge in the subterranean depths of the unconscious is based largely on this sort of civilizing of aggression. While in one sense I am still incensed at the Nazis, I also would like to nourish my ethic of psychological-mindedness and seek to understand their deeds.

For many who eschew understanding in favor of condemnation, however, there is a fear that knowing why someone does something is tantamount to excusing or condoning that person's actions. After all, sometimes explanations sound all too much like rationalizations, even justifications for wrongdoing. When smooth-talking people use language to charm and explain away their behavior, we call such persons slick, for we suspect that they are employing words, reasons, and understanding to slip away from moral responsibility for their actions.

215

Perhaps a more fundamental reason for the antipathy felt
toward understanding our enemies is that to know the reasons
behind a person's evil doings is to risk dissipating our sense of
righteous indignation. As clinicians, many of us are well aware of
patients who, not wishing to have their resentments toward parents softened, do not want to hear or know the reasons why parents did or did not do the things they did. Indeed, we may become suspicious that when patients do attempt to understand the
motives of their parents, they are protecting their idealized image
of them.

When the motives of perpetrators are understood, they
are transformed from straw targets for our anger into three-dimensional persons. The further we probe into the depths of the
human soul, the more we find, as Nietzsche said, we are all "human, all too human." Perhaps our recriminations soften the deeper
we understand someone because we begin to discover a bond of
common humanity with someone who, like us, was a child once.
It is discomfiting to imagine Adolf Hitler as a little boy in nursery
school, asking his teacher for permission to go to the bathroom
and then walking there with her hand-in-hand.

In this sense, we cannot isolate understanding from its ethical
underpinnings of empathy and compassion. In ways that words
cannot describe, human beings often seem to have a deeply rooted
understanding of each other's suffering. To understand another
person in depth is to recognize our kinship and to feel responsible for what we know. We cannot consciously injure others in
good conscience when we remain true to the memories of ourselves being hurt in similar ways.

Perhaps nowhere is this identification with the suffering of
others more evident than in the parent–child relationship. The
passionate concern of parents for their children's well-being has
been well documented. What is not as widely accepted or discussed
is that children take their parents' emotional pain very much to
heart as well. Searles (1975) suggests that already in the earliest
months of life human beings manifest "psychotherapeutic" strivings
to each other.

Time and again we hear of children who, no matter how neglected or abused, cannot abide to leave their parents' side, precisely because they sense that their parents are in trouble. With a Christlike forbearance such children see through to the unhappy person underlying the parent's sins. With regard to their parents, perhaps these children would implore us to adhere to the biblical maxim, "Forgive them for they know not what they do."

Not long ago in my own life I was surprised to learn of my son's close acquaintance with my conscience. Once when I was about to lose patience with him and say something I'm sure I would have regretted, he stopped me in my tracks and said solemnly: "Dad, don't lose your temper. You know you'll be sorry later."

Recently, Lisa, a 42-year-old wife and mother of a teenage son and preadolescent daughter, came to see a female colleague of mine regarding a deepening sense of depression and lethargy that was enveloping her daily life. Lisa had always held tightly to the idea that she had grown up in an intact, churchgoing Catholic family with a hard-working father and a stay-at-home mother. It quickly became clear, however, that she had perceived her mother to be emotionally detached and unavailable most of the time, and that Lisa had enclosed herself in a substitute world of fantasies, wishes, and food. She has struggled with obesity all her life.

After several years of therapy, Lisa grew increasingly intolerant of being on the receiving end of the treatment relationship, a position that made her feel less in control and more vulnerable. She was grateful for the new direction her life was taking—she had returned to school for a master's degree in counseling and was enjoying life in many new ways, and wanted to give something back to her therapist.

One day during the spring of their fourth year of working together, Lisa shared a fantasy. She was aware that my colleague had taken a short trip to Texas. Several months later, my colleague's 13-year-old son had ear surgery and the hospital put identical name tags on his wrist and her own. That same evening my colleague was still wearing the band when she saw Lisa.

During the following session Lisa confided that she had connected my colleague's trip to Texas with the hospital band and wondered if she had gone to Texas originally for cancer treatment at a top medical institution. She went on to say that if my colleague was indeed sick and in need, that she would finally find a way to take care of her, nurse her, and give back to her.

This clinical illustration may have profoundly radical implications for the way we conduct psychoanalytic psychotherapy. Is Lisa's wish to take care of her therapist just part of a compliant false self that must be worked through, or is it evidence of healthy psychotherapeutic strivings? Sometimes patients may be helped most when they feel that they can help us. I am not speaking here about the compulsive person's compliant giving, alluded to by Winnicott with his notion of the caretaker False Self, but a genuine wish on the part of patients to be of use to those they care about. Indeed, it often is not easy to make clear distinctions about who is giving and who is receiving in any human interchange. Some of the stalemates and resistances often encountered in psychotherapy may be due to misunderstanding these ambiguities. We may feel we are there to offer help to patients, but they, to feel worthy enough to receive, may feel they have to give to us first. They may do all they can to transform the professional relationship into a personal one to make us more accessible to their offerings while we may at times employ our technical know-how to resist these forays into our private lives. Perhaps, however, it is the patient's opportunity to gain entrée into the life of the person behind the professional mask that ultimately is most therapeutic. We would be well advised to take the psychotherapeutic strivings of patients seriously, and as therapists be open, receptive, and gracious to our patients.

THE BURDEN OF KNOWING WITHOUT BEING ABLE TO DO ANYTHING ABOUT IT

When parents do not accept who their children are or what they have to offer, the children may feel excluded from the intimacy of their parents' life. Forever knocking on the door without being able to get in, such children remain bound to their parents. If parents are in distress but still do not permit easy access in and out of their emotional lives, it is very difficult for their children to free themselves from the chains that bind.

As many attempts to give something of value come to a dead end in one who cannot or will not receive care, a child's hopes to be of special use to the parent are compromised. When each wish to give of himself and to be included in the parent's inner life has been constricted by numerous rebuffs and has nowhere to go, the child is confronted with the predicament of knowing about the parent's unhappiness and wishing to affect it without being able to do so.

Such children, however, do not give up on their caretaking task so easily. On the contrary, they become increasingly desperate to be included in the parent's life so they can be released finally to embark on their own developmental path. As their frustration mounts and their wishes to offer their services intensify, the attention of these children becomes ever more fixed on the parent's emotional state.

Through the insulated lens of his mind's eye, a child may fall back on a sense of infantile omnipotence to compensate for his actual helplessness to affect his parents. To the extent that such omnipotence is never modified, even in later years, he may feel that it is ultimately up to him to do something about the parent's unhappiness. There is no room for defeat. Failure simply is evidence that he has not done enough—he must persevere and do more.

When parents do not receive in actuality, children may relegate their caretaking attempts to the mental spheres of knowing, imagining, and thinking. Because of the parent's lack of emotional accessibility, the child's doing is necessarily restricted to mental activities such as obsessional ruminating and worrying. As a child's imagination and thoughts are enlisted into mandatory service by the desperately busy work of worry, we are reminded of the wisdom of Winnicott's (1960b) assertion that the caretaker false self is primarily a mental self. Phillips (1993), too, describes a 10-year-old boy whose worries "were like gifts he kept for his mother." Because such care is hidden from public view, little does anyone suspect how feverishly these children labor inside their minds on the parent's behalf.

Tormented by a perfectionistic sense of omnipotence that knows no bounds, a child may drive himself mercilessly to do more, always more, to alleviate the parent's misery. His frenetic attempts to give by way of obsessional worrying, however, since they are not received and remain unused by the parent, never reach their desired destination. Stalemated between the parent's continued rebuff of his offerings and his refusal to take the parent's "No" for an answer, the child is left with an unremitting sense of owing the parent. The burden of knowing or feeling the mental responsibility for the parent's unhappiness continues to weigh heavily like the pressure of a debt that never gets repaid.

For children who have been made aware of a parent's distress too early in life, knowing may become automatically linked with a mandate to fix the difficulty. Then, as the choice to care voluntarily gives way to a desperation to solve the parent's problems, the ethic of understanding and being compassionate about what one knows is confused with the moralistic duty of compulsive caretaking.

Frequently, we see individuals in psychotherapy with presenting complaints of depression, fatigue, and work burnout. Such patients may act out at their jobs by initiating an unwise argument with a boss, by procrastinating in completing an assignment, or simply by poor attendance. Unbeknownst to all onlookers, these individuals feel they have labored all their lives to please. When they should have been playing, they were worrying about a parent's emotional upsets. Now as adults, when it is time to fulfill their destinies, they attempt instead to catch up with the playtime that was missed. And what made the work of worry so especially exhausting was that it was always in vain. Even the least uplift of the parent's mood would have been sufficiently replenishing to relieve the unrelenting heaviness and laboriousness that pervaded their thinking as children. Instead, they are left only with inner demons

of self-recrimination and a sense of failure for not doing enough
good for the parent.

As adults, the consciousness of such individuals may become
so burdened with the perfectionistic command to take care of what
they know about their parents that these people yearn to be innocent not only of knowledge in general, but also of the accompanying pressures to do something about it. They may then impulsively
seek refuge in the carefreeness of unconscious action. All too often,
the mea culpas of self-blame, designed to foreclose further attacks
from the outside world, take on the *appearance* of understanding
and assuming responsibility, only to be then followed by impulsive actions that call for the same post-hoc apologies. Rather than
take stock of what they are doing, such individuals may feel they
are justified and licensed to continue to fend off the ogres of
self-recrimination by escaping into their unconscious actions
once again. In the meantime, the alternation between these
strange bedfellows of self-blame and unconscious action serves to
obscure the deeper ethical roots and implications of genuine
understanding.

When we do understand right and wrong, it becomes difficult
to look ourselves in the mirror and repeat what we know to be
wrong. Rank (1936) makes the simple but profound point that
had Oedipus known he was sleeping with his mother ahead of time,
he would never have been able to act on it.

I am reminded here of how when Gary first came for therapy,
he would put himself down in one way or another at the beginning and end of his sessions. Sandwiched in between this self-
critical framing of his treatment hour, he sometimes would launch
into an emotive, often rageful tirade against all those in his life
who had wronged him as well as all those people whom he had
not yet met, but who he imagined were more fortunate than he.
These tirades had a spontaneous, uncensored quality. If I inter-
posed by asking him to reflect on what he was saying, he would
resent my interruption of his flow, seeing it as my attempt to inhibit his free, emotional expressiveness. For Gary, to observe or
know himself in the midst of his self-expansive glory was not an

ego function but an introjection of what he called his "parental voice" for the sin of expressing himself passionately. His conscious focus—his knowledge and its caretaking obligation—was supposed to be devoted to the well-being of others, specifically his mother's needs; for himself, he could only hope to steal unnoted moments of spontaneous expression.

THE SELF-RECRIMINATIONS OF ALONENESS AND THE SENSE OF ISOLATION

The urgency with which Gary addresses the care of his mother's emotional being reflects how much is at stake. What is crucial for a human life to have meaning beyond the bare bones of existence is to have something to live for. An individual may adapt and survive through any number of terrible experiences, but those experiences exact a price if the survivor is forced to distort what it is to be a person.

When children's offerings are continually rebuffed, they often turn inward behind a defensive facade of self-sufficiency. Within their self-enclosed hermitage, however, children still may labor with worry over their acceptability to their parents and to the wider human community. Searles (1975) asserts: "The patient is *ill because, and to the degree that* his own psychotherapeutic strivings have been subjected to such vicissitudes that they have been rendered inordinately intense, frustrated of fulfillment or even acknowledged" (p. 380, emphasis in original).

Without the capacity to internalize, people may become helpless or literally without help. They continue to become bound in dependence to others precisely because they cannot take in whatever may be offered to them. And as their incompleteness as individual human beings becomes painfully and humiliatingly obvious, such individuals may feel even more unworthy to sustain themselves or to stand alone, if only temporarily.

As clinicians, we often hear our patients speak of their dread of being alone. These individuals are so intent on not being with themselves that they often compromise the quality of the company they keep. Perhaps this is because when human beings are alone, they are not really alone. The human psyche is peopled with myriad images, voices, and memories of real and fantasied relationships, all of which influence how a person copes with the experience of being alone. Solitude is never a neutral experience.

Children who have been rebuffed in their attempts to offer care to and contribute to their parents' intimate lives often carry those experiences into adulthood in the form of negative introjects, where they often surface in solitude. Thus, when these persons find themselves alone, it is not by happenstance or even by choice. Rather, a sense of unacceptability conspires with a chorus of self-castigating voices to declare incessantly that they are not worthy or good enough to fit into the lives of others, such that aloneness comes to signify the loneliness of isolation and exile. It is not aloneness itself that is unbearable; it is the relational meaning of rejection as an imagined punishment that is superimposed on the experience that renders it intolerable.

The empty spaces and times that permeate aloneness may be dreaded when they are felt to be an infinite void of meaninglessness that separates one from the life-sustaining contact with something or someone beyond oneself. Or, alternatively, solitude can be welcomed as a potential opportunity to use the freedom of creativity to shape one's life and one's relationships. The way one experiences solitude has much to do with one's approach to the question of freedom.

For the innumerable individuals whose frustration in gaining caretaking access to parents and to loved ones has been relegated to the self-enclosed impotence of worrying about others, the fear of failure hangs heavily. Freedom of choice is not very enlightening when each thought entertained and each decision taken occurs under the watchful, critical eye of a perfectionistic consciousness. For many, the kind of freedom exercised under the coercive pressure and threat of punishment for making a wrong move resembles an invisible slavishness to a demanding dictator. It is no wonder, then, that human beings would opt, as Erich Fromm (1941) pointed out, to escape such freedom. For perhaps, in that escape, they are ~~seeking a freedom from care or a state of carefree~~ness.

THE IMMEDIACY OF LOVE AND THE CHALLENGE OF RESPECT: THE GRAND INQUISITOR AND THE BURDENS OF FREEDOM

"The Grand Inquisitor" is the name of a chapter in Dostoevsky's (1880) great novel, *The Brothers Karamazov*, but it has been studied as an independent essay in its own right as well. The disciplines of psychology, sociology, philosophy, theology, and politics all congregate around its monumental subject: Is freedom of choice an aid or hindrance in the attainment of happiness? The setting is the time of the Spanish Inquisition, and the Grand Inquisitor speaks to a prisoner whom he strongly suspects to be the resurrected Christ. "Is it Thou? Thou? . . . Why, then, are Thou come to hinder us? . . . I know not who Thou art and care not to know whether it is Thou or only a semblance of Him, but tomorrow I shall condemn Thee and burn Thee at the stake as the worst of heretics" (pp. 3–4).

The Grand Inquisitor proceeds to lecture Christ (called the Prisoner) how he misjudged human nature. He scolds him for overestimating the capacity of people to cope maturely with the gift of freedom of choice: "Thou wouldst go into the world, and art going with empty hands, with some promise of freedom which men in their simplicity and their natural unruliness cannot even understand, which they fear and dread— for nothing has ever been more insupportable for a man and a human society than freedom" (p. 7).

For people who are hounded by their inner demons of worry and care, it is too great a distance to the heavens above and too long a wait until they reveal their mystery. After enduring the weight of self-enclosed isolation wearily, there is too much tension and restless urgency for release to bear with the silent abstinence of the cosmos. A trust in the invisible ambiguities of long-term promises gives way quickly to the grasp of tangible rewards in the here-and-now. The Grand Inquisitor continues, "Seest thou these stones in this parched and barren wilderness? Turn them into bread, and mankind will run after Thee like a flock of sheep, grateful and obedient, though for ever trembling, lest Thou withdraw Thy hand and deny them Thy bread" (p. 7).

People who are cut off and who feel incomplete in and of themselves, seek to lighten their load with what is nearer. The Grand Inquisitor speaks for all those long-suffering souls who have been forsaken by their abandoning gods: "Feed us, for those who have promised fire from heaven haven't given it!" And he continues: "In the end they will lay their freedom at our feet, and say to us 'Make us your slaves, but feed us'" (p. 8).

It is no longer enlightening enough just to partake in a give-and-take with another person. Self-enclosed individuals have suffered their burdens for too long. Now they would like only to collapse their isolation into the firm grip of a powerful other. The Grand Inquisitor points out a particular irony about freedom: "So long as man remains free he strives for nothing so incessantly and so painfully as to find some one to worship . . . I tell Thee that man is tormented by no greater anxiety than to find some one quickly to whom he can hand over that gift of freedom with which the ill-fated creature is born" (p. 9).

It is perhaps only when a person lies securely in the embrace of a powerful other that he can let drop the perfectionistic torments driven by omnipotent thinking and yield to the restfulness of unconsciousness. Maybe then finally he will not have to answer to the harsh taskmaster of his conscience: "Didst Thou forget that man prefers peace, and even death, to freedom of choice in the knowledge of good and evil? Nothing is more seductive for man than his freedom of conscience, but nothing is a greater cause of suffering" (p. 10).

The Grand Inquisitor accuses Christ of not loving human

beings enough, with their many frailties. Although Christ *respects* the potential that humans have within and could activate with their freedom of conscience, does he *love* human nature, warts and all? The Grand Inquisitor says:

> Thou didst choose what was utterly beyond the strength of men, acting as though Thou didst not love them at all . . . [p. 10] By showing him so much respect, Thou didst, as it were, cease to feel for him, for Thou didst ask far too much from him—Thou, who has loved him more than Thyself! Respecting him less, Thou wouldst have asked less of him. That would have been more like love, for his burden would have been lighter. [p. 12]

In fact, it is in the name of a "love" for humankind that the Grand Inquisitor insists that freedom must be eliminated so as to ensure prospects of human happiness:

> We have corrected Thy work and have founded it upon *miracle, mystery,* and *authority.* And men rejoiced that they were again led like sheep, and that the terrible gift that had brought them such suffering was, at last, lifted from their hearts . . . [pp. 13–14] We shall show them that they are weak, that they are only pitiful children, but that childlike happiness is the sweetest of all. [p. 16]

Christ's silent presence is so palpable that the essay leaves the reader with the impression that a dialogue is taking place, but He never utters a word. In this sense, the Grand Inquisitor's monologue before Christ is not unlike a stream of free associations that a patient brings to a silent analyst. From this point of view, the opposing positions expressed by the Grand Inquisitor are a projective manifestation of his own conflict. His scolding of Christ can be interpreted as a bitter confession of frustration at being abandoned to his keenly felt caretaking charge. Near the end of the essay the Grand Inquisitor hints at the solitary misery of his caretaking burdens: "The most painful secrets of their conscience, all, all they will bring to us, and we shall have an answer for all. And they will be glad to believe our answer, for it will save them from their great anxiety and terrible agony they endure at present in making a free decision for themselves . . . only we, we who guard the mystery shall be unhappy" (p. 17).

Like many individuals who have been abandoned to their tasks and who have then turned inward in their disillusionment, the Grand Inquisitor is laden down with the hubris of overestimating the omnipotent reach of his power; he carries the weight of the world on his shoulders. His tragic flaw, like that of many patients I see, is that he does not realize that he does not have to go it all alone. In his disenchantment and disidentification with Christ for leaving his flock bereft, the Grand Inquisitor determines to take up the mantle of power too stoically.

The Grand Inquisitor does not live in an interdependent world of give-and-take with others, one in which the burdens of every-day living and caring are continually released and relieved. He has enclosed himself in a sequestered world in which he has taken the cares and abdicated freedoms of others onto himself. In so doing, he has unnecessarily confused an idea of freedom with the lonely weight of his own polarized predicament. Perhaps we could also say that the Grand Inquisitor is not speaking only of the slavish needs of the masses to worship, but of his own unmet desires to surrender himself as well.

Like a son who has taken care of a mother after being left to that task by his abandoning father, the Grand Inquisitor confronts Christ, his long-lost father, with a host of recriminations, but also a subtle yearning to be released of his burden of freedom. Let us then return to the drawing room and imagine that the Grand Inquisitor, the analytic patient, is lying before Christ his analyst and experiencing the powerful emotions of the idealizing trans-ference of which he speaks: "When the Inquisitor ceased speak-ing he waited some time for his Prisoner to answer him. His si-lence weighed down upon him. He saw the Prisoner had listened intently all the time, looking gently in his face and evidently not wishing to reply. The old man longed for him to say something, however bitter and terrible" (p. 21).

What does the Grand Inquisitor want from his analyst? How should Christ be? How should he, as analyst, respond or not respond?

THE POSITIVE TRANSFERENCE AND THE YEARNING TO SURRENDER

In our clinical work, we see how the lonely frustrations of patients may be transformed into the dammed-up churning of obsessional rumination. The mental strain and heaviness of holding onto their own center may culminate in a pressure to break down the self, as manifested in declarations such as "I can't take it anymore," or "I'm reaching the end of my rope." Ultimately such patients, weary of thinking for themselves and desperate to find relief, may opt for the mental passivity of collapsing into the holding environment provided by a therapist. In this sense, a holding environment may be viewed as a place or person that provides a home to receive and contain the self's surrender. Becker (1973) makes an eloquent case for this deep yearning to surrender in all of us: "How sweet it must be to let go of the colossal burden of a self-dominating, self-forming life, to relax one's grip on one's own center, and to yield passively to a superordinate power and authority—and what joy in such yielding; the comfort, the trust, the relief in one's chest and shoulders, the lightness in one's heart, the sense of being sustained by something larger, less fallible" (p. 116).

The Grand Inquisitor's pronouncements about the needs of the masses for a powerful other parallel closely the structure of the positive transference in classical psychoanalysis. In certain ways, the power of the transference attachment is maintained also through "miracle, mystery and authority." In the implied promised miracle of characterological transformation, the withheld mystery of the analyst's personality, and the authority provided by the setting of the analytic frame, we can see how these qualities abound in the transference, and may be especially pronounced in the abstaining analytic relationship. Traditionally, maintaining the anonymity of the analyst's personal identity has been considered a cornerstone of the analytic cure. By fueling the illusion of the transference and ensuring that the patient has what Freud (1919b) calls "unfulfilled wishes in abundance," the analyst stimulates the patient's "expectant faith" (Freud 1905a) that he, the analyst, possesses a magically redemptive power shrouded in the cloak of abstinent mystery. In so doing, he accentuates his magnetic appeal to the patient as one who can perform miracles.

We know from observing young children, for example, that the act of withholding mystifies and deepens the value of that which is withheld and elevates the withholder of the mysteriously valuable possession to an idealized position, thus perpetuating the child's clinging to the now-idealized withholder. As Ferenczi (1932a) wrote in his personal notes, "The transference has become so passionate—as a result of my *coldness*" (p. 262).

Once the patient's "expectant faith" has been called forth and mobilized in the transference, it is to be transformed by the hypnotic authority of the analyst in the service of self-exploration. The harnessing and sublimation of this transference passion is then intended to engender the freely associative pursuit of psychic truth through the elaboration of unconscious fantasy, until finally the veil of the transference is lifted and self-understanding is reached with the aid of a still essentially unknown analyst. Throughout, the analyst is to use the technical tools of personal anonymity, abstinence, neutrality, and interpretation to shroud himself in mystery, maintain his authority, and to keep up the faith in the possibility of miracles.

FREUD'S TENSION-REDUCTION MODEL: FROM ABSTINENCE TO INSATIABILITY

In this sense, the patient's search for a transference love, as manifested in the patient's surrender to what might be called the mana power of the analyst, has been viewed traditionally both as an unfortunate impediment and a necessary spur to the higher aims of the analytic work. The crucial implicit assumption here is of a *natural* mental inertia on the part of patients; the curiosity for self-knowledge is not as potent as the resistance against it. Thus, in classical analysis, the analysand's regressive longings for a surrendering love of the analyst must be redirected toward more appropriate analytic aims by means of the analyst's abstinence and neutrality. Ferenczi and Rank (1925)—before they deviated from Freud later in their careers—state the principle clearly in their classic monograph, *The Development of Psychoanalysis*: "To consciously become aware of any thing is, in general, a mental phenomenon which human beings never produce except under the pressure of a privation-situation, that is in order to avoid pain" (p. 27).

These assumptions regarding the psychic inertia of human beings—assumptions that have had a major impact on the practice of psychoanalysis—stem directly from Freud's metapsychology, and more indirectly from his life. In Freud's early thinking, pleasure is attained through tension-reduction. Then in 1920, in "Beyond the Pleasure Principle," Freud posits an inherent death drive to repeat, to restore an earlier inorganic state of things; in contrast, organismic life and growth are triggered only by "external disturbing forces" (p. 36). He says: "The elementary living entity would from its very beginning have had no wish to change; if conditions remained the same, it would do no more than constantly repeat the same course of life" (p. 35).

Freud's (1920) metaphysical view of organismic inertia parallels his earlier notion of an "adhesiveness of libido" (1905b) when he suggests that if gratification from incestuous loved objects were available, human beings would never want to give up that gratification and move on with their lives. Freud (1912b) states: "For what motive would men have for putting sexual instinctual forces to other uses if, by any distribution of those forces, they could obtain fully satisfying pleasure. They would never abandon that pleasure and they would never make any further progress" (p. 190). Indeed, so adhesive is the libido that new relationships are always revisited editions of old ones; thus, Freud (1905b) states that "the finding of any object is in fact a refinding of it" (p. 222). Perhaps because tension-seeking is minimized in Freud's thinking, he is not able to find a voluntary impetus within human beings to move from refinding an object to creatively discovering a new one, as when one graduates from a mother to a wife, or emerges with curiosity from unconsciousness into consciousness.

Becker (1973) sheds interesting light on how the huge burdens of Freud's own life may have led him to his theoretical idealization of seeking the lifelessness of the inorganic. Becker suggests that Freud used psychoanalysis as a vehicle by which to become father to himself and to thus transcend death. In fathering and carefully nurturing the growth of his psychoanalytic movement, Freud was heavily invested in the reflected immortality of his progeny. He could not easily relinquish control over the product of his creative genius. To do so would mean to acknowledge his death and profound dependence on others to continue his labors. Thus, Freud's conflicts with Jung and Rank, two surrogate sons in line to inherit the mantle of his leadership, have been well documented (Gay 1988, Roazen 1984).

As Becker says, "To yield is to disperse one's shored-up center, let down one's guard, one's character armor, one's lack of self-sufficiency. . . . To yield is to admit that support has to come from outside oneself and that justification for one's life has to totally come from some self-transcending web in which one consents to be suspended" (p. 107). Becker continues: "That is why Freud had to fight against yielding—he risked effacing his whole identity. He was spinning his own web; how could he suspend himself in someone else's?" (p. 116).

As Freud discovered, however, there is a price to be paid for being the undisputed genius of a transcendent movement: it is lonely at the top. Perhaps nowhere is this aloneness of being father to himself more evident than in the pride and burden of his pioneering self-analysis. As creative overseer to his own analytic process, here, too, Freud fathered his wakeful transformation from an old unconscious self into a newly conscious one. During this analysis, however, unlike any other since, Freud had no one but himself to lean on or to whom he could surrender. It is worth noting here Roazen's (1984) observation that "Freud came back again and again to the fantasy of being raised fatherless" (p. 180).

From this perspective, the wish to surrender that was not lived out in Freud's self-sustaining life may have become resurrected as an ideal for which Freud himself yearned unconsciously. This ideal then became the theoretical basis for Freud's metapsychological ideas about the drive toward the respite of tension-reduction. We can only imagine how pleasurable that elimination of tension may have seemed for Freud's overburdened life as a fatherless creator.

Becker (1973) relates Freud's two fainting spells in Jung's presence to Freud's emotional ambivalence about the *causa sui* (self-creation) project of being father to himself. Jones (1953) points out that as Freud was coming to after his second fainting, he was heard to say: "How sweet it must be to die" (p. 317). Becker quotes Jung's report on the same occasion: "As I was carrying him, he half came to, and I shall never forget the look he cast at me as if I were his father" (p. 116).

At certain times—perhaps in the presence of men whom he respected—Freud may well have been tempted to abdicate his ever-expansive throne of kingly creator in exchange for the unburdened peace of being one of the king's creatures. In this sense, his desperate unconscious search to surrender and reconcile with a father who was not there may have been manifested in Freud's fainting spells.

Perhaps it is because Freud sensed how quickly self-denial could lend to insatiability in his own life that he was moved to comment that transference gratifications encourage the patient to be "insatiable" (Freud 1912b). From this viewpoint, Freud's assumptions concerning the insatiability of patients may have been an extrapolation of his own unmet transference yearnings. Insatiability, rather than deriving from the natural power of drives, thus can be understood as a polarized reaction to one's own extreme self-restraint.

THE HOPE FOR MIRACLE AND THE WISH NOT TO KNOW

When we play with the fiery passions of transference fantasies, by calling them forth and then attempting to dissolve them by rational means, we risk becoming singed by flames that are not so easily doused. Patients are not only passive objects whose transference fantasies we manipulate and control. They also have a stake in participating and maintaining the transference illusion, but perhaps for a different reason than we intended.

For when a person's freedom to think, imagine, and be curious to know has been constricted by tormenting self-recriminations and worries over his capacity to care for those he loves, there is no time to waste. Desperate to be delivered from his mental travails, he will do anything to put his mind at rest. Waiting for Godot to make an appearance has been to no avail.

In his haste to bring heaven down to earth, he falls for the temptation, as Dostoevsky's (1864b) Underground Man notes, "to mistake the nearest and secondary causes for primary causes" (p. 276). That is, he displaces his spiritual needs to devote himself to something or someone beyond his omnipotence onto the cultural realm. In so doing, he seeks transcendence in the consensus of the crowd with conformity as his primary form of worship. Rather than think and decide for himself, the tyranny of the majority reigns, as he sorts through lists of Top 40 songs, best-sellers, and the newest videos. Or he may seek simply to extinguish the burdens of consciousness by going to a movie comedy so that he will not have to think too much. In keeping up with the cutting edge of cultural evolution, he keeps himself from perishing in the isolation of abandoned extinction. In acting as if the consensual agreements of a given culture are transcendent truths, he surrenders his burdened consciousness in an idealizing transference to the crowd.

Alternatively, he may seek release in the enveloping grasp of a strong, powerful other—one who is closer than the gods, but yet silently stoic about his own mortal failings. Only such an other as the charismatically mysterious healer can be accorded the idealized due usually reserved for a god.

As long as there is mystery about the promised cure of psychoanalysis, hope springs eternal for the miracle that painful losses and disillusionments are not final but can be undone. From this viewpoint, the positive transference is an intensified constellation of wishes, fantasies, and hoped-for modes of relating to a future in which one's suffering is to be ultimately redeemed. It is this hope to miraculously undo the disillusioning past and to form a new beginning that may animate patients' voluntary surrender to the hypnotic sway of the positive transference.

Thus, Macalpine (1950) has termed the transference a "slow-motion hypnosis." And Becker (1973) has emphasized that the person who is held hypnotically in the spell of the positive transference is doing so willingly out of a "slavishness in his own soul" (p. 129). The anonymity of the analyst's personality lends projective space to the patient's fantasied yearning—and entitled demand—to claim from the analyst that which is withheld, and which the patient may consider his therapeutic birthright to receive. The dialectic between the mystery of the analyst's personality and the patient's expectant faith in miracles forms the core of the positive transference. In this sense, transference love and the wish to surrender to the analyst are not preordained urges rooted in Freudian metapsychology; they are manifestations of a relational hunger that can be maximized or minimized by an analyst's technical stance.

Yet the phrase "positive transference," as used here, is a misnomer. Because the positive aspects of idealizing transferences are born in the shadow of unfulfilled longings and disillusionments, and based only on the fantasy of future fulfillment, they carry within themselves the hidden seeds of an actual negative transference. Old disillusionments and their self-recriminations have left scars of bitterness in their wake, as well as an underlying demand that one should not have to wait any longer before being delivered to a better place. If the mortal god of the analyst does not create miracle out of the mystery of the idealizing transference in good time, he can suffer the same fate as her sacred predecessor. Dostoevsky's (1880) Grand Inquisitor is well aware of this fickleness of the positive transference when he says, "And the very people who have today kissed Thy feet, tomorrow at the faintest sign from me will rush to heap up the embers of Thy fire" (p. 4).

In a sense, classical analysis and analysts have withheld their idealized magic for too long; they have been deposed by the advent of self-psychology, and more recently, by relational and intersubjective psychoanalysis. Patients now may claim the miracles of undoing disillusionments more immediately in the selfobject transference. Thus, the patient's demand for the redemptive magic of time reversal, by forging an illusion of a new beginning through the selfobject transference, may be viewed as an acted-in follow-up to the deposed idealization of the analyst.

In both the idealizing and selfobject transferences, analysts contrive to some extent to fill a professional role and to be someone other than who they are. Their immersion in one or another technical guise may be calculated to keep their personal reactions anonymous and under disciplined control. Time and again (to the point of being satirized in books and film), a patient's questions concerning the analyst's personhood are deftly parried and skillfully deflected into return questions. The patient is left to grope endlessly in a relational void. In the wake of this sort of object silence, Lipton (1977) was moved to assert that "such technique incurs the danger of fostering iatrogenic narcissistic disorders by establishing an ambience in which the patient has little opportunity to establish an object relationship" (p. 272). There is something disingenuous, however, about a fundamental analytic injunction that encourages the patient to "know thyself," while discouraging a curiosity to know about the person of the analyst. The unruly passion of curiosity, manifested in a wish to discover and know, is not so easily tamed and redirected.

The treatment relationship is a paradoxical one; it is both professional and personal. Whereas some patients play up the personal aspects of the relationship and would rather forget that it is also professional, others are more comfortable adhering to the straight and narrow working focus of the professional. In fact, I find it somewhat peculiar when patients do not seem to be interested in the person with whom they are engaged so intimately.

Perhaps there is a clue in the statement made by one of my students, who said, "I don't want to know anything about my analyst. Then I would have to take care of him." Here we see that knowing about the foibles and frailties of another person is still tangled up with the mandate to take care of what one knows. The patient's sense of what Searles (1975) calls "guilty responsibility" may have been so disillusioning historically that he may conclude that it is better not to know anything about the person of the analyst. How can analysts perform the miracle of reversing time and delivering patients from their caretaking burdens if they themselves need care? To know the imperfect human being behind the controls of therapeutic wizardry ruptures the illusion of miracle and opens up the treatment relationship to the patient's previous experiences of failed caretaking and self-recrimination in all their transference manifestations.

THE TRANSFERENCE: A FREEDOM FROM TO A FREEDOM WITH

When relational wishes are disillusioned, it takes but a small step of rationalization to transform the defenses of narcissistic self-sufficiency into a utopian ideology of psychic liberation such as psychoanalysis. Through the rational tools of analysis and interpretation, it has been believed that neurotic individuals may gain some measure of independence from unconscious conflicts underlying the compulsion to repeat. In this regard, clinical psychoanalysis has assumed historically that the compulsion to repeat, and its most pervasive exemplar, the transference, is and should be an eradicable neurosis of the human condition. Thus, the vice of disillusionment and defensive detachment may be turned into a virtue, when such terms as "autonomy," "maturity," "self-actualization," and "rationality" come to signify a freedom *from* the messy emotionality of relational entanglements.

This traditional psychoanalytic ideal of mature adulthood and freedom is an illusion, however, to the extent that it is based on an image of humans as self-sufficient beings. The transference can be viewed also as a universal dynamic of the human condition that is based in wishes to belong, to be an integral member of an interdependent community. In this sense of give-and-take, we can speak of an enlightening freedom *with* others. It is precisely because no man can be a self-enclosed island unto himself, that repressing one's relational/transference wish to devote oneself to something greater than oneself may lead to an intensified return from the repressed in the form of idealization. It is too burdening to maintain an enclosed self-sufficiency; hence, the need to surrender oneself to an idealized other. In the Grand Inquisitor's monologue, we see how a potential freedom with others is distorted into a polarization between a wearying, self-reliant notion of freedom and its intensified opposite, a slavish need to worship.

To whatever extent the classical prescriptions of abstinence, neutrality, and anonymity still are present in contemporary psychoanalytic treatment, we are apt to see this polarized dialectic brought to transferential life. The shroud of professional role that covers the analyst's personal identity in mystery colludes with the patient's wishes not to know the imperfect person who may disillusion him again as his parents did. As Singer (1971) asserts, "The lack of authenticity in parent–child relations, the child's inadequate opportunities to express constructive relatedness, finds an analogue in the traditional analytic relationship" (p. 67). The analyst's abstinence from personal relating begets patient fantasies of insatiable transference hunger that may, in turn, cause the analyst to immerse herself self-protectively in the technical prescriptions of her professional role. As a result, the patient may never get the opportunity to work through the disillusionments that led him to conflate knowing about another's woes and the compulsive need to fix them.

When analysts, in pursuit of psychic truth, do strive to rid patients of their illusory transference props through their analyses, they may attempt to remain above it all in their role as observer and commentator. They may find, much to their chagrin, that the analysis of the transference leads only to a multiple regress in which patients cling tenaciously to the idealizing transference with ever-greater urgency in silent defiance of analysts' attempts to divest them of it. Thus, Ferenczi (1932b) has suggested

that: "The precocious overburdening of the patient with as yet unwanted knowledge, responsibility and seriousness of life goes hand-
in-hand with a regression to infantile dependence" (p. 262).

But is it inevitable that the freedom to know, think, and decide be overburdening? Knowing certainly is oppressive when it is
coupled with a pressured call to caretaking action for any sufferings in others that our curiosity may unveil. It is a shame, however, when patients complete an analysis and are never able to
liberate themselves from this burdensome pressure of compulsive
indebtedness by learning to give and to receive from the analyst
in a different way.

Singer (1971) comments that "strict psychoanalytic anonymity would have reduced my patients' opportunities to see their own
strengths; and certainly I would have limited my knowledge of their
caring and compassionate qualities" (p. 62). Indeed, Searles (1975)
goes so far as to say that "The more ill a patient is, the more does
his successful treatment require that he become, and be implicitly acknowledged as having become, a therapist to his officially
designated therapist, the analyst" (p. 381).

It has been my own experience that the longer a psychotherapy
goes on, the more the therapist's professional persona wears away.
In my treatment with Gary, personal information that was originally kept private has seeped out gradually. Whereas in the early
stages of treatment I was the idealized therapist ("I wish I could
sit on your lap so you could tell me about life"), little by little I
have come to be viewed as another human being in Gary's eyes.
To the extent that I am viewed as "weaker" and have come off my
pedestal, Gary has gained strength and confidence in his own
abilities.

Perhaps this evolution in Gary's view of me could have been
anticipated from our earliest sessions together, when, in addition
to referring to me by the properly formal Dr. Shabad, Gary often
would just drop the "Dr." Rather than be put off by Gary's familiarity, I always saw this as Gary's attempt to be chummy, as if I were
a frat brother. Seeing me as an open, accessible buddy whom he
just refers to as "Shabad" has been an indispensable aspect in a

dialectic (Hoffman 1999) of a more informal, expressive participation and a more formal disciplined reflection on the therapeutic process.

This informal, personal aspect of our relationship has become
more pronounced through the years in the form of humor. Gary
has a good-natured, gently teasing wit that he calls "giving shit"
that I find very funny. On a number of occasions I have laughed
heartily with him, and even tried my own hand at creating levity.
At these times, Gary has laughed, but punctuated his fun with a
"Shabad, how many times do I have to tell you. You do the therapy,
and leave the comedy to me."

I tend to think comedy is one way that Gary is expressing his
psychotherapeutic strivings toward me. He is having a "corrective
emotional experience" (Alexander 1946) by making me laugh in
ways that he was never able to coax out of his mother. Rather than
let me hog the spotlight in the realm of comedy and therapy know-
how, Gary is letting me know in no uncertain terms that if there
is any entertaining to be done, he will be doing it. That is how he
brings *his* worthiness and usefulness to our relationship.

The initial years of Gary's and my relationship reflected his
history of burdened isolation and self-enclosure, his own failed
attempts at caretaking for his mother. He sought to hand over his
shames and sense of guilty responsibility to me; he would know
nothing and I would know everything.

Gradually, however, my idealized shroud of professional anonymity has come down to reveal more and more of my personality
and aspects of my life. This evolution in our relationship has syn-
chronized, I believe, with Gary's conviction that he is genuinely
accepted and well liked by me. He, in turn, is able to take a chance
on participating in an open give-and-take once more. I do the
therapy; he does the comedy.

10

Confidence and Doubt: The Therapist's Sense of Lovingness and the Use of the Personal in Psychotherapy

This above all: to thine own self be true
and it must follow, as the night the day,
thou canst not then be false to any man.

—William Shakespeare

Nothing ever becomes real till it is experienced
—even a proverb is no proverb to you till your life
has illustrated it.

—John Keats

WORD MAGIC AND THE FEAR OF THE
TALKING CURE

Many of the inner-city adolescents with whom I work, struggling through the numerous losses of their lives by means
of violent rage or suicidal depression, have difficulty understanding the advantages of talking through their problems. What they
do know is that it is intensely painful to voice their worst experiences in the here-and-now. If they do not think about or discuss
what ails them, maybe it will disappear. Or better yet, it never
happened.

Perhaps, then, it is not surprising that many parents calm their
children's nightmares with phrases such as "Don't think about
anything bad now. Just have sweet dreams." To speak of one's
suffering conjures up the partial reexperiencing of one's traumas;
it calls those experiences into being again. Many patients may express their resistance to the talking cure with refrains such as
"What's the point of dredging up the past? It has nothing to do
with me now." To which, I, at times, familiar with the haunting,
persecutory quality of the repetition compulsion, have replied, "I
wonder if you have been saying that to yourself for twenty years,
and you still find yourself facing the same problems. Maybe it would
be worthwhile to try something different at this point."

When we deny that suffering is an inevitable aspect of the
human condition and can be eliminated by simple avoidance, we
are taken aback when our problems resurface again. If our suffering does not have to be, then others must be bringing it into our
lives. When very young children or animals experience pain, they
may strike out at whatever is nearest. Or when a person walks into
a dentist's office feeling fine and trudges out with aching teeth,
she may believe that the dental treatment manufactured a problem that would have remained dormant had it been ignored. In
psychotherapy, too, where language is the medium, we often are
witness to the magical belief in the power of the word to make

reality; the implication is that talking creates rather than uncovers emotional suffering. One patient was so suggestible that the mere mention of the phrase "panic attack" began to produce symptoms. Why not just let sleeping dogs lie?

The narcissistic wish to perfect one's self-image and find the problem elsewhere is a seductive temptation. Denial can quickly lead to projection, as we attribute blame for our troubles to an external source. Projection may then give way to displacement as the hot potato of culpability is lifted off the loved ones we need the most, and placed on others who live outside our circles of familiarity. Hitler placed a portrait of his beloved mother above every bed that he slept in during his adult life; somebody else, other "devils" had to pay for the whitewashing of his mother into an angel. Coping with suffering and sin by ignoring, isolating, displacing, and eliminating it in this way has had a very long history. Killing the messenger who brings bad tidings, burning witches at the stake, kicking the dog after a bad day at work, beating up a little brother, and ethnic cleansing all are examples of ways in which we heap our unwanted demons onto a scapegoat whom we then send unceremoniously into the wilderness never to be heard from again. Before we cast stones of blame, however, I think it is important that we heed Jung's caution—one that he did not always take care to follow himself—that when we find ourselves disliking another person, we first must look to the hidden shadows within and give these shadows expressive life.

In speaking of their suffering, patients are acting in good faith—a faith that the acute pain of imaginatively and symbolically reenacting their worst experiences through words will lead to a lifelong liberation from the demons that haunt them. In this regard, I believe it essential that the therapist share this same faith and conviction in the freeing effects of the talking cure. All too often, however, it seems to me that therapists' superstitions concerning word magic collude with those of patients, such that both participants may fear articulating and naming the worst dreads and fears experienced by patients. When therapists hesitate before offering an interpretation to a patient and say to themselves, "I don't know if he's ready to hear that" or "I don't think she will be able to tolerate that," they, like many patients, may also be subscribing to the superstitious belief that their words will make problems rather than articulate them.

What do we, as therapists, really mean when we declare that a particular patient will not be able to tolerate an insight? Do we really mean that the patient will decompensate before our eyes and end up in a psychiatric hospital? If that is true, then what are we to make of it when therapists become anxious about bringing up difficult topics even within the confines of a hospital setting? Perhaps the most valuable aspect in understanding our patients' sufferings is that we keep them company with difficult truths. I am concerned that our most sincere intentions to protect patients from the realization of their own experiences only leaves such individuals, who already have been alone too long with their suffering, in their self-enclosed solitude still longer. Not to speak directly, sincerely, and fearlessly, and finally name the hidden monster lurking inside, colludes with the patient's dread that to speak is to reexperience a trauma full force all over again.

It is true that it may be counterproductive to bring an issue up at an inopportune time, but in my opinion that usually has more to do with knowing the difference between ordinary human tact and tactlessness. I suspect that a great deal of the anxiety about a patient's capacity to tolerate the therapist's words has to do with the therapist's fantasies concerning her destructive omnipotence, as well as fantasies about the patient's fragility. When a therapist has not worked through her own disillusionments with sufficient hope still intact, she may have doubts about whether her love is stronger than her hate. It may then be difficult to trust that what will come out of her mouth will help more than hurt the patient.

THERAPISTS' DISILLUSIONMENTS AND THEIR COMPENSATING IDEOLOGIES

It is of fundamental importance that when human beings emerge from childhood they feel that their love toward others is stronger than their hate. As children, our relative success in making the significant people around us feel better goes a long way toward establishing some confidence about what we have to offer. This confidence is indispensable to clinical work, for it enables therapists to trust the unconscious and to use themselves in a spontaneous fashion. When self-doubt replaces confidence, and therapists must think twice about their basic capacity to love, they then have to embrace the certitude of prepared technical applications to convey their love.

It is impossible for anyone to be neutral with regard to their illusions and disillusionments. We all use some mode of defense to cope with significant disappointments. Although therapists may partly work through the disillusionments experienced with their parents, the core of helplessness that lies at the basis of those interactions probably never is resolved entirely. That helplessness instead may become manifested implicitly in the compensatory ideologies and values of the therapist's adult character. The substance of these ideologies, the therapist's implicit view of human nature, and the idealized images she envisions would improve that nature, may then be direct outgrowths of the therapist's personal disillusionments.

A therapist's image of a character ideal is a very personal matter, for it is designed to master the experience of helplessness one feels in interacting with persons who fall short of that ideal. To a large extent, therapists cannot help but perceive, theorize about, interpret, and create patients in their unarticulated image of a preferred character. Rank (1936) viewed therapists as creative types who have a powerful urge to fashion a personal artistic project out of the treatment process. In this sense, each cure, at one and the same time, may be the therapist's attempt to heal her own wounds while also improving the patient's lot in life. How therapists come to terms with their personal disillusionments, then, has major implications for their theories of cure and the methods used to effect that cure. Although therapists may analyze their personal countertransferences scrupulously, they may not be as aware of the way the residue of disillusionments, the subsequent attempts to master those disillusionments, and their ideology of cure are intertwined. On the contrary, rather than being examined thoroughly, a therapist's ideology and technique may be passed down from one analytic generation to the next through indoctrination and training.

The treatment relationship is a complex constellation of mutual gropings to shape and to be shaped, to use the other and to be of use to the other. Patients, depending on their relative need to be a creature or a creator, may either attempt to mold the therapist to specification, or offer themselves up to be influenced by the therapist's creative strivings or, of course, both. When therapy proceeds almost too smoothly, we might conclude that the patient has not found his creative voice, but has agreed tacitly, for reasons good or bad, to go along with the therapist's vision of a curative ideal. On the other hand, a patient's dogged resistance may be a way of saying "no" to the therapist's vision, without yet being able to articulate his own ideal of self-healing.

Is it really necessary that one participant within the treatment relationship be the creative person and the other the created object? A sadomasochistic relationship can be defined through the dimension of control, one in which one individual claims creative dominion over another person who then is perceived to be his "colonized" object. From an ethical viewpoint, it is important that we, as clinicians, examine the myriad ways in which this theme of sadomasochism plays itself out in the psychotherapy relationship as a defense against the experience of helplessness. When therapists have moments (or longer) of disappointment, impatience, and even irritation because their patients persist in their symptomatology, it becomes evident how much of a personal stake they have in the treatment process.

For those therapists, in particular, who have been frustrated previously in being of use to significant others in a consistent way, the need to be needed may be especially charged and fraught with vulnerability. If they lack confidence in their lovingness, such practitioners may find the naked spontaneity of a person-to-person interchange tremendously anxiety-provoking. They may then seek to control the proceedings so as to guarantee a recep-

tive audience for their offerings, and thus prove their essential
worthiness and all of this must be done from afar—out of reach
of being rebuffed personally by the patient. Perhaps there is no
better way for therapists to remain at a safe remove from the high
emotional states of intensive psychotherapy than to lose themselves
in the professional role of rational, self-contained analyst and interpreter of the patient's transferences. As Renik (1993) suggests,
however, because everything analysts do in the analytic setting is
based upon personal psychology, they cannot escape their irreducible subjectivity.

COMPLIANCE WITH TECHNIQUE AND THE
EMERGENCE OF SELF-CONSCIOUSNESS

From its inception, the discipline and practice of psychoanalysis
has been informed by an underlying fear of the unconscious and
idealization of conscious thought. The analytic function of dissect-
ing underlying motives into their constituent parts, and of pro-
moting thinking before acting, reflects a radical mistrust of unconscious impulses. The process of making the unconscious
conscious, of rendering the hidden manifest, may be viewed as a
counterphobic attempt to calm persecutory anxieties concerning
the unknown and the invisible. By exposing the beast in oneself
to the light of day, the mind attempts to master a fear of the unpredictable and spontaneous emotionality of the body.

Individuals who place great value on gaining rational governance over their emotions have traditionally been attracted to the
practice of psychoanalysis. It is not surprising then that psychoanalysts have been well aware of the pathologies of compulsive
action, but not as concerned with the dangers of obsessional thinking. Such phrases as "acting-out," "acting-in," and "flight into
health" attest to the keen eye that psychoanalysts cast on the neurotic foundations of unconscious actions. But obsessionals also have
their own unique set of problems. Their tendency to flee the
mercurial unreliability of their bodies through mentation or think-

ing-in may result in a split between mind and body. The anxieties of some obsessional analysts concerning their own dark underworld of concealed passions may then be projected onto the patient who they can then attempt to tame and cure through the raising of consciousness.

Such a relationship between analyst and analysand is exemplified in the prototypical analytic dyad of the obsessional male analyst and the hysterical female patient. In a scene reminiscent of Henry Higgins's refrain of why a woman can't be more like a man, the obsessional analyst attempts to teach, by his abstinence, the wisdom of rational self-discipline and mental curiosity to an overly expressive emotional being ruled by the irrationality of her unconscious drives. Perhaps more humorously, this analytic dyad bears a strong resemblance to the married couple that presents for marital therapy. Quite commonly, the wife accuses her husband of silent withholding and insensitivity to her tears, whereas he explains dispassionately that it is difficult to attend to her when she is so irrational. By putting the classic analytic dyad into the context of the marital relationship, we immediately see the relativism in the respective pathologies of its participants such that rational thought is not healthier than but complementary to irrational action.

What happens when this one-person psychology in which there is an overvaluation of self-reliance and rationality is put into clinical practice? To a large extent, the classic psychoanalytic image of an ideal of mental health has shaped both its vision of cure and the therapeutic technique used to effect that cure. Thus, the unquenchable pursuit of psychic truth, based upon a self-exploration in the face of the analyst's interpersonal abstinence, may be viewed as a microcosm created in the idealized image of a stoic, truth-laden individual braving alone the various miseries, disillusionments, and conflicts endemic to the human condition (Shabad 1991).

Rather than respond to the patient's various requests, tirades, flattery, or other provocations for a more real relationship with the analyst, the analyst, by his professional demeanor of abstinence, anonymity, and neutrality tacitly discourages the wish for a more personal relationship. The patient may come to realize that it is not considered appropriate to expect the analyst to respond in certain ways. Consequently, the relatively healthy wish of the patient to maintain and deepen the unconscious relationship with the analyst may be buried, obscured by a subtle compliance with the therapist's technique. This sort of compliance may be difficult to detect, especially when working with the analyzable, higher-functioning neurotic. Precisely because we expect neurotics to bear and tolerate analytically induced frustrations more capably, we may be less apt to take note of how they subtly transform unconscious transference wishes for a more personal relationship into further narcissistic grist for the mind. Thus, Renik (1995) points out that far from being able to associate freely, what may be most salient to patients in such austere, interpersonal circumstances is to wonder what the analyst is thinking.

It is ironic that patients produce associations self-reliantly with the unconscious hope that their efforts will bear relational fruit with the analyst. Because the search inward for the whys and wherefores of their motivations does not and cannot yield the realization of that desired relationship, the involuted journey of associating freely may take on the quality of an endless quest in which patients attempt to capture something essential that remains ever-elusive. One might view the self-absorbed obsessional quality that sometimes accompanies patients' associations as an unsuccessful, and therefore repeated, intellectualized attempt to incorporate the indigestible reality of relational frustration in the analytic setting.

From my viewpoint, psychoanalysis cannot afford to treat the unveiling of the unconscious only as an analytic research investigation. The process by which patients come to understand themselves is not conducted in an emotional vacuum and patients are not information-processing machines. To be considered a genuine therapeutic endeavor, psychoanalysis must also be concerned with the evaluative attitudes and meanings that the conscious explorer of the unconscious imposes on her new discoveries. In short, psychoanalysis must provide patients with a usable self-knowledge to live by.

By virtue of the fact that none of us can escape our essential humanity, people always come to know themselves with a particular emotional valence. Each new insight is flavored immediately with a feeling of its being good or bad, such that all self-knowledge may be viewed at least to some degree as either self-acceptance or self-condemnation. Moreover, the emotional valence of these self-evaluations is never constructed outside of a relational context. Thus, Bollas (1987) has pointed out that a person's attitude toward herself is very much created in the introjected shadow of a history of object relationships. This is equally true of relationships in the here-and-now.

This leaves us with the all-important clinical question of what the implications are when patients find out about themselves within the highly charged, passionate context of the relationship with the analyst. Patients' evaluations of their new self-discoveries as acceptable or not are interwoven with the fate of their transference wishes. Specifically, their relative acceptance or condemnation of themselves may be directly affected by the felt presence or absence of a relationship with the analyst.

When a patient's unconscious stream of associations is interspersed only by an analyst's interpretations, psychological-mindedness may become an unusual blip on the analytic screen. Because the interpretive consciousness of the therapist is not tied to the patient's unconscious material by an embodied relationship, sharp discontinuities may arise between minds and bodies, and between the conscious and unconscious. Without the bridging link of a person-to-person dialogue, the patient may come to perceive the analyst as a disembodied talking head. And if this is the only show in town, a patient may have no choice but to grab on hungrily to the analyst's interpretations for relational sustenance. In this sense, patients may cling to an analyst's disembodied pronouncements to keep themselves company in the absence of any other sort of relationship.

The patient's emerging self-consciousness, born of the necessity of relational frustration, will be tinged with that frustration. She will look more shamefully upon transference wishes that are being thwarted by the analyst's silence, neutrality, or formality. The analyst's technical demand on the patient to associate freely, and in a sense to be on her own, may bring with it a self-knowledge colored by the patient's contempt for her dependent longings. To call these unconscious wishes for relationship into awareness then exposes the patient to a sense of shame before a condemning self-consciousness. The paradox is that this emergent self-consciousness has an opposite effect on the patient than what was therapeutically intended, as she attempts to cover over rather than reveal the source of her shame.

Such self-consciousness, lacking the foundation of relationship to bridge conscious and unconscious, mind and body, offers the semblance of self-awareness without its essence; it is an involuted hyperconsciousness superimposed on but not integrated with desires based in an unconscious, unaccepted body. As a reflex triggered by a sudden, rude awakening to the unconscious, it is a defensive reaction designed to shelter rather than reveal the deepest strata of the person's self. It is noteworthy that Rank (1936), who considered an inhibiting self-consciousness to be a hallmark of neurosis, was led to assert provocatively, "The neurotic has long since been where psychoanalysis wants to bring him" (p. 251).

REMAINING ABOVE THE FRAY: ENGENDERING TRANSFERENCE INTENSITY AND ANALYZING THE TRANSFERENCE

Whereas in the one-person psychology of a more traditional analysis much attention is placed on the internal life of the freely associating patient, in many contemporary two-person psychologies the focus of the analytic searchlight has shifted from the self-contained mind of the individual patient to the insulated relationship between analyst and patient. Reducing the patient's life either to her fantasies or to her participation in the treatment relationship, however, risks rendering other dimensions, historical and extra-transferential, to an unreal secondary status. Although Freud recognized the importance of engendering the illusion of transference love for the purpose of furthering the analysis, it is ironic that the transference may now be viewed as where the action is and other aspects of the patient's life are viewed as illusory.

When the transferential here and now is viewed as the primary field of therapeutic action, and any discussion of the patient's history is considered a defensive flight from the intensity of the transference, the patient's life outside of treatment may be reduced to a dreamlike epiphenomenon. By not recognizing the substantive reality of the patient's external life, the analyst may accentuate a transferential intensity that has the perhaps not coincidental effect of binding the patient to the analyst. In thus reducing the patient's other relationships to mere subsidiary shadows of the primary transference, the analyst is able to take creative possession of a patient who has now been transformed from a person into a case.

At conferences and staffings the objectification of patients runs rampant in the shorthand exchanges among the various clinicians. It is commonplace, for example, to hear therapists refer to the significant others in a patient's life without using personal pronouns, such that "his mother" becomes just "mother" or "her father" is rendered into "father." In omitting the personal pronouns in the description of a patient's significant relationships, therapists denude patients of their personhood in order to re-create them as case specimens to be controlled, diagnosed, and treated.

Thus, it may feel safer for therapists to take notes about a case to be observed, than to speak with a person whom they engage firsthand. No matter how much this simple practice of note-taking is rationalized as a necessary means of gathering useful information, there is no denying that the very process of jotting something down on paper during the session transforms the patient into an object of scrutiny. The problem here is that many patients come for therapy in the first place because they have felt depersonalized or exploited as objects for much of their lives. They may even introduce themselves to us by way of that sine qua non of objectification, the diagnostic label: "I'm a borderline . . ." or "I have bipolar illness." Therapists risk colluding with the self-objectification of such persons when they view patients as cases as soon as they walk in the door.

Sometimes these patients demonstrate through their descriptions of experiences with others the degree to which they have felt objectified. Their narratives are filled with descriptions of themselves as seen through the eyes and desires of others: "My wife didn't think I talked enough last night when we had company." If such individuals are queried about their own wishes, they seem taken aback by the notion and may be at a loss as how to respond. They filter any questions concerning their wants through the possessors of their souls—the persons to whom they are currently giving their devotion. For such individuals there is something forbidden about the assertive subjectivity of desiring, something that endangers the nice-person status of being someone else's object.

Rather than respect the patient's manifest, conscious declarations as substantive in and of themselves, the analyst may interpret the patient's experience in terms of unconscious transference needs. Here we see the fine line that exists between the therapist discovering the patient's unconscious transferences via interpretation on one hand, and creating the patient's unconscious via suggestion. In this sense, excessive transference interpretations, having the effect of binding the patient to the therapist's possessive control, may be a vehicle by which therapists master their doubts about their essential usefulness. The engendering of a transferential intensity illustrates a paradox inherent in a treatment that is predicated primarily on an analysis of that transference. The patient's conscious receptivity to the therapist's interpretive attempts to work through the often disillusioning implications of the transference is motivated by the patient's continued wish to please and win over the person behind the therapist's professional mask.

The analyst's transcendent role of interpreter-commentator

may actually have the effect of enhancing his mystique, and thus of redoubling the strength of the transference. As long as it is only the analyst who primarily inhabits the creative, godlike role of dispassionate observer and interpreter of the transference, there is a risk that the patient will feel the onrush of shame that arises when a heretofore unconscious person is made suddenly conscious of herself. The resulting shame and self-consciousness may only foster a paradoxical urge to hide from this sense of exposure by clinging to and even merging with the analyst. The patient's repressed wish to elicit the personal in the therapist, without any other appropriate outlet, may end up being acted-in by way of a mystical union with the interpreter-creator of relational meaning.

Through a subtle and sometimes not so subtle imitation of the analyst's mannerisms, jargon, intonation, and general analytic stance of self-containment, poise, and authority, the patient can flee from her sense of shame by becoming the analyst. This imitation may have the aim of finally building a relational bridge across the chasm created by the analyst's anonymity and abstinence. Perhaps it is this sort of imitative outcome that Ferenczi (1928) had in mind when he declared, "It is the business of a real character analysis to do away, at any rate temporarily, with any kind of superego including that of the analyst . . . successes that consist in the substitution of one superego for another must be regarded as transference successes; they fail to attain the final aim of therapy, the dissolution of the transferences" (p. 98).

THE NARCISSISM AND SELF-CONSCIOUSNESS OF THE PROFESSIONAL MASK

Ferenczi's insight concerning "transference successes" has fundamental implications for psychoanalytic treatment and training. To the extent that imperfectly resolved transferences in training analyses are cured by "the substitution of one superego for another," the overvaluation of a disembodied consciousness is perpetuated from one generation of trainees to the next. And when imitation is employed to bridge the person-to-person gap between patient and analyst, such cures may resemble indoctrinations that are coerced by the analyst's abstinence.

As an unconscious creature who has incurred the shame of being caught with his pants down once too often by the analyst's interpretations, a trainee may seek to regain control and dignity by identifying with the aggressor of the training analyst's consciousness. By showing that he already knows about himself first, the trainee can foreclose the analyst's creative molding of him into a case. Without the mutual trust provided by an embodied personal relationship, however, the trainee may use his newly acquired consciousness of himself more as a defensive shield of sympathetic magic (an eye for an eye) to combat his analyst's intrusive consciousness rather than to discover his own truth. In this sense, self-consciousness is the protective mask of self-awareness, without its substance.

With the acquisition and possession of the power of consciousness, trainees now may imagine that they can transcend previous experiences of helplessness. By anticipating and detaching from anticipated attacks on the emotionality of the body, self-conscious persons can escape from the frustration of relationships gone wrong. With a counterphobic alertness they can cover over the shame of being taken rudely by surprise. With impregnable cerebral magic such as this at one's disposal, it is easy to see why it is possible to lose perspective on one's human limitations.

Thus, budding analysts may invest their training and training analyses with all of their harbored yearnings to be saved from their childhood disillusionments. With the salvation magic of consciousness as their medium, they can put the insults and shames of humbler times behind them. Their new parents—supervisors and the training analyst—may lead them through an incubation period until they have mastered the art of self-observation, at which time they may be reborn into a brand-new professional identity. With this tempting offer to redeem and undo one's childhood disillusionments, it is no wonder that so much importance is attached to the locus of one's training as the source of one's rebirth.

I would thus suggest that the intermingling of self-consciousness and narcissistic inflation of our professional identities has become the scourge of clinical psychoanalysis. There is an unspoken hierarchy that pervades the entire profession—ranging from the keenly self-observing training analyst at the top to the nonfunctioning unconscious patient at the bottom—that is based on the degree to which one is conscious of oneself. In between are the large bulk of psychologists, psychiatrists, social workers, and trainees who bask in the glorified shadow of their idealized masters of consciousness and who in turn distance themselves from the unconscious blindness of their patients. The street-smart, with-it person who anticipates the problems of the real world and therefore masters them, at least in his head, is the paragon of mental health. The unconscious, impulse-ridden child who knows not whence he came nor where he is going, and whose innocence is in danger of being blindsided by rupture is the shameful, vulnerable underbelly for all of us.

This hierarchy is reflected, I believe, in the distinctions that we make between them and us, between our patients and ourselves. Although it is true that some insights garnered from the depths of psychoanalytic treatment cannot be matched in any other area, it seems strange to me that psychoanalytic theorists so commonly use clinical examples rather than observations from everyday life to illustrate their thinking. In doing so, we are able to keep the arena of psychopathology, in which our patients and we as professionals reside, safely distinct from the outside world where we as private citizens live. This may account, at least partially, for the discomfort some clinicians feel when they encounter their patients in an off-guard moment in their private lives. Theories that are derived only from the clinical laboratory and constructed in professional jargon lose their vital tie to the English language. Such jargon then proliferates in case conferences, seminars, and supervision, greatly influencing the way we think about patients.

To the extent that a central feature of an observing consciousness is to analyze or to tear apart the object of focus into its constituent parts, self-consciousness has a deconstructive effect on the
constructed holism of our creations. The created products of our
self-revelations, both verbal and nonverbal, that provide us with a
sense of kinship to other persons become subject to the nihilistic
doubts cast by the second-guessings of self-consciousness. When
our creative animus is thus objectified and paralyzed, it is difficult
to construct a bridge of generalizability from our unique experiences to the lives of others. Caught in an internal web of our own
making, we become locked in an involutional prism of wondering
whether our experience is nothing but our experience. In this most
isolated of worlds, we lose a sense of belonging to something real
beyond our self-preoccupations.

In a sense, we are too smart for our own good; our self-
consciousness penetrates our illusions with annihilating skepticism,
leaving the machinery of our creativity exposed in its deadened
parts. We then question the usefulness or accuracy of our perceptions to such an extent that our creations are shadowed constantly
by an anxiety of collapsing into the trivial (reinventing the wheel)
or the idiosyncratic (ideas as reflective of self-absorbed psychopathology). It is disheartening to hear trainees, inundated with the
double-takes of self-consciousness, preface their contributory re-
marks at case conferences and seminars with the disclaimer "This
may be my fantasy, but . . ." When the generalizing, relational glue
of creative insight is undone and reduced to the individual psychopathology of hallucinatory fantasy, it is difficult to find one's
place within the common fabric of human experience. Self-
consciousness thus leaves each of us with our own set of unique
experiences in a lonely internment of self-doubt.

As the overvaluation of disembodied thinking becomes institutionalized and transmitted from one generation of students to
the next, trainees may be propelled into a professional role at
the cost of their personal participation. Laboring under the exacting perfectionism of a watchful self-consciousness, they unlearn
the best of what they have to offer. They become overly invested

in not making mistakes, in presenting the appearance of doing all the right things so as to gain entrée into professional respectability.

SELF-DOUBT AND THE BUFFER OF TECHNIQUE

Although to outside observers therapists may exhibit an image of professional self-importance, inwardly they may suffer uncertainty about their capacity to love, to create, and to care effectively for others. To ward off doubts about whether they have something useful to offer personally, some analysts may seek to ensure their influence on treatment outcome by emphasizing the trappings of their role. Rather than lend themselves to the depths of spontaneous interactions with patients, such analysts may assert control over the frame, setting, and technical rules that circumscribe the treatment.

The analyst's overconsuming faith in the therapeutic efficacy of rationality, emergent as a defensive bulwark against fears of the spontaneity of emotion, has had a major impact on the psychoanalytic method. For example, the analyst may use precocious thinking or what Romanyshyn (1989) calls the "mathematical" to prepare for the human encounter. Romanyshyn describes the mathematical as a mapping of the world "in advance of our experience of things, the conditions according to which things will appear" (p. 51).

Psychoanalytic technique, an example of what Schon (1983) calls "technical rationality," is a planned, systematic application of a therapeutic technology that adheres to specific rules and principles. In a general, formal sense, analysts, equipped with their foreknowledge of technique, may enter an analytic session ahead of time, before the session makes its actual appearance. With their correct technical principles in hand as a protective buffer, they can counter the phobia of sinking into an unpredictable intimacy of being alone with a person in need. Historically, many

psychoanalysts have thought it advisable to observe before participating, to heed caution before plunging into the transference–
countertransference morass. It is assumed that it is wiser to wait
twenty minutes or twenty sessions and mull over an interpretation
before expressing it. Thus, the discipline of observing, listening,
and waiting has taken precedence over learning how to think and
speak on one's feet while in the midst of participating. It is assumed
that this use of rational self-examination, of thinking twice before
speaking, will enable the analyst to say something more helpful or
profound than if she were to speak spontaneously.

Are various interpretations and interventions really more therapeutic for patients if they have been thought about ahead of time
rather than offered spontaneously? Are we not adding another
inhibiting superego, one derived from the analyst's training, on
top of the superego already acquired in the process of normal
socialization? I often ask my trainees to imagine how they would
feel if they were placed, without the technical and professional
know-how of their graduate and analytic training at their disposal,
in a room with a person in emotional distress whom they were
simply told to help. Who would they be? What would they say or
do, or not do? Many students, already well initiated into the sanctuary of the observing ego, are lost as to what resources to fall back
on in this nakedly person-to-person situation. This is a shame, for
they have forgotten what they once knew as children, and what
motivated them to enter the helping professions in the first place:
how to use themselves to care for others.

Perhaps we would not fear drowning in transference love if
we did not also have a corresponding countertransference love that
pressures us to fulfill the patient's entreaties. If transference love
has to do with seizing another chance to receive what was not
gotten from a parent, then countertransference love has to do with
new opportunities to make offerings that were not accepted by our
parents. Countertransference love thus can be viewed as a residual
sense of indebtedness that propels us to give ourselves to others.
When analysts are not aware of the disillusioning sources of their
indebtedness, they may justify expressions of countertransference

love through the self-protective guise of proper technique. Because such love is essentially transferential, it is also impersonal and abstract and can easily be applied to any individual. For good reason, many of us mistrust the motives of those who repeatedly fall in love too quickly, suspecting that they are more in love with the idea of being in love than they are in love with us as concrete individuals. The self-conscious calculatedness of using empathy as a therapeutic technique, for example, may detract from its quality of spontaneous generosity. The underlying love that motivates emotional understanding (Orange 1995) or an identification with the experiences of others cannot be prescribed.

The ready-made indebtedness of the therapist's countertransference love, prepared as it is professionally for general usage, is ultimately empty because it lacks the credibility of the personal. The therapist's ministrations by technical rote may be viewed instead by the patient as an infantilizing love that has been coerced omnipotently out of pity. Because the patient may not believe this sort of love originates outside of his omnipotent making, it has an unbelievable, hallucinatory quality. And a love that becomes unreal because it cannot be believed also cannot be internalized. The insatiability of transference love may not derive so much from therapeutic indulgences as much as from an inability to internalize a technical love that is impersonal. For love to be credible, it must be personal and real; that is, it must come from a therapist who is acting out of her own freedom of will, beyond the controlling reaches of the patient's omnipotence. As anxiety-provoking as it may be for the patient not to control the therapist, the therapist's freedom to be herself provides a sanity of the real for the patient, the credibility of which cannot be second-guessed.

THE USE OF THE PERSONAL: BUILDING A SANITY OF THE REAL

I believe that the importance of a sense of the real as a psychological category has been underappreciated. Often, reality has the connotation of something noxious that has to be confronted or accepted only with great reluctance. It then follows that the experience of safety derives from finding protective harbor in illusions that buffer the unpleasantness of difficult truths. Certain therapeutic techniques, especially those influenced by object relations theory, have emphasized the need to cultivate the illusion of a holding environment (Winnicott 1960a). Self psychology similarly has emphasized the need to foster the illusion of the analyst as a selfobject. According to these viewpoints, clear images of reality should be introduced only in gradual doses.

I would suggest however that, more often than many therapists would suspect, a patient's sense of psychological safety is very much linked to the therapist's realness, forthrightness, sincerity, and authenticity. For paranoid patients, in particular, it is not the negative or positive content of a communication that eases suspicion, but whether the communication is clear, direct, and aboveboard. In this sense, a person's experience of safety is restored when she locates a containing sanity of the real. For example, an envious person may harbor destructive wishes and fantasies about her friend's upcoming marriage. If she kept silent about her envious thoughts, those wishes would subsist and perhaps even intensify during the wedding. By confessing her envy out loud to her friend beforehand, she, at one and same time, reveals and contains her wish to do harm.

To the extent that we all live in the burdensome shadow of an omnipotent sense that we create and are responsible for all our experiences, good and bad, there is a relief in knowing that some things cannot be helped, that it is out of one's hands. In speaking of the sense of the real, then, I am referring to the experiential dimension of realization: at one end of the continuum is the hallucinatory, crazy-making sense that the discovered world is a created figment of our imagination; at the other end of the continuum is the conviction that we are finding a solid world of other experiences that are not controlled by us.

Perhaps a fundamental aspect of good psychotherapy is to help patients make the transition from adhering to their self-enclosed fantasies to opening up to the reality of others. Many patients hold onto their wish-fueled illusions for dear life because of an underlying despair about how little the real world has to offer them. After suffering through many experiences in the person-to-person school of hard knocks, such individuals may view people whom they have never met before through the transferential lens of wariness, sarcasm, and cynicism.

It is all too easy to face reality with the resignation of bitterness, to brace constantly for new hurts with one's own tough hide. It is quite another matter to face down one's hardships and weather one's sufferings with a faith in the possibilities of the real still in place. The therapist's capacity to cultivate hope is crucial here; the conviction that the future can be better in spite of previous sufferings provides patients with the needed courage to open up to the unknown beyond their omnipotence and to give real people another chance.

In this regard, it is of utmost importance that analysts understand not only what their own disillusionments are, but also the specific defenses they have resurrected to guard against a repeat of more pain. It has been my impression that many psychoanalytic therapists tend to use counterphobic defenses to come to terms with their personal disillusionments. The pursuit of truth at all costs can be viewed as a counterphobic defense that reflects an urgency to confront the frustrations of reality head-on, actively and consciously, rather than fall passively and unconsciously under the deceitful spell of illusion—only to be disillusioned once again. In this sense, counterphobia reflects a fear of being lulled dumbly by the seductive sway of wishful illusions only to be caught suddenly unaware. Whereas phobia has to do with the fear of hopelessness, counterphobia fears the trickery of hope. In this sense, some analysts may have fully acknowledged the inevitability and truth of their disillusionments without fully mourning and recovering from them with hope intact.

The maintenance of a hope-filled encounter with reality is influenced greatly by the relative acceptance or rejection with which patients view themselves. What is the quality of the voices in their heads? How do they speak to themselves? If a critical self-consciousness does indeed emerge from a transference–countertransference dynamic in which patients look for something personal from the therapist only to find impersonal professional responses, it is important to alter that dynamic. For patients to be able to come to know themselves with some degree of benign tolerance, the therapeutic endeavor must facilitate a self-accepting awareness that has its basis in the actual relationship.

Instead of depersonalizing themselves in technical preparation for their role as the patient's created object, or, alternatively, depersonalizing the patient as their case, therapists can lend a sense of the real to the patient's experience by retaining their own personhood. Renik (1998) suggests that this sort of interpersonal "reality testing" helps further the treatment. Therapists who retain their own personal center of gravity demonstrate that they can contain the patient's destructive attempts to transform them from a person into a created object. In so doing, they enable the patient to internalize and use their freely given, credible love.

In my view it is as important that the authentic personal participation of the therapist precede her observations as it is that a sense of psychosomatic unity precede the emergence of a self-reflective mind. As many contemporary writers have suggested, it is through the mutual participation of patient and therapist that the patient learns that the fruitfulness of his being is not to be found in a reliance on the mind and its fantasy derivatives, but in the embodied actuality of real relationships. In this sense, the mutual participation of an I and Thou (Buber 1958) dialogue becomes the needed interpersonal event sought by the patient to objectify his experience.

A psychologically minded treatment dialogue provides a substantive basis in interpersonal reality from which the patient can enter the isolation of his own experience in order to observe it. These self-observations are based in the body of spontaneous, mutual participation of therapist and patient. Self-awareness, in contrast to the disembodied self-consciousness of talking heads, emerges from the concrete grounding of a living dialogue between two persons—a dialogue in which the patient can imagine relatively easily that the therapist is made of flesh, blood, and guts, as well as a mind. It provides the patient with the courage to work through his disillusionments, while still unashamedly accepting the validity of his desires despite the fact they never came true.

From this perspective it is not so much the therapist's technical continuum of gratification and frustration that may matter, but rather the sincere personal quality of the therapist's participation. In contrast to the planned application of technique in "technical rationality," Schon (1983) proposes a model of "reflection in action" for the helping professions. Hoffman (1999) similarly suggests that a dialectic between insight and some form of "expressive participation" on the part of the analyst may further the analytic work. He notes that the analyst cannot help but express something personal about himself in one way or another in the treatment relationship. What is sacrificed in ever-deeper elaborations of unconscious fantasy is gained in the fostering of a usable self-knowledge grounded in interpersonal reality.

The process of discovering oneself always carries with it the ethical imperative to act upon or to be what one knows. Therapists, too, must follow who they are. With self-awareness and a deeply abiding respect for the freedom to be, we have no choice but to use ourselves sincerely and spontaneously. When all is said and done, ourselves are all we have.

11

Haunting Echoes of Personal Truth: The Pangs of Regret and Remorse

The might-have been with tooth accursed
Gnaws at the piteous soul of man.

> —Beaudelaire, "The Irreparable"

Something I've not done
is following me
I haven't done it again and again
so it has many footsteps
like a drumstick that's grown old and never been used.

In late afternoon I hear it come closer
at times it climbs out of a sea
onto my shoulders
and I shrug it off
losing one more chance.

Every morning
it's drunk up part of my breath for the day
and knows which way
I'm going
and already it's not done there.

But once more I say I'll lay hands on it
tomorrow
and add its footsteps to my heart
and its story to my regrets
and its silence to my compass."

—W. S. Merwin, "Something I've Not Done"

"THE ROAD NOT TAKEN"

No matter how often we determine to seize life passionately and shake it until we have distilled its vital essence, somewhere along the way we invariably lose our initial resolve. We may very much intend to appreciate those persons who mean the most to us, reminding ourselves that they will not be around forever, but we can do so only for so long before lapsing into forgetfulness once again. By nature we seem to be limited in our capacity to realize fully the vivid contrast between life and death, and between the presence and absence of loved ones.

It is only after the fact, when it is too late to alter the course of events as they were lived, that we torture ourselves with fantasies of what we could have done or should have done differently. Regrets are characteristic not only of the later stages of life; they are part of the very essence of each person's developmental journey. For each age passed through, reverberating echoes of regret and remorse pursue us mercilessly. A 23-year-old woman may rue her missed opportunities to be a more confident teenager, whereas a 14-year-old boy, acutely aware that his one and only childhood is nearing completion, may suffer from a vaguely gnawing melancholy.

Perhaps because the ideal of a fully appreciated and realized life remains so frustratingly elusive, we should be grateful for those down times when we do not think about who we are and who we have been. If not for these restful moments of unselfconsciousness in which we are concerned only with overcoming the hurdles that lie immediately before us, we would go crazy from the perfectionistic insanity of second-guessing ourselves.

Sometimes, however, we go too far in dulling our capacity for self-reflection. When we overindulge the automatisms that constrain our growth, we give in to the inertia of not thinking about what we do, and so we do it again. The habits of an unconscious creature conspire with a dormant consciousness to maintain and perpetuate more of the same.

The obsessional person may become so immersed in a private, eternal life of the mind that potentially enriching experiences with others pass by unnoticed. The depressed person may become so preoccupied with nostalgic ruminations about the past that she forfeits control over her life in the here and now. The anxiety-ridden person may worry about the potential dangers in the future so single-mindedly that the actual pleasures of the moment are lost.

In the midst of these sleeping repetitions of character, such individuals are oblivious to their mortality, to the fact that there is only so much time to become what they would become. In his poem "The Road Not Taken," Robert Frost (1915) writes of the necessity of choosing only one of the many roads that life offers. Frost emphasizes the need to embrace that choice and affirm the chosen path as one's own.

Many persons, however, refuse to accept the limitations inherent in living only one of many potential lives; they resist the urgency to choose, to create, and to live out a road of their own making. Preoccupied with unfulfilled yearnings or unconsummated rages, and lulled by the illusion of limitless life, the passivity of psychic drifting replaces the activity of individual development. By stepping outside the mainstream of development, of the inevitable juxtaposition of life and death, these persons drift indefinitely, attempting to bring time to a standstill. Meanwhile time of course marches on, indifferent to the desperate manipulations of its human captives, and precious life goes undeveloped.

For some, not being able to seize the moment may be of relatively little consequence, such as when one misses a movie because of indecisive dawdling. For others, however, passing up one-time opportunities may have repercussions so far-reaching and profound that the meaning of their lives seemed to have disappeared along with the chance that was lost. The example of the one true love that got away is all too familiar not only in fictional characters, but for nonfictional ones as well.

Many years ago my grandmother warned me of the sins of omission, when she declared that if given a choice between doing something or standing pat, then to just do it, commit yourself to action. For her, wondering about what might have been was far more tormenting than any remorseful feelings for sins actually committed. In a letter to Hugh Walpole, Henry James (1913) echoes these sentiments when he says, "I think I don't regret a single 'excess' of my responsive youth—I only regret, in my chilled age, certain occasions and possibilities I didn't embrace." Although I think there is a wise kernel of truth in my grandmother's advice to opt for the virtues of activity over passivity, perhaps the either/or aspects of the choice are not quite as distinct as she had suggested. In some ways, regret and remorse are complementary sides of the same coin; a regret for an idealized life that had not been lived out may imply a remorse for those actions that were taken instead.

Sometimes it is years before intimations of mortality spur on a person's sense of urgency to finally enter treatment and confront the increasingly audible echoes of unlived truth that plague her. Landman (1993) suggests that the metaphor of the "ghost" is a predominant one for regret. The person wishes to put the ghosts that haunt her to rest. The process of reflecting on one's life, however, is a double-edged sword; newly acquired insights also may be accompanied by a regretful despair over bygone, wasted years.

From the patient's point of view, it is too late to change, to grow, and to live meaningfully anyhow. Faced with the impossibility of turning back the clock of a precariously short life, the patient becomes invested in shutting down any awareness of her regret-filled predicament by continuing to maintain her symptoms. Thus, the laudable therapeutic project of enhancing self-understanding may have the paradoxical effect of strengthening a patient's resistance to change; that is, she may be tempted to perpetuate her mistakes to justify the road that was indeed taken.

re: "my own" + me deepening

ANNE: NOT STRIKING WHEN THE
IRON IS HOT

Anne is a 49-year-old single woman who came to treatment with the presenting complaints of anxiety, fatigue, somatic problems, and a general desire "to find herself." Although she was living with an elderly woman at the time she first came to see me, Anne expressed the wish to move into her own apartment eventually. In addition, she mentioned that she was about to begin a job as an occupational therapist, and declared that she did not want to "blow it."

Anne is the youngest of three children; she has two older brothers. She reported having a very close relationship with her mother until the age of 23, at which time her mother had a mild heart attack. Her mother then died suddenly of a second heart attack two years later. Anne was painfully shy as an adolescent, electing always to stay by her mother's side. An early attempt at art school proved unsuccessful because of "tension" and "fatigue." She described her alcoholic father as a "poor, pathetic man" with whom she had little to do as a child. He was a hard-working man, but also a shadowy figure whom her mother often "kept in the basement."

For the twenty-four years since her mother's death, Anne had not been able to work or love successfully. She had remained a virgin, and did not have any significant relationships during that period. She went to singles' dances with her girlfriends until she was in her late thirties, only to continue encountering the "lost souls who go to those things." She drifted from one secretarial job to another, often quitting because of fatigue and somatic problems that had no ostensible physical basis. She always arranged her living arrangements such that she roomed with a single or widowed woman twenty to thirty years her senior. Although she was often friendly with these women, she frequently found them annoying as well.

During the initial phase of treatment, Anne spoke of a previous friendship with a homosexual man whom she had not seen in a year. With the unselfconscious hopefulness of a little girl, Anne spoke about her fantasies of becoming more seriously involved with this man, even though he was living with another man at the time. She guarded the specifics of her fantasies tenaciously, at times becoming coy about revealing her thoughts to me. Perhaps not coincidentally, Anne stated that she did not feel like meeting any other new men. *Sara*

As we began to explore Anne's tenacious hold on fantasied men as a means of counteracting her fear of actual men, she began spontaneously to discuss her wish for her mother to return to life. When at this point, Anne broke into tears about her desperate need to break free from her mother, it was clear that even twenty-four years later, Anne had never acknowledged the full emotional impact of that loss. Now, in the second month of therapy, Anne resumed the incomplete work of mourning the loss of her mother.

Because of the intensely symbiotic mutual dependence of her relationship with her mother, Anne was dumbstruck in the immediate aftermath of her death. She was not able to express the devastation and shock that she had experienced in any words that made sense. As she said, she had felt as if "the rug has been pulled out from under my feet."

After working through various feelings of rage and sorrow over a period of many months, more pleasant memories of a shared intimacy with her mother began to emerge. These memories seemed to provide Anne with a feeling of substantiveness that, in turn, became coupled with a burgeoning but intermittent sense of autonomy. With these new feelings of strength, however, Anne began to speak of her regret over the past and her fear of the future.

At this point, perhaps significantly, Anne shifted her focus from regret to a long-hidden resentment toward her father for not being the loving paternal figure she had wanted. She recounted his habit of walking around naked at nighttime, one hand holding a candle and the other one covering his genitals. Although she was not allowed out of her room, she remembers peeking through the keyhole of her door at this scene with a mixture of curiosity and revulsion.

In the void left by the absence of fatherly affection, Anne was particularly susceptible to the stimulation of oedipal fantasies in which she could grasp hold of anything she could about her mysterious father. Because her father's nocturnal wanderings exposed her prematurely to the world of grown-up sexuality, he became a frightening, intimidating representation of the outside world to her. In reaction, Anne retreated to the safe confines of her tight-knit relationship with her mother. This retreat perhaps was accentuated also by the maternal retaliation Anne imagined she had coming to her for her sexual curiosity. There was too high a price to pay for entering the full bloom of womanhood; it was far safer to remain her mother's daughter.

Eighteen months after treatment began, my return from a vacation sparked a great deal of anger. Anne expressed her rage and fear of men in general, and of her father in particular. Each week, in one way or another, she expressed her resentment of how her father had "screwed me up." On one of these occasions, I prodded Anne to elaborate on what she meant by "screwed up," specifically with reference to her fatalistic feeling of being doomed.

Hesitatingly, and with great difficulty, Anne began to talk of her regret over the years in which she did not develop herself—of not relating adequately to men, of not having children, and of not following through with her artistic potential. The particular pain of this last regret was brought to consciousness by a dream in which Anne dropped out of college to enter art school. In associating to this dream, Anne wistfully expressed her misgivings about losing the possibility of an artistic career. In reality, she had entered college two years *after* she dropped out of art school. The dream thus could be seen as the expression of a wish to reverse the course of events as they had been lived.

The task of treatment now became one of mourning the road not taken. In light of the heavy burden that Anne took upon herself for the conduct of her life, I reminded her that she was reviewing her past inertia with the help of current revelations. Thus Anne remembered again the almost blithe innocence with which she had remained under her mother's protective wing. She remembered again her father's bizarre behavior and lack of emotional availability. And she remembered again the genuine helplessness and shock she had felt immediately upon her mother's death. Anne realized slowly, as she struggled to forgive herself, that she had neither been able nor prepared to cope with the demands of growing up and the emotional reality of the later loss of her mother. She began to understand that she was scanning her past with 20/20 hindsight. By relieving herself of excessive responsibility over the omissions of the past, Anne began to be better able to cope with the problems of her life in the present.

Nevertheless, this was slow, painful work that was in no way complete. Throughout this latter phase of treatment, Anne's concerns centered around the allocation of responsibility for her life as dramatized through the transference. She clung to her symptoms tenaciously, continuing to report fatigue, anxiety, and insomnia. She indicated subtly that it was I who seemed most invested in her being symptom-free. Sometimes she would remark defensively that these symptoms were not due to any psychological causes, even though she had undergone a thorough physical recently. On another occasion, Anne mentioned almost apologetically that she still harbored much hatred toward her mother. When I asked her whether she felt I was rushing her to health, she quickly backed down, saying it was she who was frustrated with herself.

Anne was not entirely off the mark, of course. I was frustrated with the circularity of what seemed to be two steps forward and two steps backward. And I have no doubt that Anne was sharply attuned to my countertransferential zealousness. In fact, she probably used my active interest in her progress to flee from her own sense of regret and guilt about her life.

To relieve herself of intolerable regret over wasted years, Anne projected responsibility for her therapeutic fate onto me. In doing so, she viewed me through the lens of the revisited maternal transference, for at one time she had perceived her mother also to be the proprietress of her life. It soon became clear that Anne's symptoms worsened the few days before our weekly appointment. In a sense, she presented her symptoms to me as an offering, as a

sacrifice of her health and autonomy, as she had once felt compelled to do with her mother.

Two important breakthrough dreams enabled Anne to see that
she was an active agent in her own life. On one occasion, as she
spoke again of the circumstances surrounding her mother's death,
I remarked that she was born in the same hospital in which her
mother died, and where our sessions took place. Anne seemed
surprised, cracked a wide, sheepish smile and said, pensively, "I
never thought of that before." Nothing more was said at that time.

That night, Anne dreamt of having a baby. Despite her
mother's protestations in the background of the dream, she said
she was determined to follow through with the birth. In climactic
contrast, on the eve preceding her next session the following week
Anne dreamt of being an ugly insect with clipped wings. When
asked what she thought of the dream, Anne was stymied, immobilized like the paralyzed insect. After a few moments she remarked
disgustedly about the dark, repellent ugliness of the clipped bug.
Whereas the first dream was relatively joyful in its feeling tone,
the second dream was depressingly empty.

There was a clear parallel between the flavor and content of
the dreams on one hand, and Anne's yearning to break free from
her mother, from me, and from her neurosis in one fell swoop by
giving birth to herself on the other. Thus, the dreams also brought
to light the issues of choice and responsibility within the transference. As Anne became aware of her projection of a suffocating
maternal image, she experienced a dawning realization that she
had ultimate say over her comings and goings with great relief.
Choosing to come to therapy each week of her own free will, she
no longer felt obligated to report, to apologize, and to give her
independence and health away as she once had.

Anne terminated treatment six weeks later, two years after it
had first begun. She never completely mourned the undeveloped
time of her life, but she attained sufficient self-acceptance to meet
life on its own terms; she has learned to derive small but substantive pleasures from her everyday activities. Although her job as an
occupational therapist had fallen through early on because of her

fatigue and anxiety, she has worked steadily as a secretary for the past three years, with a minimum of absenteeism. Her symptoms have abated considerably, to the extent that she no longer takes antianxiety medication. Living in her own apartment for the last two years has enabled her to achieve a degree of independence and self-respect. And perhaps most significantly she has begun taking figure drawing classes through continuing education curricula.

FATALISM: THE LIFE-STUNTING TOLL OF FIXATION

When people experience a significant disillusionment or trauma, there is often an almost automatic reflex of the psyche to curl inward into a defensive ball to protect against the prospect of further wounds. No longer feeling able to afford the pursuit of whatever path their heart desires, they mobilize around the self-preservative mandate to safeguard the security of their survival. As a result, they may become preoccupied with fantasies of undoing the harm that has befallen them. Moreover, because this sense of endangered survival is constant, due to introjecting the experience of trauma, their emotional resources are continuously diverted to cope with the perceived threat.

But the core of a person's developmental being resides in the guiding desires of her heart. When an individual detaches from or renounces wishes that never came to fruition, it engenders an inertia with regard to all matters that do not have to do with healing herself. In spite of what appears to be active or independent behavior, her growth is compromised by the compulsion to restage the drama that precipitated the original hurt.

Anne had experienced both the shock of acute trauma (the death of her mother) and the cumulative buildup of chronic trauma (lifelong dependency on her powerful mother; bizarre behavior of her father). Perhaps we could say also that whereas a sudden trauma elicits a preoccupation or fixation at a particular point in time, the preoccupations of the more chronic traumatic theme reflect a relational fixation on the character flaws of parents. In contrast to the acute trauma and circumscribed fixation of a parental death, for example, fixation on the insidiously evolving traumatic theme can weave its way subtly but pervasively into the fabric of character.

Without a governing voice in consciousness, this exiled dynamic of fixation typically exacts a life-stunting revenge: the future is held hostage by the denied trauma of the past. The essential passivity of waiting for losses to be undone and disillusionments to be redeemed saps life of its developmental passion. When people fixate on prior experiences, they forsake a genuine, open interchange between themselves and others in order to lick their wounds in their own shut-off world.

Because the implicit demand to transform (through a fantasied undoing) the real event of trauma into a wished-for pretraumatic state or ideal parent is never satisfied, the demand itself becomes a source of stuckness or fixation. Each failed attempt to undo what is real is repeated indefinitely. The repetition compulsion may thus reveal the fact that one has not accepted one's trauma as an experience that must be.

Since waiting and searching is to no avail, these individuals' sense of having a fantasied control over their future gradually gives way to a feeling of hopelessness that their lot will ever improve. In a sense, they develop a deep sense of themselves as being fatally wounded, irreversibly injured by conditions beyond their control. Anne's use of the phrase "screwed up" refers to a conviction that her injuries are so devastating that they are beyond repair. This feeling of being doomed by her unfortunate circumstances, then, is manifested in a fatalism in which she is resigned to the fact that life will continue to be as it was, regardless of her participation in it. And in one sense she is right, for as long as she is caught in the grip of the compulsion to repeat, she is fulfilling her own prophecy.

As they remain stuck on a treadmill, such persons watch enviously as others actively pursue their destinies. They punish their parents spitefully with their crippled lives, so that at some point they will be able to say, "I hate my parents for doing this to me." But even this solution of spite reflects a despair of ever finding their own effective voice, as it means they are reduced to negating the ideals of their parents.

In Anne's case, the premorbid experiences of her traumatic theme—dominated as a child by her mother and little relationship with her father—complicated the problem of mourning the physical loss of her mother. Anne's mother was such a pervasive presence that Anne was rendered speechless at news of her death. It is understandable that she could do nothing but deny the incomprehensible reality of her motherlessness in self-enclosed silence, while adapting to her ongoing world with the skeletal mask of a smiling face. Similarly, in his paper "Splitting of the Ego in the Process of Defense," Freud (1940) describes a woman who spoke matter-of-factly about her mother's death, while at the same time waiting with unconsciously bated breath for her immanent return.

People's lives sometimes seem to be dictated by unspoken preoccupying fantasies about healing their assorted wounds—so much so that many psychologists refer to encapsulating diagnostic labels such as "anal personality" or "preoedipal character" to comprehend an individual's level of developmental organization. Individual lives, however, are not pigeonholed so tidily. Indeed, a crucial question then becomes, "What does become of a person's life after the original fixation to a trauma?"

One major problem is that in forever seeking a perfectibility that is not and never can be found, certain individuals with their *idée fixe* of self-cure, lose a perspective of finitude. In their insulated world, they become seduced, without the benefit of reality testing, by fantasies of time standing still. Lichenstein (1977) thus notes that repetition is an attempt to annul the flow of time. In this sense, fixation and the eternal circularities of the repetition compulsion are a dreamlike sanctuary from time and loss.

Meanwhile such persons act out the same patterns of living: relationships are mischosen, distorted, or ended, and the autonomy represented by work is sabotaged in one form or other. When these individuals, unbeknownst to themselves, squirrel away the passions they have regarding unacknowledged ideals, they are not playing the game of life with all their cards on the table; success in love and work is then a daunting challenge indeed.

As years go by, a coldly indifferent world imposes its necessities and limitations upon these individuals. The hope-filled wait for the materialization of an impossible dream gives way to a spiritless disillusionment. Undermined by an unconscious passivity, life is experienced as a lengthy, superficial exercise devoid of meaning. The surprise and novelty inherent in the active developmental process of self-creation is traded in for the mechanized routine of the repetition compulsion. What was once a dream-filled slumber, fueled and impassioned by unconscious hope, increasingly resembles a pointless nightmare from which one prepares to awaken.

REGRET: WAKING UP TOO LATE

When we grow disenchanted with habitual patterns of living that have proved fruitless in achieving an ideal end, sooner or later a personal crisis may trigger a whole reevaluation of how we have conducted our life. Some people, of course, never go through a crisis of awakening to what matters to them, and remain in their automated patterns of existence until they die. For others, however, a divorce, a job failure, or disappointment in one's children may precipitate reflections on lifelong patterns that have not succeeded. The death of a parent and the growing independence of one's children may acquaint one with new glimmerings of a heretofore denied mortality and the uneasy realization of time slipping away. In Tolstoy's (1886) *The Death of Ivan Ilych*, a fall from a ladder becomes a metaphor for Ivan's descent from the dumb innocence of leading a "most ordinary life" into a spiritual crisis of reassessing his life's meaning.

The confrontation with death stirs long-dormant passions that never had been expressed—a self that has not yet unfolded, a road that was not taken. The dawning realization of having but a limited lifespan spurs an urgency to live out a personal truth, and finally to live before dying. After drifting passively through years of ennui, these persons may now be drawn, almost as if by an irresistible internal pressure, into a climactic reopening of their lives. In seeking out psychotherapy, they are implicitly requesting help in order to return to the flow of their life once more.

It is evident that mourning and working through the fixation(s) on the original traumatic situation are of paramount importance in the treatment of patients. The establishment of the transference relationship enables patients to distinguish between the fantasied ideal of undoing previous trauma and the provision of something genuine in the present. The real attentions and ministrations of this nonparent—the therapist—for example, may enable patients to relinquish the necessity for attaining an ideal parent. Working through fixations on the past thus becomes a type of compromise with life's exigencies as they are funneled through the therapeutic process. With a newly discovered awareness of life's brevity and fragility, patients may return with urgency to their own particular path of destiny.

A price is to be paid, however, for this renewed alertness to life's preciousness. The acquisition of self-understanding may confront patients with the realization of many lost years devoted to the pursuit of an illusory ideal. Whereas previously a patient may have passively and repeatedly sloughed off responsibility for his life upon the vagaries of fate, now, filled with the shock of self-revelation, he is overburdened with regret over missed opportunities. Acknowledging the realistic limitations and loss of both life and time leads to an unbearable truth: the attainment of personal responsibility and agency could have occurred years earlier.

Sullivan (1956) suggests that the profound sadness of regret has much to do with the patient's emergence from an obsessional uncertainty as to the source of his suffering. He says: "Grieving is over the many opportunities for possible happiness that were wasted because the patient was so puzzled as to whether he was right or wrong about the savage interference of the significant parent" (p. 268). This tortured sentiment of regret often is voiced by patients, sometimes poignantly, sometimes reproachfully, in the question, "Where were you when I needed you?"

Balint (1968) points out that such patients experience a kind of regret that the original defect or fault has "cast its shadow over one's whole life, . . . the unfortunate effects of which can never fully be made good. Though the fault may heal off, its scar will remain forever, that is some of its effects will always be demonstrable" (p. 183). By the time the regretful person enters treatment, there is a well-entrenched despair that it is already too late, so what is the point of change and growth? Toward what end?

In Dostoevsky's (1864a) *Notes from the Underground*, the Underground Man gives voice to this despair:

> The enjoyment was just from the too intense consciousness of one's own degradation; it was from feeling oneself that one had reached the last barrier, that it was horrible, but that it could not be otherwise; that there was no escape for you; that you never could become a different man; that even if time and faith were still left for you to change into something different you would most likely not wish to change; or if you did wish to, even then you would do nothing; because perhaps in reality there is nothing for you to change into. [p. 5]

A profound guilt toward oneself for committing the supreme error of omission—an unused life—overlays the original trauma on which the patient is fixated. Because the overwhelming burden of responsibility for the undeveloped intervening years is too heavy to bear, the patient does everything to evade a reflective confrontation with himself.

Let me illustrate this crisis of self-reflection with a small example: the neglect of writing a letter to a loved one. Some of us would-be letter writers have had the frequent experience of losing touch with a close friend or relative for an extended period of time. Although we may have promised each other when we parted that we definitely would write, the letter continues to go unwritten. We may tell ourselves that it is imperative to sit down to write the long overdue letter. Despite the best of intentions, however, we do not follow through. The longer we wait, the more difficult it is to alter the habit of omission and write the letter. Perhaps this is because when finally we do sit down to write the letter, we realize we could have done so much earlier. Thus the first sentence of the yet-to-be written letter might read, "I'm sorry it has taken eons for me to write to you, but . . . " By continuing not to write, we try to forget that we have been untrue to our relationship with the loved one.

If we magnify this example to one that has life-altering implications, such as missing a chance to have a family, children, or a desired career, we can understand why it is so difficult to muster a courage of necessarily heroic proportions to face one's omissions. Insight brings with it the responsibility to act on what one knows— that is, to grow from this day forward. But what if it is too late? Regret is not for easygoing consciences. Dinner is to be served on time, and latecomers who amble in after the meal need not bother to sit down. Better late than never is only for those who are forgiving of heart, and rarely characteristic of those who feel regret. With a self-reckoning too unbearable for this Rip Van Winkle, it is better not to wake up at all, but to just continue with business as usual, to act as if one were still helpless to alter one's destiny.

REPETITION OF THE SAME AND JUSTIFYING THE ROAD TAKEN

Patients now may become caught in a paradoxical situation of continuing to act out the very behavior that precipitated guilt and regret in order to deny any awareness of those feelings. Repetition of the same is a tactic frequently employed to ward off a vague sense of shame, deficiency, or guilt. This is one way of understanding J. M. Barrie's (1922) observation of the perverse tendency to repeat errors: "What really plays the dickens with us is something in ourselves. Something that makes us go on doing the same sort of fool things, however many chances we get" (p. 109).

Frequently, when we suspect that we are in the wrong but

cannot bring ourselves to admit it, we implicitly attempt to prove the righteousness of our cause to all those who would judge us harshly. Shakespeare's well-known phrase, "the lady doth protest too much," fits well as a description of those situations in which we attempt to justify ourselves through the conspicuous repetition of the same actions. Self-justification here is not verbal; it is conveyed through action. In self-justification, we repeat our actions as if we were employing an imaginary arbiter to see that we had no other choice than to do what we did. What had to be, had to be; the proof is in the pudding of repetition. In the meantime, however, our very lies to ourselves mire us ever more deeply in regret. As Scheler (1912) says: "The eternal fugitive from the past sinks deeper and deeper into the dead arms of that very past."

Patients may ward off the threat of change by continuing to display a fatalism within the context of the transference. Responsibility for engendering insight and change may be laid at the door of the therapist. By projecting their urge toward health onto the therapist, patients perpetuate the illusion that it is first the exploit-ative parent and then the all-powerful therapist who determines the outcome of their fate. They can then rebel silently against the power with which they have imbued the therapist, and maintain a self-image of themselves as fatally scarred. The psychic passivity, originally consequent on the fixation to previous trauma, is thus extended through the projection of responsibility in the transference.

In this way, patients may attempt to justify lost time by prolonging treatment. Even after they seemingly have worked through many of the emotions connected with the original trauma, the therapist may notice that the therapeutic process begins to drift. Rather than complete the process of internalizing and being internalized by the therapist, patients may externalize their guilt by continuing to blame parental figures for their predicament. By immersing themselves in memories of what someone else did to them, patients can take a stance of victimized righteousness that may be a means of warding off a more immediate self-disgust. Indeed, the continued retention of symptoms can be viewed as a form of self-punishment for not striking while the iron was hot.

Anne retained the very same symptoms of anxiety, fatigue, and lack of stamina when she first came to therapy that had been responsible for her quitting art school prematurely. She desperately looked for an external target to blame to account for the manner in which she had lived her life. Initially, she focused on her mother's death, then on her mother taking over her early life, and then on her father's spooky nighttime sojourns. And she continued to return to the hatred for her mother.

Something, however, was eluding us. And I suspect it was what Buber (1965) referred to as the illumination of a real guilt (versus neurotic guilt)—a real injury that she had perpetrated on her life. As long as she externalized her self-hatred, the cleansing of her conscience eluded her. In *The Death of Ivan Ilych* (Tolstoy 1886), Ivan also seeks to justify the life he led until the very end. His physical and spiritual pain continued to get worse, but he still refused to admit his mistakes. Only in the very end when he confesses his regret does he attain the enlightenment of release: "He felt the agony was due to his being thrust into that black hole and still more to his not being able to get right into it. He was hindered from getting into it by his conviction that his life had been a good one. That very justification of his life held him fast and prevented his moving forward, and caused him most torment of all" (p. 154).

Up to this point I have been referring to a regret for past mistakes of omission. However, what is being omitted, missed, or passed over? Regret refers to a desired or idealized course of life that has never been lived out. Many individuals frequently harbor fantasies of a parallel life in which they imagine how it would have been if their wishes had come true. I have found this dynamic to be especially characteristic of individuals who have not mourned a parent's death. As children wait indefinitely for a parent to come back to life, their what-if life of dissociated fantasy may drain away the passion necessary to make a deeper commitment to the living. Such children may initiate a leave of absence from their lives without realizing that they have done so until they speak about their loss many years later. In their self-enclosed melancholic haze, they lost their way. Seduced by the what-if world of wishful fantasies, they turned their backs on an open process of give-and-take with the living and abdicated from their consciences.

THE FLIGHT FROM REMORSE: DESTROYING THE EYE OF CONSCIENCE

There are two complementary sides to the abdication from one's conscience. In a sense, every omission and every action that we do not give ourselves over to imply that we have committed ourselves to another action that we have taken instead. Perhaps, then, when the primary reason for fleeing one's conscience has to do with omitted actions, we can speak of the mis-givings of regret; when we refer to committed actions, we can speak of the mis-takes of remorse. Taken further, regret may refer to a feeling of wrongdoing against oneself, whereas remorse stands out when it concerns harming others.

There often is a profound relationship between doing harm to another person and not holding faith with oneself. In the silently reflective aftermath of doing malicious destruction to another, aggressors may be haunted by the realization that they have not held true to the memory of their own suffering. In this regard, it is interesting to note that the word *remorse* derives from the Latin *remordeo* or "to bite again," as in the biting or gnawing of conscience. From the vantage point of the present and laden with the retrospective knowledge of conscience, remorse takes the form of a vague echo that bites one from the back side of one's life, from the past.

Sometimes the burden of a remorse-filled consciousness may become so heavy to bear that people flee from all semblance of self-reflectiveness through action and externalization. The flight from the reverberating echoes of conscience may be seen in the literary theme of the Double, a topic that has been examined comprehensively by Rank (1925).

The Double often is depicted as an unwanted intruder into the otherwise peaceful existence of the protagonist. In this sense, the Double can be viewed as a projected embodiment or personification of one's conscience; it is the embodiment of the disowned shadows of one's life returning to mercilessly pursue its regretful and remorseful prey. In "The Uncanny," Freud (1919a) thus speaks of the eerily haunting quality inherent in the "return of the repressed."

Not surprisingly, the protagonist in many depictions of the Double typically grapples with fits of persecutory anxiety in response to the intrusion of his mirror image. When all desperately panicky attempts to escape his alter-ego fail, the cornered person may finally lash out violently to silence the relentless pursuer. When the persecutory anxiety deriving from the internal foe of one's conscience is thus transformed into a focused fear of an external enemy, it becomes easier to scapegoat and destroy this reflective mirror of one's personal truth.

To confess sincerely that we have done wrong is a difficult and courageous act because, at least momentarily, we are in the weakened, vulnerable position of being divided against ourselves. For those of us who are already predisposed to viewing life in terms of polarized dynamics such as winning and losing or strength and weakness, the inhibitions of guilt and the mortification of shame may feel annihilating. When we are determined to flee any admission of guilt, offense is the best defense.

Piers and Singer's (1953) concept of the shame–guilt cycle well describes the self-perpetuating quality of the flight from conscience by means of aggression. They state that aggressive actions generate a sense of guilt, resulting in feelings of inhibition and weakness. The resulting sense of one's own passivity then arouses a feeling of shame that one attempts to combat by committing aggression again. In this model, the perpetuation of aggression is a way of defending against the shameful weakness of owning up to one's guilt.

In a fascinating study of Hitler, Stierlin (1976) uses the shame–guilt cycle to explain the mass murders committed by the Nazis.

Once a person or group embarks on a path of slaughter, each new murder is committed in order to justify the righteousness of the first transgression. Rather than admit our collective mistake of becoming involved in Vietnam, for example, many argued that as long as we were there, we might as well stay there and "finish the job."

One is reminded here of the declaration of Hercule Poirot, Agatha Christie's famous detective, that the first murder is always the most difficult one. After breaking that fundamental commandment, "Thou shalt not kill," a person may become preoccupied with annihilating any reminders of the original crime. The compulsive killing of eyewitnesses is a doomed and therefore repetitious attempt to close the internal eye of conscience once and for all.

Here is a *New York Times* excerpt from a September 1997 interview with a Croatian militiaman responsible for the death of eighty-six people: "I go to bed with this thought and, if I sleep at all, I wake up with the same thought. I killed 72 people with my own hands. Among them were nine women. We made no distinctions, asked no questions. They were Chetniks and our enemies. The most difficult thing is to ignite a house or kill a man *for the first time, but afterwards everything becomes routine*" (p. 1, my italics).

Implicit in what I have been saying is the view that every human being has a conscience, although there may well be stronger and weaker ones. As long as a person has any minimal experience of his desires being fulfilled, which he has had at least in the relief of biological needs, he knows also that the bad (drive tension) can be made good (drive relief). It is true that this knowledge of conscience, of good transcending and containing the bad, may sometimes be imperceptible, especially when it has been derived primarily from physiological experiences. When juxtaposed with experiences of deprivation and exploitation, conscience may be covered over by great suffering and bitterness. In such instances, a person can become as hardened to the pain of others as he is to his own.

In contrast with the prevailing view of psychopaths as individuals who have deficits in superego functioning, I believe it more useful to view them as persons whose conscience is obscured by an externalizing flight into action. It is too convenient to create a separate category of conscienceless beings who do not resemble us in any familiar human way. It is not difficult to rationalize isolating and imprisoning creatures who seem to have no remorse, in some far off place where they cannot disturb and stir the doubts we have about our own souls.

Psychoanalysis can and must do better. As a profession interested in understanding and treating all things human, we have yet to catch up with Martin Luther King Jr.'s redemptive vision of concern with the "spiritual degradation of white people." We have yet to develop and systematize any ideas of how aggressors mourn their crimes.

In an important paper, "Guilt and Guilt Feelings," Buber (1965) distinguishes between neurotic guilt and real guilt. He takes the community of psychotherapists to task for paying too much attention to the breaking of conventional taboos. What, however, of the person who must come to terms with the existential guilt of doing real injury to the human order?

For Buber, a person's world is "his share in the human order of being, the share for which he bears responsibility" and "injuring a relationship means that at this place the human order of being is injured. No one other than he who inflicted the wound can heal it" (p. 122).

That person, possessed by the regret and remorse of existential guilt, is at war with himself as long as he does not listen to the soundings of his conscience. Buber thus notes that the reflective clarity of *self-illumination* is a first step toward a reconciliation with both oneself and the world. In Buber's words, "From no standpoint is time perceived so like a torrent as from the vision of the self in guilt. Swept along in this torrent, the bearer of guilt is visited by the shudder of identity with himself. I, he comes to know, I, who have become another, am the same" (p. 116).

Recognizing how difficult it is for this individual to retain the stamina to face his mistakes and misgivings, and how tempting it is to flee from what he knows, Buber posits that *perseverance* is a second "action of the conscience." Finally, Buber emphasizes that the person with existential guilt can achieve a third stage of *reconciliation* when, "in the given historical and biographical situations, [he is able] to restore the order of being injured by him through the relation of an active devotion to the world—for the wounds of the order-of-being can be treated in infinitely many other places than those at which they were inflicted" (p. 126).

In my experience working with regretful individuals, I have found also that themes of generosity and reparation are fundamental to patients reconciling with their consciences. It might seem that it would be useful to point out to patients filled with regret that their self-torments for what could have been are filtered through the prism of 20/20 hindsight. I have thus attempted to remind such patients what circumstances must have been like back then, that they were not as aware as they are now, and that what had to be had to be.

This sort of intervention has proved not to be very effective at times. Perhaps these guilty patients, yearning for the clarity of self-illumination, have no patience for the lie embedded in this merciful appeal to forces beyond their control. On the contrary, if one takes the notion of conscience seriously, it implies that they *did* know better and did have the freedom of choice to act on what they knew, but failed to do so. Coming to terms with guilt requires at least a privately confessional truth-telling and acknowledgment of falling short of the best that they could do.

Winnicott (1960a), like Buber, notes the clinical ineffectiveness of attempting to lift the burden of guilt from a patient through interpretations. Guilt has to be assumed and then worked through reparatively through compensatory actions toward others in cases of remorse, and through self-forgiveness in cases of regret. In the end, it is generosity that moves people toward apology and forgiveness sufficiently so as to reconcile themselves with their errors of commission and omission.

Thus, it is fortunate that patients tend to view the past through the lenses of the present; they have multiple opportunities to refashion meanings of bygone events. I think this is true because, at bottom, human beings are creatures governed by the mood of the moment. For example, when we have been in a humiliated or shamed position for a long period of time, it is all the more difficult to look someone in the eye and make a requisite apology from the one-down position of felt unworthiness. Once in this bad mood, we are more apt to wall ourselves in, conserving as much for ourselves as possible. Or we may take our bad mood out on our neighbor.

On the other hand, when we are in a good mood, we are more likely to let bygones be bygones and forgive ourselves for our imperfections. With an inner sense of fullness and integrity, we can transcend, at least temporarily, the deep sense of shame that keeps us in cycles of denial of our guilt. It is in that transcendent moment of regained integrity, when we have refound our better half, our conscience, that we are moved to make genuine reparations to others.

All of this highlights the clinical importance of enhancing the quality of the here-and-now for patients. The quality of personal relationship between the therapist and the patient is of the essence. Liking and being liked, respecting and being respected consistently in an authentic, spontaneous dialogue can provide patients with the generosity and courage necessary to drop their now obsolete defenses and mourn what has to be mourned.

remorse – what we have done to others
regret – what we have done to, or not done for ourselves.

12

Self-Acceptance and the Generosity of Letting Go: The Experiences of Mourning and Growth

I cannot say what portion is in truth
The naked recollection of that time
And what may rather have been called to life
By after-meditation.

—Wordsworth, "The Prelude"

Give sorrow words; the grief that does not speak
Whispers the o'er fraught heart and bids it break.

—Shakespeare, *Macbeth*

HANK: HOLDING ON IN MEMORIAM

Recently, a 48-year-old man, Hank, came to me for psycho-therapy because he has not been able to become intimate with any woman in his adult life. He said he had once wanted to get married and have children, but now he feared time was running out. Four months earlier, he had reunited with a now-divorced woman whom he had dated during his senior year in high school, and for whom he carried a torch many years thereafter. This woman, herself a psychologist, suggested strongly that Hank get help because of her concerns about his ability to become emotionally intimate. A friend then referred him to me after attending a workshop I gave on loss and mourning.

Hank is the youngest of five children, two of whom were born before World War II. When his father returned from the war, three more children were born. When Hank was 8 years old, his mother died of breast cancer. Immediately in the first session, Hank wondered whether her death might have something to do with his fear of intimacy and consequent fear of being abandoned again. He said he probably had been depressed for a long time. When I asked him if he remembered any of his own interactions with her, he could recount only one.

A few days before she died, he was sitting and playing at his mother's feet. He noticed that her legs were puffy, and he asked why they were so "fat." She responded with what looked like a hurt expression and asked, "Are they?" Hank cried audibly as he re-called this scene that was as vivid to him as if it were occurring right then and there. He said he felt bad for what he said to her, but almost as if to justify himself, he added that he had not known what was wrong with her since he had not been told anything. Although soon after that he remembered visiting her in the hospital together with the rest of the family, he never spoke to her alone again.

Soon after that he was told that his mother had died, but no one spoke again about her death in the ensuing years—with one exception. The family's housekeeper, Anna, and Hank reminisced frequently about his mother's life and the circumstances surrounding her death. But she, too, soon disappeared. Indeed, when he was 11 his father and stepmother changed his birth certificate so that it would read as if Hank had been born to his stepmother, who did not have her own biological children. Ostensibly, this was done for inheritance reasons.

Soon after Hank's father remarried, his stepmother took control of the household; in came a new regime and out went the vestiges of the old, including Anna. For unknown reasons, Hank's stepmother fired Anna. With her departure, he lost his only remaining confidante and shared memory of his mother. Instead, Hank was left to his own company, and he made lonely sojourns into the woods near his house, silently cursing under his breath against the God who took his mother away from him.

Eventually, cajoled partly by the flattery of his stepmother making him her favorite, and also intimidated by her arbitrary wielding of power, Hank became an agreeable, compliant teenager. He was uncomfortable around girls, but a very good athlete. During his senior year, however, he became very anxious about the prospects of graduating from high school. This was not helped by the fact that he sensed that his father and stepmother wanted to be rid of him already. This sense of being evicted has been deeply hurtful to Hank, and to this day tears of indignation well up in him when he thinks of that time. This indignation has been buttressed as well by the fact that Hank received no financial support to go to college from parents who were relatively well-to-do.

From then on, Hank's life went downhill. He became heavily involved with drugs in college and thereafter until finally he ended up in prison for drug possession for nine months. When he came out, he swore off drugs and opened his own business.

Hank lives alone in a rural community. He has his share of friends, and is a devoted uncle and brother, but there is something profoundly sad and lonely about him. He is self-conscious about dancing, and plays down the importance of his birthday when it comes around. Here, too, he associates his birthday with the time of his mother's death. I was clued into the desperate depths of Hank's isolation when in the third session he admitted, somewhat sheepishly, to voyeuristic tendencies. He said there had been a number of occasions dating back to the time near his mother's death in which he would use a telescopic lens to spy on girls undressing in their bedrooms. In general, though, he claimed he had a number of good relationships with women, but said that none of them ever worked out.

His current re-found girlfriend was a high school sweetheart whom he dated during the eighth grade and then again in the twelfth grade. After she went away to college, he thought about her constantly when he was in his twenties but never contacted her—believing that he was not good enough for her. Now nearing the age of 50, he finds himself getting tongue-tied with her quite often, unable to articulate what he feels inside and leaving her quite frustrated.

For the past forty years, Hank has not forgiven himself the innocent remark he made as an 8-year-old to his dying mother. The guilt stemming from this remark is compounded by the fact that he has very little else to remember her by. The distance between him and his ailing, dying mother replicated the veil of World War II separating Hank from what he imagined to be a happier, healthy pre-war mother. His guilt and sense of being peripheral to his mother's life may have been reflected in his voyeuristic tendency to unveil women from afar. He can look but not speak his passions. Without the reality testing of speaking with adults like Anna, he never was able to modify his omnipotent sense that he had done irreparable verbal harm to his mother. If anything, Anna's dismissal only reinforced Hank's fantasy that he hurts women when he speaks to them.

The theme of refinding his mother after a lengthy separation has repeated itself in the loss and then reconciliation with his girlfriend. Unfortunately, Hank has discovered that pursuing the ideal of reunion is a far easier matter than exposing himself to the conflicts and vulnerabilities of human intimacy. Things have not worked out with this girlfriend; since then they each have gone their own way.

Even though Hank's mother died when he was 8 years old, he never reconciled himself to her permanent disappearance. He, alone, carried the weighty mental burden of propping up the unreal, ghostlike existence of a person whom no one ever discussed. He, alone, must light a candle to her memory by recreating and holding onto her again and again in his fantasies. If he let go of her, who would be there to catch the fact that she ever existed?

Recently Hank has had numerous opportunities to ask women out on first dates, but has talked himself out of them at the last minute. He then becomes frustrated with himself for not following through to try to improve his life. He reports these struggles in therapy and concludes matter-of-factly, as he often does, with "Well, I guess I'm back to my old patterns." At these junctures, it has seemed to me that Hank takes a secret pride in showing me how he holds onto the past so tenaciously. And perhaps he is proud. For unlike everyone else in his family who went on with their lives after his mother died without so much as a glance backward, Hank has always sacrificed himself in the service of remembering. In holding himself as still as a statue with regard to new women, Hank has rendered himself into a devotional monument to his mother. Through his example, perhaps he would teach the rest of the family a moral lesson in loyalty.

I thus suggested to Hank that to move toward another woman with any kind of emotional depth would be to forsake and betray his mother as the others had. But why did Hank elect himself for this self-sacrificial duty of memorialization? Why did *he* have to give his life up for her? Maybe it was only through a devotional act of heroic proportions such as this that Hank could make up for the destructive effects that he imagined his unkind words had on her. All these years he had reserved a place for her return; to give his heart to someone else was to close off the possibility of his mother coming back and his chance to redeem himself with her.

THE EVASION OF MOURNING
AND THE PROBLEM OF ADAPTING TO
THE FACTS OF LIFE

Much of this book has been concerned with the different ways in which people become and remain stuck in their lives. Now the question remains, How do people finally leave their difficulties behind? How does a child come to terms with the experience of hearing parents bicker constantly? How does a little girl ultimately reconcile herself with the fact that her father molested her? Or another little girl that her mother died? When a 14-year-old boy catches a glimpse of other dads embracing their sons, how can he accept that he does not even know the name of his own father? The problem of how to help people work through and overcome hardships endured and losses suffered is perhaps the most vexing, important question facing the psychotherapy community.

In this final chapter, I will explore the conditions that promote a willingness to let go of those experiences that individuals hold onto for dear life and that continue to impede their development. Although grieving and mourning often have been used interchangeably in the loss literature, I think it useful to distinguish between the two terms. Whereas grief is an emotion of overwhelming sadness, mourning can be viewed as a process of internal transformation by which the old is relinquished and the new is engaged with an open heart. Although it often does involve grief, mourning is more generally at the crux of how human beings change and grow.

I use the phrase "open heart" advisedly because I would like especially to emphasize how it is the private, internal quality of letting go that defines mourning. All too often, outside observers and the bereaved alike, like Hank's father and stepmother, believe that mourning is and should be only a brief process corresponding to the course of external events. When a person loses a loved one to death, for example, uninvolved onlookers may expect that as a practical matter he would adapt to the fact of loss and get on with his life. And as a practical matter, the survivor may be ready to accede to what is expected of him, although adaptation to the facts of life is very different from mourning. Indeed, he may be only too willing to use a superficial acknowledgment of external events to sidestep the difficult internal work of mourning with all its concomitant pain.

Compliant with but not fully open to the world around them, these are the functioning people who compartmentalize their losses and proceed onward, somewhat mechanically and stoically, with the tasks of everyday life. No one would ever suspect that they had not mourned their losses until it was too late, until numerous opportunities for intimacy had played themselves out unsuccessfully in their lives because, as human machines, shut off to their most profound longings, they were not emotionally equipped to handle love.

In matters of mourning, as Hank discovered, merely adapting to the practical is more a deceitful hindrance than a help. Human beings are not merely reactive machines with the practical aim of adaptive functioning. When the external world does not allow for even the voicing of unrealizable wishes and indicates that it is more rational to forget someone who dies, the bereaved hold on all the more tenaciously.

Survivors of loss and disillusionment do not really turn away from their most cherished desires, they merely divert them inward. In the deepest reserves of their heart, the bereaved rebel secretly against the facts of loss that have been shoved down their throat, and hold on to what they supposedly had given up. In such circumstances, some survivors do not accept that the loved one is lost permanently; they may say that they have worked through the loss, but somewhere inside they may save a place for the loved one's eventual return. In a meeting between the pragmatic and the defensive, survivors use the mandate to adapt to external reality precisely so as *not* to mourn; they cover over and maintain an inextricable link between their unfulfillable wishes and the necessity that those wishes be fulfilled.

In psychotherapy, incomplete mourning, where wish has never been disentangled from its fulfillment, may be glimpsed from the following exchange:

Therapist: Would you like your father to be more affectionate?
Patient: That will never happen.

The patient's response is something of a non sequitur, in that the therapist does not ask how affectionate his father is or will be, but rather what the patient would wish for. This relatively commonplace example reveals how the patient automatically connects his wish for physical affection to the actual fulfillment of that wish, as if he could not even imagine one without the other.

Paralleling this unconscious fluidity between wish and fulfillment is also a fluidity between thought and action. When patients are finally able to express a deeply held desire, they may, in the next breath, add, "Okay, so what do I do now?" Here we can see how a previously defensive preoccupation with external reality gives way immediately to a call to some action toward fulfilling the wish once it is revealed. Thus, Freud (1911) notes that "unconscious processes equate reality of thought with external actuality, and wishes with their fulfillment" (p. 225).

Language and the superstition of word magic (a belief that the utterance of a word has an immediate transforming effect on the external world) reflect many of these unmourned linkages between wish and fulfillment, as well as between thought and action. The spoken word is a midwife between a wish (thought) and its consequent fulfillment (action). Freud (1913) referred to this conviction that words lead automatically to action as "motor hallucinations." Not being able to mourn means one is unable to modify one's omnipotent conviction that one's desires lead to immediate fulfillment if uttered. Because a heavy burden of responsibility goes hand-in-hand with the transforming power of magic, the unfortunate ironic consequence is that the possessors of such omnipotence must inhibit their imagination, thinking, and verbal expression for fear of hurting the ones they love. In harnessing their passions, however, they may compromise their in-depth participation in the interpersonal world of human intimacy.

Perhaps we can say that rather than conform to the hard facts of loss and disillusionment, people take up the slack narcissistically. Winnicott (1949) notes that when the environment fails in

its caretaking provision, individuals develop the omnipotent conviction that they are responsible for providing for themselves. Thus,
when people lose a bridging link between themselves and a substantive world of others, they may take up the slack for this rupture by denying a reality beyond their control. In this sense, an
individual frequently reconstructs the objectivity of a traumatic
event into the subjectivity of a self-created experience, and as
Winnicott (1960a) states, "There is no trauma that is outside of
the individual's omnipotence" (p. 37).

I supervise the treatment of many inner-city children who have
been removed from neglectful, drug-addicted mothers. Time and
again, these children imagine that it is they who have betrayed
and left their mothers behind to a lonely misery. A sexually abused
girl may wonder to herself whether it was really she who seduced
her father and brought the molestation on herself. A physically
abused child is convinced that the beatings he receives are punishments for his badness. The bereaved, too, not acknowledging
even the finality of death, sometimes may assume an inordinate
burden of control over bringing the dead back to life.

One of the problems with this conviction of omnipotently
creating one's own reality is that a real world that is constructed
can just as easily be deconstructed or reduced to subjective experience, where it is but a figment of one's imagination. Once individuals reduce the objective events of their lives only to their constructions of them, they may begin to lose any sense of a substantive
reality beyond their control. For example, when people lose a loved
one to death or suffer the breakup of a romantic relationship, they
may find it too painful to re-imagine a passionate love that was
shared with someone who is no longer there. In detaching defensively from their wishes to remember and restore the good, they
also lose an essential sense of the relationship as real. In their own
mind, they have analyzed the relationship to such an extent that
they may have doubts as to whether the intimacies they exchanged
really occurred or whether they were hallucinatory products of
their wish-filled imaginations. From within these dizzying,
derealizing circles of their own making, such persons now have
the impossible task of proving the objective existence of their own

[handwritten margin notes: "reaction formation w/ me compulsively"]

experience; they bear the burden of bringing those experiences to realized life by re-conceiving and reenacting them repeatedly. From this perspective, the repetition compulsion may be viewed as an attempt to hold on to and, through duplication, to keep alive experiences in order to make up for a missing quality of the real. Repetition is self-perpetuating because one searches for a sense of the real where it cannot be found—in one's own mind's eye.

I do not know in what direction Hank's treatment will evolve. For many years within a private mental prison fueled by obsessional doubt, Hank has hung on to memories and fantasies tinged with guilt, shame, sadness, and yearning. I see a man now, however, who is coming to life, as images, long frozen in dark silence, begin to thaw out in the shared light of a human dialogue. Each day I am learning anew that the inner life has a will of its own; a person lets go when he is good and ready, and not before. *[handwritten: not through any specific technique of the therapist.]*

ENTRUSTING ONE'S EXPERIENCE TO AN ENDURING HOLDING ENVIRONMENT

So what does facilitate this internal process of letting go? How does the shared expression of spoken words facilitate the mourning process? If we take Winnicott's notion of omnipotence as seriously as it deserves, mourning does not so much resemble the process of a child's separating and walking away from his mother as it does giving up a fantasized hold on the life and death of one's experiences.

When a master of ceremonies attempts to solicit generous applause from an audience for a particular performer, he may say "give it up for . . ." In a similar way, the mourner's giving of his possession to a world outside of his control can also be viewed as an act of generosity. Perhaps what inspires the sort of generosity involved in mourning more than anything else is the person's trust that there is an environment out there that cares enough to hold his experiences if he drops or gives them away—a real world that endures beyond the subjectivity of his whims.

Here trust entails that a person locate a place for himself in an awaiting world beyond the one he has created. Only then can he emerge from the absurdity of self-relating and form a meaningful relationship with a real other. In the ongoing quest for meaning, we may say that a universal dynamic of the human condition involves a search for this transcendent reality that lies beyond one's omnipotent grasp; for some, the culmination of this search for the limits to one's powers may be found embodied in the absolute being of God, while for others it may lie in the fundamental otherness of a different person. Although the notion of limits is usually associated with an inhibiting restrictiveness (as in setting limits, or a curfew), these need not be negative at all. On the contrary, the receptivity of another human being may have a containing effect on one's sense of omnipotence.

When we speak then of a therapeutic holding environment, we are speaking of a relationship that overcomes the patient's sense of meaningless isolation and incompleteness, one in which he feels he belongs to the therapist. Once the therapist's credibility as a freely willing other (credibility of the absolute) has been established, the degree to which he resonates with the experiences of the patient also gain him credibility as one who understands (credibility of the relative). Taken together, both types of credibility help provide patients with the conviction that they are revealing and giving their experiences away to an enduring posterity rather than to the oblivion of deaf ears.

The impetus behind mourning, creativity, and even development itself is an inspired passion to transform and objectify experience into something real and enduring. The various ways by which a person reveals and expresses himself in a relationship with a genuine other become the medium by which these transformations occur. Niederland (1989) has documented how creative writers, artists, and scientists have turned their losses and defects into enduring works, monuments that will be lasting testaments to their experiences. Pollock (1989), too, has described a "mourning–liberation" process in which creativity is used to free the mourner from his losses. Finding and securing a real ground of being inspires a movement of generosity on the part of the mourning individual that enables him finally to relinquish his valued possession. It is in this romantic but powerful psychological sense that a brief moment, once revealed and alive, lives forever.

A number of years ago I saw Charles, an acutely suicidal 40-year-old man in treatment, who, along with his other problems, struggled with the cancer of his beloved girlfriend as well as her subsequent breakup with him. In his early sessions he would walk in and before even sitting down would exclaim, "I don't care; I don't care; I just don't care anymore." He then would launch into obsessional tirades in which he ragefully disavowed the woman's significance to him, interspersed only rarely by nostalgic, dream-like reminiscences of better times they had shared together. There was some quality of tenderness, however, in these brief instances of remembered intimacy that prompted me to believe that Charles had rewritten history so bitterly that he had taken away something precious from himself.

Sensing that he was killing off his experiences of passionate love once shared with his girlfriend, I said that no matter what had happened since, no one could take away the genuine intimacies he had exchanged with her at one time. They were not part of a dream but a reality that had existed and would always exist, and one to which I could now bear witness because of his communicating it to me. His obsessional rage subsided immediately, giving way to bittersweet tears as he said rather proudly, "We did have something pretty good, didn't we?"

GEORGE BAILEY: SEEKING RELIEF FROM BEING A GOD UNTO HIMSELF

Although perhaps initially disillusioning, ultimately it may be calming to come up against and to be contained by insurmountable limits. To give up the burdens and pressures of ambition that accompany a sense of omnipotence often is relieving. Frank Capra's well-known film, *It's a Wonderful Life* (1946), regarded generally as a nice, sentimental entertainment, is, in my view, a profound depiction of a man learning to accept the limitations of his mortal life.

It's a Wonderful Life may be thought of as a moral fable about a modern world in which God has been declared dead, and in which, therefore, as Ivan Karamazov says, "everything is permitted." In this godless world, young men and women, flush with the freedom and ambition to fill the void, dream of being anything and everything their hearts desire, or as Marlo Thomas once put it, "free to be you and me." James Stewart's character in *It's a Wonderful Life*, George Bailey, is one of those young men whose energy and passion know no bounds. His ambitions to be everywhere—reflected in his intense desire to explore the world—and to build cities from scratch would be more appropriate for the powers of a god. To be everywhere and to do everything is more than the life of any one individual can handle.

Inevitably George Bailey's dreams of grandeur yield to rank necessity; he remains bound to his home as circumstances and responsibilities require that he serve his community and family. As is so often the case with ambitious people whose high ideals are crushed by disappointment, George becomes despondent and despairing; his impulse is to give up and take his ball and go home. With his aspirations of something greater fast eroding, and faced with the shame of bankruptcy, George's initial sense of omnipotence has soured into a nightmare of humiliating unworthiness. Unable to live up to the ambitions that nurtured his self-image, he is on the brink of taking his life when a guardian angel answers his prayers.

It is of great significance that George Bailey, who by his own admission is not a praying man, prayed at all. For in that pivotal moment of prayer in which he begs for help, he is opening up and searching for a larger power that transcends his own, a containing, holding environment that will provide reason and courage for him to emerge from his burdened despair.

As a psychotherapist may embody the culmination of a patient's idealized search for an absolute, the earthly arrival of Clarence, the guardian angel, may be seen as a resonating response to

George's quest to move beyond his isolating predicament of self-preoccupation; like a therapist who earns trust through a very personal, empathic understanding of the patient's experiences, Clarence gains credibility because he reveals his thorough acquaintance with George's ambitious dreams and their eventual collapse.

In one moment of bitter self-pity, George declares to Clarence that he would have been preferred it had he never been born. Clarence then uses the imaginary, fantastic elaboration of George's wish to demonstrate the value of a human life. He does this metaphorically by illustrating how the contrast between living and not living parallels a person's relative alienation or participation in an interdependent human community. From his unborn perch of isolated observer, George is guided through a world of family and friends who do not recognize him; he can look, but not touch or be touched. Without any familiar faces to anchor himself by, George's fantasy turns into a hallucinatory nightmare of eerie alienation.

Clarence teaches George a frightening object lesson in appreciating the worth of the life he actually has lived but had taken for granted. George's preoccupation with being a god unto himself is so self-involving that he overlooks his effect on the community of which he is an indispensable part. In imploring Clarence to let him return to life again, George is also asking to be brought back to his senses. He is asking to be brought out of his crazy-making isolation and to an attunement to the reality of human interdependence. With reborn grace, George then gleefully embraces the newly redeemed world of the familiarly human, basking in the thank-yous coming his way—and that he might have heard earlier if only he had been open to them.

Fifty years after it was made, *It's a Wonderful Life* has caught on with the public imagination in vivid fashion. It delivers a therapeutic message about the possibility of attaining acceptance within the real world of human relationships: don't try so hard to be more than you are; just be yourself, one vital link in an interdependent human community and that is enough.

Strictly speaking, it would seem from an outsider's point of view

that the intersubjective meeting between two persons, such as
Clarence and George or between a therapist and patient, would
not be sufficient to attain a sense of meaningful transcendence;
after all, there would seem to be nothing absolute about a dialogue between two different sets of subjectively constructed experiences. Perhaps ironically, however, from the vantage point of each
person in such a dialogue, the other is perceived to be inhabiting
an objective world beyond his own making. It is this resonating
otherness of freely acting human beings that allows people to serve
as effective limits, containers, and as holding environments of the
real for one another.

REINTEGRATING ONE'S WISHES AND
LETTING GO OF THE NECESSITY OF
THEIR FULFILLMENT

For the purposes of mourning, it is essential that a person internalize a sense of belonging to and being contained by the enduring quality of a holding environment. The feeling of being contained allows people to return to their primary task of being
themselves, of being true to their own nature. They can then get
to the crux of mourning: to accept their wishes, while simultaneously relinquishing the omnipotent burden of fulfilling those
wishes themselves. The process of reintegrating disowned wishes
and their imaginative elaborations engenders the generosity
needed to let go of the demand for their fulfillment.

If we view mourning as a process whose aim is to become relatively free from the compulsions to repeat the past, then we see
how the disintegrating consequences of suffering chronic disillusionments alone work against that process. The detachment defenses that arise in the wake of trauma stymie growth and mourning in their tracks. The resulting sense of disintegration has a
derealizing effect on a person's memory, leading her to search
repeatedly for a lost integrity or sense of continuity. To go forward
a person must first gather up these disillusioned but potentially

vital wishes for the ideal childhood from which she had detached herself. The reintegration of disillusioned wishes and the reestablishment of a sense of integrity is intrinsic to both self-acceptance and mourning.

This becomes clearer if we view a person's self metaphorically as an extended family. All the wayward children and relatives that had been disowned and evicted must be welcomed back into the lifeblood of the family. It is especially the black-sheep children who never found their way in the real world who have to be brought back into the fold. If we agree with Freud (1933), who, in speaking of the id, noted that "no alteration in its mental processes is produced by the passage of time" (pp. 73–74), then it would be far wiser to join with our wishes than combat them fruitlessly. Mourning need not, indeed, cannot entail that a person be rid of her desires. On the contrary, mourning is a paradoxical process in which a person must affirm precisely those orphaned desires that are most unrealistic and impossible to fulfill in order to relinquish the irrational demand for their fulfillment. By consciously recognizing the dignified, if irrational voice of those wishes—whether or not they are fulfillable—we lend those wishes an inclusive life within. Let me illustrate with a brief clinical vignette.

Max, a 42-year-old Jewish man, presented with anxiety and insomnia that worsened on the Sunday nights before he was to become, in his words, a "faceless bureaucrat" on Monday morning. As an only child, Max had felt extremely catered to by his mother. His childhood fear of independence—his fear of going to school, his returning home frequently from college—was his attempt to repay his mother by forming a dependent false self that had the function of catering to *her* need to be needed. At the cost of being called a "nebbish" and "mama's boy" by his father, Max sacrificed many boyhood initiatives and autonomous pleasures to enhance his mother's sense of her irreplaceability to him.

As an adult, Max believes only a supreme gift of immense professional success and fame would be sufficient to repay his mother for her past ministrations—or would be sufficient to buy himself free of her. However, this gift of professional success continues to elude him, in large part because he feels compelled to make an equally significant offering to his father to repair the rift he imagined his closeness to his mother caused between the parents.

It has only been in middle age, as he searches to root himself concretely in a network of communal and generational continuity, that Max has belatedly come to discover that the cost of his early oedipal victory was an alienation from his previously devalued father. Because his father failed at many jobs, Max's reparative gift to him has taken the form of his own work inhibition. In this way, he can, in identificatory fantasy, keep his father company in his downtrodden state of professional failure and bridge the chasm between them. In order for Max to be able to liberate himself from his fixation on his actual father, he would have to retrieve in his imagination the ideal father he had once wished for.

On one occasion immediately following Passover Max came to his session in a more depressed mood than usual. He and his wife, who had converted to Judaism, had invited only non-Jewish friends to their seder. Max said that he often became "down" the day before Passover and thought that it was because he missed being part of a Jewish community. He felt that the guests who were at the seder could not fully appreciate him as the rabbi. He recounted that he had been leading Passover seders since he was 13 because his father had never been interested in conducting the ceremony. I asked him if he had missed his father being in attendance at Passover since his death ten years earlier, and specifically at this last one. Max replied that "it would have been nice" to have had his father there. I then continued, "How would you have liked for your father to watch you lead the seder, come up to you after dinner, put his arm around you, and tell you how proud he was of you for the job you did as rabbi?"

Max's face reddened and his eyes teared up a little. After a brief pause, he cleared his throat, smiled barely perceptibly, and said: "Yeah, I'd love that." A few seconds later he roused himself from his reverie and added, "But that will never happen." A person can get lost in a world of make-believe for only so long before becoming anxious about losing contact with reality.

For just two or three minutes, Max was able to suspend disbelief and forsake an external reality in which his father had been dead for ten years. In its place he, not unlike the infant who conjures up an imaginary breast via hallucinatory wish fulfillment (Freud 1911), was able to reconstitute (Loewald 1980a) a more ideal world within; one in which his father was still living.

During the few brief moments of this constructive illusion, Max was able to fill the emptiness left by disowned wishes with the sweetness of their imagined fulfillment. This inner fullness, in turn, provided him with the strength to encounter the bitterness of a fatherless reality, and to let go of the necessity that his father actually be alive and present at the Seder. The generosity of mourning the loss of a loved one—relinquishing a demand that the dead person be present in the flesh—depends on these internalizations of the imaginary.

Max's reconstitution of an idealized father within allowed him more easily to let bygones be bygones; that is, he did not demand as urgently or resent as bitterly in retrospect that his actual, deceased father never lived up to his idealized image. He could let his father lie in peace in more ways than one. Perhaps more importantly, Max was also able to mourn his flawed relationship with his father, because he realized finally that his father's deficiencies did not relate to his own wish to love and to be loved. The conscious reintegration of wishes for what could have been or for what should have been can go a long way toward softening a person's image of his own capacity to love and to be loved.

A woman may hate herself because she thinks of herself as habitually nasty or bitchy, and is aware that other people view her in that light as well. In the silences interspersed between her words and her actions, somewhere she knows that she is more resentful and hateful toward men than other women are. She hates her own bitterness, but feels it to be an intrinsic part of her entrenched character and identity. It is only when she tells her tale of dashed hopes and crushing disappointment with a father who abandoned her when she was 4 and an alcoholic husband who left her for another woman, does her bitchiness unravel into a story of disillusioned wishes to love and to be loved. It makes all the difference in the world whether a person believes that she was not loved because of something fundamentally defective about herself, or because the other person simply was not capable of it. Perhaps ironically, once one's underlying self-recriminations are softened, one may be more forgiving of the person who disappointed one so much.

The re-creation of an imaginary world that elaborates on one's unarticulated desires is among the most mutative processes in psychotherapy with regard to mourning and psychic growth. The bittersweetness of owning up to wishes that cannot be fulfilled is far more satisfying than the despair and cynicism that fill the otherwise empty void. It is through the retrieval of long-buried wishes for what could have been and should have been, along with their imaginative elaborations, that at least something of the eternal spark of a lost childhood can be salvaged. The recapturing of a vision of one's ideal childhood can then become the internalized and therefore nonrepeated source of a new beginning for the rest of one's life. With this constant access to an inner source of rejuvenation, one may be able more easily to let go of the fantasized necessity of perfectly repairing the defects of one's traumatic themes or other traumas that have been endured. In so doing, one may discover paradoxically that one's life can be renewed by partaking in the better life that one is generating for one's children.

In this way, the process of losing and mourning may be experienced as if it were voluntarily coming from within, as part of the natural shedding and outgrowth of one's psychic skin. As this mourning process evolves, in large part self-willed and self-created, one is spurred to meet the unidirectionality of life generously on its own mortal terms.

Mourning thus implies some recognition of the necessity of compromising with the passage of time. I am reminded here of the question my son posed to me when he was 5 years old, "If God is so great, why did he make death?" I was left momentarily speechless. Groping for an answer, I replied finally, "Everyone gets a turn at life, but then we have to make room and share with someone else, so others get a turn, too." Sharing was a concept I hoped my son could understand.

Psychotherapy has provided humankind with the tools to fulfill Kierkegaard's (1843) ethical injunction of self-acceptance, "to choose oneself." Although I still have some distance to travel myself, I believe there is something profoundly satisfying about attaining integrity in the twilight of one's life, and in facing oneself in all one's unembellished truth and accepting what one sees with a degree of serenity. In the end, we must look back and answer for how we have conducted ourselves during our life's journey. Have we used our lives fully with the fires of our passion? Have we been open enough to use the opportunities available to us? Have we kept faith with our conscience that weaves together our mutual destinies? We are ultimately responsible for realizing the personal truths that connect us to others—nothing less.

References

Aberbach, D. (1989). *Surviving Trauma.* New Haven: Yale University Press.

Adler, G., and Buie, D. (1979). Aloneness and borderline psychology: the possible relevance of child development issues. *International Journal of Psycho-Analysis* 60:83–95.

Alexander, F. (1946). The principle of corrective emotional experience. In *Psychoanalytic Therapy: Principles and Applications,* ed. F. Alexander and T. French, pp. 66–70. New York: Ronald.

Angyal, A. (1965). *Neurosis and Treatment.* New York: Viking.

Balint, M. (1968). *The Basic Fault.* New York: Brunner/Mazel, 1979.

Barrie, J. M. (1922). *Dear Brutus: A Comedy in Three Acts.* New York: Scribner.

Becker, E. (1973). *The Denial of Death.* Glencoe, IL: The Free Press.

——— (1975). *Escape from Evil.* New York: The Free Press.

Benjamin, J. (1988). *The Bonds of Love.* New York: Pantheon.

Bergson, H. (1889). *Time and Free Will.* New York: Harper & Row, 1960.

Bollas, C. (1987). *The Shadow of the Object.* New York: Columbia University Press.

——— (1989). *Forces of Destiny.* London: Free Association Books.

Boris, H. (1994). *Envy.* Northvale, NJ: Jason Aronson.

Bowlby, J. (1958). The nature of the child's tie to the mother. *International Journal of Psycho-Analysis* 39:350–373.

——— (1979). *The Making and Breaking of Affectional Bonds.* London: Tavistock.

Buber, M. (1952). *Eclipse of God.* New York: Harper & Row.

——— (1958). *I and Thou.* New York: Scribner.

———— (1965). Guilt and guilt feelings. In *Selected Essays of Martin Buber*, ed. M. Friedman, pp. 111–138. New York: Harper and Row.

Camus, A. (1955). *The Myth of Sisyphus*. New York: Vintage.

Carse, J. (1980). *Death and Existence*. New York: Wiley.

Danieli, Y. (1989). Mourning in survivors and children of survivors of the Nazi Holocaust: the role of group and community modalities. In *The Problem of Loss and Mourning: Psychoanalytic Perspectives*, ed. D. Dietrich and P. Shabad, pp. 427–460. Madison, CT: International Universities Press.

Dinnage, R. (1978). A bit of light. In *Between Reality and Fantasy*, ed. S. Grolnick and L. Barkin, pp. 366–378. New York: Jason Aronson.

Donne, J. (1624). *John Donne: The Complete English Poems*. London: Penguin Educational, 1975.

Dostoevsky, F. (1864a). *Notes from the Underground*, trans. C. Garnett. New York: Dover, 1992.

———— (1864b). *Notes from the Underground*. In *Great Short Works of Fyodor Dostoevsky*, pp. 263–377. New York: Harper & Row.

———— (1880). *The Grand Inquisitor*. New York: Continuum, 1993.

———— (1880). *The Brothers Karamazov*. New York: Vintage, 1990.

Dundes, A. (1981). Wet and dry, the evil eye: an essay in Indo-European and Semitic world view. In *The Evil Eye: A Casebook*, ed. A. Dundes, pp. 257–312. Madison: University of Wisconsin Press.

Eissler, K. (1955). *The Psychiatrist and the Dying Patient*. New York: International Universities Press.

Eliade, M. (1971). *The Myth of the Eternal Return*. Princeton, NJ: Princeton University Press.

Ellworthy, F. (1895). *The Evil Eye*. New York: Collier, 1970.

Erikson, E. (1949). *Childhood and Society*. New York: Norton.

———— (1964). *Insight and Responsibility*. New York: Norton.

Fairbairn, W. R. D. (1941). A revised psychopathology of the psychoses and psychoneuroses. In *An Object-Relations Theory of the Personality*, pp. 28–58. New York: Basic Books, 1954.

Farber, L. (1966). *The Ways of the Will*. New York: Basic Books.

Ferenczi, S. (1909). Introjection and transference. In *First Contributions to Psycho-Analysis*, ed. M. Balint, pp. 35–93. New York: Brunner/Mazel, 1980.

———— (1927). The adaptation of the family to the child. In *Final Contri-*

butions to the Problems and Methods of Psycho-Analysis, pp. 61–76. New York: Brunner/Mazel, 1980.

———— (1928). The elasticity of psycho-analytic technique. In *Final Contributions to the Problems and Methods of Psychoanalysis*, pp. 87–101. New York: Brunner/Mazel, 1980.

———— (1932a). The analyst's attitude to his patient. In *Final Contributions to the Problems and Methods of Psychoanalysis*, pp. 261–262. New York: Bunner/Mazel, 1980.

———— (1932b). The vulnerability of traumatically acquired progressive faculties. In *Final Contributions to the Problems and Methods of Psychoanalysis*, pp. 262–263. New York: Brunner/Mazel, 1980.

Ferenczi, S., and Rank, O. (1925). *The Development of Psychoanalysis*. New York: Nervous and Mental Diseases.

Flores-Meiser, E. (1976). The hot mouth and evil eye. In *The Evil Eye*, ed. C. Maloney, pp. 149–162. New York: Columbia University Press.

Foster, G. (1965). Peasant society and the image of limited good. *American Anthropologist* 67:293–315.

Freud, A. (1936). *Ego and the Mechanisms of Defence*. London: Hogarth.

Freud, S. (1895). Project for a scientific psychology. *Standard Edition* 1:283–397. London: Hogarth Press. 1966.

———— (1905a). On psychotherapy. *Standard Edition* 7:257–268.

———— (1905b). Three essays on the theory of sexuality. *Standard Edition* 7:125–245.

———— (1908). Creative people and day-dreaming. *Standard Edition* 9:143–153.

———— (1911). Formulations on the two principles of mental functioning. *Standard Edition* 12:218–226.

———— (1912a). On the universal tendency to debasement in the sphere of love. *Standard Edition* 11:179–190.

———— (1912b). Recommendations for physicians on the psycho-analytic method of treatment. *Standard Edition* 12:109–120.

———— (1913). Totem and taboo. *Standard Edition* 13:1–161.

———— (1914). Remembering, repeating and working through. *Standard Edition* 12:145–156.

———— (1915). Thoughts for the time on war and death. *Standard Edition* 14:275–300.

———— (1916). On transience. *Standard Edition* 14:303–307.

—— (1917). Mourning and melancholia. *Standard Edition* 14:243–258.

—— (1919a). The uncanny. *Standard Edition* 17:217–256.

—— (1919b). Lines of advance in psycho-analytic therapy. *Standard Edition* 17:157–168.

—— (1920). Beyond the pleasure principle. *Standard Edition* 18:7–64.

—— (1923). The ego and the id. *Standard Edition* 19:3-166.

—— (1925). Negation. *Standard Edition* 19:235–239.

—— (1926). Inhibitions, symptoms and anxiety. *Standard Edition* 20: 77–175.

—— (1930). Civilization and its discontents. *Standard Edition* 21:59–145.

—— (1933). New introductory lectures in psycho-analysis. *Standard Edition* 22:3–182.

—— (1936). A disturbance of memory on the Acropolis. *Standard Edition* 23:239–248.

—— (1940). Splitting of the ego in the process of defense. *Standard Edition* 23:275–278.

Fromm, E. (1941). *Escape from Freedom*. New York: Avon, 1972.

—— (1947). *Man for Himself: An Enquiry into the Psychology of Ethics*. New York: Rinehart.

Frost, R. (1915). The road not taken. In *Selected Poems*, ed. I. Hamilton. London: Penguin Educational, 1973.

Gaddini, E. (1969). On imitation. *International Journal of Psycho-Analysis*, 50:475–484.

Gaddini, R., and Gaddini, N. (1970). The transitional object and the process of individuation: a study of three social groups. *Journal of the American Academy of Child Psychiatry* 9:357–365.

Gay, P. (1988). *Freud*. New York: Norton.

Green, A. (1978). Potential space in psychoanalysis: the object in the setting. In *Between Reality and Fantasy*, ed. S. Grolnick and L. Barkin, pp. 170–189. New York: Jason Aronson.

Greenspan, S. (1992). Lives as texts: symptoms as modes of recounting in the life histories of Holocaust survivors. In *Stoned Lives*, ed. G. Rosenwald and R. Ochberg, pp. 145–164. New Haven: Yale University Press.

Heidegger, M. (1927). *Being and Time*. New York: Harper & Row, 1962.

Heinicke, C., and Westheimer, I. (1966). *Brief Separations*. New York: International Universities Press.

Hoffman, I. (1999). *Ritual and Spontaneity in the Psychoanalytic Process.* Hillsdale, NJ: Analytic Press.

Horton, P. (1981). *Solace.* Chicago: The University of Chicago Press.

Hyde, L. (1979). *The Gift.* New York: Vintage.

Ionesco, E. (1960). *Rhinoceros.* New York: Vintage.

Joffe, W., and Sandler, J. (1965). Notes on pain, depression and individuation. *Psychoanalytic Study of the Child* 20:394–424. New York: International Universities Press.

Jones, E. (1953). *The Life and Work of Sigmund Freud,* vol. I. New York: Basic Books.

Khan, M. (1963) The concept of the cumulative trauma. In *The Privacy of the Self,* pp. 42–58. New York: International Universities Press, 1974.

Kierkegaard, S. (1843). *Either/Or.* Vol. II. New York: Anchor, 1959.

——— (1846). *The Present Age.* New York: Harper & Row, 1962.

Klein, M. (1940). Mourning and its relation to manic-depressive states. *International Journal of Psycho-Analysis* 21:125–153.

——— (1957). Envy and gratitude. In *Envy and Gratitude, 1946–1963,* pp. 176–235. New York: Dell, 1975.

Klein, M., and Riviere, J. (1953). *Love, Hate and Reparation.* London: Hogarth.

Kohut, H. (1977). *The Restoration of the Self.* New York: International Universities Press.

Kohut, H., and Wolf, E. (1978). The disorders of the self and their treatment: an outline. *International Journal of Psychoanalysis* 59:413–424.

Kris, E. (1952). *Psychoanalytic Explorations in Art.* New York: Schocken, 1974.

——— (1956). The recovery of childhood memories in psychoanalysis. *Psychoanalytic Study of the Child* 11:54–88. New York: International Universities Press.

Landman, J. (1993). *Regret.* New York: Oxford University Press.

Lewis, O. (1951). *Life in a Mexican Village: Tepoztlan Restudied.* Urbana, IL: University of Illinois Press.

Lichenstein, H. (1977). *The Dilemma of Human Identity.* New York: Jason Aronson.

Lifton, R. J. (1968). *Death in Life, Survivors of Hiroshima.* New York: Random House.

Lipton, S. (1977). The advantages of Freud's technique as shown in his analysis of the Rat Man. *International Journal of Psycho-Analysis* 58:255–273.

Loewald, H. (1962). Internalization, separation, mourning and the superego. In *Papers on Psychoanalysis*, pp. 257–276. New Haven: Yale University Press.

——— (1978). *Psychoanalysis and the History of the Individual.* New Haven: Yale University Press.

——— (1980a). Some considerations on repetition and repetition compulsion. In *Papers on Psycho-Analysis*, pp. 87–101. New Haven: Yale University Press.

——— (1980b). The waning of the Oedipus complex. In *Papers on Psycho-Analysis*, pp. 384–404. New Haven: Yale University Press.

Lynch, W. (1965). *Images of Hope.* South Bend, IN: University of Notre Dame Press.

Macalpine, I. (1950). The development of the transference. *Psychoanalytic Quarterly*, 19:501–539.

Mahler, M., Pine, F., and Bergman, A. (1975). *The Psychological Birth of the Human Infant.* New York: Basic Books.

Margolis, D. (1998). *The Fabric of Self.* New Haven: Yale University Press.

Maslow, A. (1967). Neurosis as a failure of personal growth. *Humanitas* 3:153–169.

May, R. (1969). *Love and Will.* New York: Norton.

McCartney, E. (1981). Praise and dispraise in folklore. In *The Evil Eye: A Casebook*, ed. A. Dundes, pp. 9–38. Madison: University of Wisconsin Press, 1981.

Miller, J. (1988). *The Way of Suffering.* Washington, DC: Georgetown University Press.

Milton, J. (1667). *Paradise Lost.* New York: Chelsea House, 1961.

Mitchell, S. (1988). *Relational Concepts in Psychoanalysis.* Cambridge: Harvard University Press.

——— (1991). Wishes, needs and interpersonal negotiations. *Psychoanalytic Inquiry* 11:147–170.

Muensterberger, W. (1969). Psyche and environment: socio-cultural variations in separation and individuation. *Psychoanalytic Quarterly* 38:191–216.

Murgoci, A. (1923). The evil eye in Romania and its antidotes. In *The Evil Eye: A Casebook*, ed. A. Dundes, pp. 124–129. Madison: University of Wisconsin Press, 1981.

Napier, A. (1986). *Masks, Transformation and Paradox.* Berkeley: University of California Press.

Niederland, W. (1989). Trauma, loss, restoration, and creativity. In *The Problem of Loss and Mourning: Psychoanalytic Perspectives*, ed. D. Dietrich and P. Shabad, pp. 61–83. Madison, CT: International Universities Press.

Odier, C. (1956). *Anxiety and Magic Thinking.* New York: International Universities Press.

Orange, D. (1995). *Emotional Understanding: Studies in Psychoanalytic Epistemology.* New York: Guilford.

Ortega y Gasset, J. (1964). *In Search of the Goethe from within.* In *The Worlds of Existenialism*, ed. M. Friedman. New York: Random House.

Phillips, A. (1993). *On Kissing, Tickling and Being Bored.* Cambridge: Harvard University Press.

———— (1995a). *Terrors and Experts.* Cambridge: Harvard University Press.

———— (1995b). The story of the mind. In *The Mind Object*, ed. E. Corrigan and P. E. Gordon, pp. 229–240. Northvale, NJ: Jason Aronson.

Piers, G., and Singer, M. (1953). *Shame and Guilt.* New York: Norton, 1971.

Pollock, G. (1989). The mourning process, the creative process, and the creation. In *The Problem of Loss and Mourning: Psychoanalytic Perspectives*, ed. P. Dietrich and P. Shabad, pp. 27–59. Madison, CT: International Universities Press.

Rank, O. (1925). *The Double.* Chapel Hill: University of North Carolina Press, 1971.

———— (1936). *Will Therapy and Truth and Reality.* New York: Knopf.

Renik, O. (1993). Analytic interaction: conceptualizing technique in light of the analyst's irreducible subjectivity. *Psychoanalytic Quarterly* 62:553–571.

———— (1995). The ideal of the anonymous analyst and the problem of self-disclosure. *Psychoanalytic Quarterly* 64:466–495.

———— (1998). Getting real in analysis. *Psychoanalytic Quarterly* 67:516–593.

Rheingold, J. (1967). *The Mother, Anxiety and Death.* Boston: Little, Brown.

Rilke, R. M. (1934). *Letters to a Young Poet.* New York: Norton, 1993.

Roazen, P. (1984). *Freud and His Followers.* New York: New York University Press.

Robertson, J., and Bowlby, J. (1952). Responses of young children to separation from their mothers. *Courier de la Centre Internationale de l'Enfance* 2:131–142.

Rochlin, G. (1965). *Griefs and Discontents: The Forces of Change.* Boston: Little, Brown.

Rogers, C. (1961). *On Becoming a Person.* New York: Houghton Mifflin.

Roheim, G. (1955). *Magic and Schizophrenia.* Bloomington: Indiana University Press.

Romanyshyn, R. (1982). *Psychological Life.* Austin: University of Texas Press.

——— (1989). *Technology and Dream as Symptoms.* New York: Routledge.

Russell, P. (1993). The essential invisibility of trauma and the need for repetition. Commentary to "Resentment, Indignation, Entitlement: The Transformation of Unconscious Wish into Need." *Psychoanalytic Dialogues* 3(4):515–522.

Rycroft, C. (1965). On ablation of the parental images, or the illusion of having created oneself. In *Psychoanalysis and Beyond,* pp. 214–232. London: Hogarth.

Sartre, J.-P. (1946). *No Exit.* New York: Vintage.

Scheler, M. (1912). *Ressentiment.* New York: Free Press, 1961.

Schoeck, H. (1955). The evil eye: forms and dynamics of a universal superstition. In *The Evil Eye: A Casebook,* ed. A. Dundes, pp. 192–200. Madison: University of Wisconsin Press, 1981.

Schon, D. (1983). *The Reflective Practitioner.* New York: Basic Books.

Schur, M. (1972). *Freud: Living and Dying.* New York: International Universities Press.

Searles, H. (1975). The patient as therapist to his analyst. In *Countertransference,* pp. 380–459. Madison, CT: International Universities Press, 1979.

Segal, H. (1981). *The Work of Hanna Segal.* New York: Jason Aronson.

Shabad, P. (1989). Vicissitudes of psychic loss of a physically present parent. In *The Problem of Loss and Mourning: Psychoanalytic Perspectives,* ed. D. Dietrich and P. Shabad, pp. 101–126. Madison, CT: International Universities Press.

——— (1991). The unconscious wish and psychoanalytic stoicism. *Contemporary Psychoanalysis* 27(2):332–350.

——— (1993a). Repetition and incomplete mourning: the intergenerational transmission of traumatic themes. *Psychoanalytic Psychology* 10(1):61–75.

——— (1993b). Resentment, indignation, entitlement: the transformation of unconscious wish into need. *Psychoanalytic Dialogues* 3(4):481–494.

Shabad, P., and Selinger, S. (1995). Bracing for disappointment and the counterphobic leap into the future. In *The Mind Object*, ed. E. Corrigan and P. E. Gordon, pp. 209–227. Northvale, NJ: Jason Aronson.

Shengold, L. (1991). *Soul Murder*. New Haven: Yale University Press.

Siebers, T. (1983). *Masks of Medusa*. Berkeley: University of California Press.

Singer, I. (1971). The patient aids the analyst: some clinical and theoretical observations. In *In the Name of Life—Essays in Honor of Erich Fromm*, ed. B. Lands and E. Tauber, pp. 56–68. New York: Holt, Rinehart & Winston.

Stekel, W. (1949). *Compulsion and Doubt*. New York: Grosset & Dunlap.

Stierlin, H. (1976). *Hitler: A Family Perspective*. New York: The Psychohistory Press.

Stolorow, R., and Atwood, G. (1992). *Contexts of Being*. Hillsdale, NJ: Analytic Press.

Sullivan, H. (1956). *Clinical Studies in Psychiatry*. New York: Norton.

Thass-Thienemann, T. (1973). *The Interpretation of Language*. Vol. II. New York: Jason Aronson.

Tillich, P. (1963). *Morality and Beyond*. New York: Harper & Row.

Tolstoy, L. (1886). *The Death of Ivan Ilych*. New York: Signet Classics, 1960.

Van der Leeuw, G. (1957). Primordial time and final time. In *Man and Time* Bollinger Series XXX, ed. J. Campbell, pp. 324–350. Princeton, NJ: Princeton University Press, 1973.

Van Gennep, A. (1908). *Rites of Passage*. Chicago: University of Chicago Press, 1975.

Wilder, T. (1938). *Our Town*. New York: Perennial Classics, 1998.

Winnicott, D. W. (1947). Hate in the countertransference. In *Through Paediatrics to Psychoanalysis*, pp. 194–203. New York: Basic Books, 1975.

——— (1949). Mind and its relation to the psyche-soma. In *Through Paediatrics to Psychoanalysis* (pp. 243–254). New York: Basic Books, 1975.

——— (1951). Transitional objects and transitional phenomena. In *Through Paediatrics to Psychoanalysis*, pp. 229–242. New York: Basic Books, 1975.

——— (1954–1955). The depressive position in normal emotional development. In *Through Paediatrics to Psychoanalysis*, pp. 262–277. New York: Basic Books, 1975.

———— (1956). Primary maternal preoccupation. In *Through Paediatrics to Psychoanalysis*, pp. 300–305. New York: Basic Books, 1975.

———— (1960a). The theory of the parent-infant relationship. In *The Maturational Processes and the Facilitating Environment*, pp. 37–55. New York: International Universities Press, 1965.

———— (1960b). Ego distortion in terms of true and false self. In *The Maturational Processes and the Facilitating Environment*, pp. 140–152. New York: International Universities Press, 1965.

———— (1967a). The location of cultural experience. In *Playing and Reality*, pp. 95–103. London: Tavistock, 1971.

———— (1967b). Mirror role of mother and family in child development. In *Playing and Reality*, pp. 111–118. London: Tavistock, 1971.

———— (1969). The use of an object and relating through identifications. In *Playing and Reality*, pp. 86–94. London: Tavistock, 1971.

———— (1971). The place where we live. In *Playing and Reality*, pp. 104–110. London: Tavistock, 1971.

Credits

The author gratefully acknowledges permission to reprint material from the following sources:

Excerpts from "The Most Intimate of Creations: Symptoms as Memorials of Lonely Suffering," by Peter Shabad, in *Symbolic Loss: The Ambiguity of Mourning and Memory at Century's End*, ed. P. Homans. Copyright © 2000 by The University Press of Virginia and reprinted with permission.

Excerpts from "Fixation and the Road Not Taken," by Peter Shabad, in *Psychoanalytic Psychology* 4(3):187–205. Copyright © 1987; and "Repetition and Incomplete Mourning: The Intergenerational Transmission of Traumatic Themes," by Peter Shabad, in *Psychoanalytic Psychology* 10(1):61–75. Copyright © 1993. Reprinted by permission of Lawrence Erlbaum Associates, Inc.

Excerpts from "Giving the Devil His Due: Spite and the Struggle for Individual Dignity," by Peter Shabad, in *Psychoanalytic Psychology* 17(4):690–705. Coypright © 2000 by the Educational Publishing Foundation. Reprinted with permission.

Excerpts from "Resentment, Indignation, Entitlement: The Transformation of Unconscious Wish into Need," by Peter Shabad, in *Psychoanalytic Dialogues* 3(4):481–494. Copyright © 1993; "Paradox and the Repetitive Search for the Real," by Peter Shabad, in *Psy-*

choanalytic Dialogues 3(4):523–533. Copyright © 1993; and "The Essential Invisibility of Trauma and the Need for Repetition," by Paul Russell, in *Psychoanalytic Dialogues* 3(4)515–522. Copyright © 1993. Reprinted by permission of The Analytic Press.

Excerpts from "The Evil Eye of Envy: Parental Possessiveness and the Rivalry for a New Beginning," by Peter Shabad, in *Gender and Envy*, ed. Nancy Burke. Copyright © 1998. Reproduced by permission of Routledge, Inc./Taylor and Francis.

"Something I've Not Done" by W. S. Merwin. Copyright © 1973 by W. S. Merwin.

Excerpts from "Gerontion" by T. S. Eliot, in *The Oxford Dictionary of Quotations*, Third Edition. New York: Oxford University Press, 1980. Reprinted by permission of the publisher.

Index

fulfillment, 206, 308–311
for ideal parent, 79, 81, 83
vs. needs, 142–144
Witches, 172–173, 184
Witness
  credible, 152–153, 157
  not-yet-located, 138–139
  to one's life, 126
  to one's own suffering, 114–118, 123–124, 132–134
  therapist as a, 154

validating, 139
Wizard of Oz, The, 91, 172
Wolf, E., 77
Wordsworth, 293
Worrying, 149, 219–220
Worship
  need to, 225, 227, 237

Youth
  inner city, 13–14, 46, 243, 302

About the Author

Peter Shabad, Ph.D., received his doctoral degree from Washington University in St. Louis and completed a post-doctoral fellowship in psychoanalytic psychotherapy at Northwestern Memorial Hospital in Chicago. He has served as Director of Training in Psychology at Michael Reese Hospital in Chicago, and is currently an Assistant Professor of Clinical Psychiatry at Northwestern University Medical School.

Co-editor of *The Problem of Loss and Mourning: Psychoanalytic Perspectives* (1989), he has written numerous journal articles and book chapters. Dr. Shabad had also taught daylong seminars nationally on loss and mourning for the American HealthCare Institute. He teaches, supervises, and maintains a private practice in Chicago.